Cultural Resources Archaeology

Cultural Resources Archaeology

An Introduction

Thomas W. Neumann
and
Robert M. Sanford

ALTAMIRA
PRESS

A Division of Rowman & Littlefield Publishers, Inc.
Walnut Creek • London • New York • Oxford

PRESS

A Division of Rowman & Littlefield Publishers, Inc.
1630 North Main Street, #367
Walnut Creek, CA 94596
www.altamirapress.com

Rowman & Littlefield Publishers, Inc.
4720 Boston Way
Lanham, MD 20706

12 Hid's Copse Road
Cumnor Hill, Oxford OX2 9JJ, England

Copyright © 2001 by AltaMira Press

British Library Cataloguing-in-Publication Information Available

Library of Congress Cataloging-in-Publication Data

Neumann, Thomas William.
   Cultural resources archaeology : an introduction / Thomas W. Neumann, Robert M. Sanford.
     p. cm.
   Includes bibliographical references and index.
   ISBN 0-7591-0095-0 (pbk. : alk. paper)
    1. Archaeology—Vocational guidance—United States. 2. Archaeology—Methodology. 3. Excavations (Archaeology)—Evaluation. 4. Historic sites—United States—Management. 5. Compliance—Evaluation. 6. Historic sites—Conservation and restoration—United States. 7. Historic preservation—United States. 8. United States—Antiquities—Collection and preservation. 9. Archaeology and state—United States. I. Sanford, Robert M. II. Title.

CC107 .N48 2001
930.1'02373—dc21

                                                              2001022917

Printed in the United States of America

∞™ The paper used in this publication meets the minimum requirements of American National Standard for Information Sciences—Permanence of Paper for Printed Library Materials, ANSI/NISO Z39.48-1992.

An abridged version of *Practical Archaeology*, Thomas W. Neumann and Robert M. Sanford (AltaMira, 2001)

CONTENTS

PREFACE

Most archaeologists do not work in an academic setting, although they received their initial training there. Rather, most archaeologists work in the private sector or for the government, either conducting or reviewing compliance work. This text is a short, general summary of what that archeological work involves and is meant to be a supplement to introductory archaeology and method-and-theory classes. It gives some sense of what a person needs to know—in addition to the standard classroom, field, and laboratory courses—to do archaeology after he or she gets out of college. It also serves as a guide for those who need to hire, work with, or review the work of archaeologists. It reflects what we have found to be useful in professional practice. A lot of that was never explained to us in college and still seems to be left out of textbooks. It is in response to that neglect that this text was written.

We have been doing Section 106–mandated archaeology for over a quarter-century. While we have taught (or again teach) in university settings, most of our careers have been spent either in archaeology firms or in government agencies overseeing environmental and historic preservation regulations. We have been fortunate to be natives of both the academic and the extra-academic worlds. Being members of these two cultures has also given us a rare perspective on what each needs from the other.

Within the university, students have told us numerous times how much they want to know where archaeology jobs are, what such work involves, and what they need to know to work in such settings. Outside of the university, employers and government regulators have time and again bemoaned the lack of exposure their new hires have to the professional archaeology workplace. Recent graduates who are hired can, indeed, excavate; and they often do recognize how to apply processed archaeological data to research problems using the latest theoretical concepts. But they are in a fog about how to set up a survey, how to respond to a bid request and structure a budget, or how to allocate organizational resources. And the vast majority have never heard of the Section 106 Process, while those who have rarely understand it.

One recurring theme we have heard from our professional colleagues has been how much they would like to have their prospective employees know how extra-academic archaeology works. There are many things that full-time archaeologists need to be aware of—if not know—to work in the day-to-day compliance world. There are many wonderful method-and-theory texts and many field and laboratory method texts that explain how to do archaeology itself. However, left out of all of that is how the majority of people doing archaeology go about translating that course material into the professional workplace. And that, of course, is what we go over here.

Similarly, environmental professionals, developers, public officials, and interested citizens often have asked us to explain just what it is that a professional archaeologist does. Sure, they may know generally that a targeted development area "needs a Phase I," but they also want to know what that entails. This text also addresses that need for an explanation of how archaeology is done in service to environmental and historic preservation laws that affect development.

Last, we did not come to know about compliance archaeology and professional practice all at once. It has been quite a learning experience, believe us. We have certainly made our share of mistakes. It only seems right that others benefit from our errors.

Acknowledgments

We greatly appreciate the extensive work done by our editor and publisher at AltaMira Press, Dr. Mitch Allen. It was his vision, energy, and patience that brought this text to completion.

Any text requires input and comment from a lot of people. We have had the good fortune of working with reviewers who corrected errors, freely gave of their advice, recommended better wording of critical passages, and pointed us to additional materials. We would particularly like to thank:

- Mr. Chad Braley (Vice President, Southeastern Archeological Services, Inc., Georgia)

- Dr. Paul Brockington (President, Brockington and Associates, Inc., Georgia)

- Dr. Dave D. Davis (University of Southern Maine)

- Ms. Hester Davis (State archaeologists, Arkansas Archaeological Survey)

- Mr. Thomas Gresham (President, Southeastern Archeological Services, Inc., Georgia)

- Mr. Scott Hoffeld (URS Corporation)

- Ms. Connie Huddleson (Laboratory Director, Brockington and Associates, Inc., Georgia)

- Dr. Benjamin Z. Freed (Research Associate, Zoo Atlanta, and Adjunct Faculty, Department of Anthropology, Emory University)

- Dr. Joseph W. Joseph III (President, New South Associates, Inc., Georgia)

- Dr. Thomas F. King (Senior Advisor and Training Consultant, National Preservation Institute, Silver Spring, Maryland)

- Mr. David Lacy (Forest Archaeologist, Green Mountain and Finger Lakes National Forests, U.S. Department of Interior)

- Dr. Samantha Langley-Turnbaugh (Environmental Science and Policy Program, University of Southern Maine)

- Dr. Francis P. McManamon (Chief, Archeology and Ethnography Program, and Departmental Consulting Archeologist, Archeology and Ethnography Program, National Center for

Cultural Resource Stewardship and Partnerships, National Park Service)

- Dr. Mary Spink Neumann (Behavioral Scientist, Centers for Disease Control and Prevention, Atlanta)

- Mr. Paul Nordman (State Auto Insurance Companies, Columbus, Ohio)

- Ms. Peggy Nordman (Breen, Winkle, and Company, Inc., Columbus, Ohio)

- Dr. James B. Petersen (Chair, Department of Anthropology, University of Vermont)

- Dr. Adrian Praetzellis (Director, Anthropological Studies Center, Sonoma State University)

- Dr. Richard S. Sanford (Professor Emeritus, Clarkson University)

- Mr. Thomas Wheaton (Vice-President, New South Associates, Inc., Georgia)

We appreciate the assistance given by Brockington Associates, Inc. (Norcross, Georgia), New South Associates, Inc. (Stone Mountain, Georgia), and Southeastern Archeological Services, Inc. (Athens, Georgia). We are especially grateful to Mr. Jerald Ledbetter (Southeastern Archeological Services, Inc.) for allowing us to use his photographs. We also are grateful to St. John Neumann Parish (Lilburn, Georgia), especially Fr. James Fennessy, Rev. Mr. Gary Womack, and Ms. Joanne Walding, for use of computer facilities in production of earlier drafts.

Dr. Nathan Hamilton (University of Southern Maine) field-tested a draft of this text with his Public Archaeology students, who provided much-appreciated comments. Neumann's archaeology students at Emory University, particularly Ms. Jennifer Carden, Ms. Angela Cronan, Ms. Amy Judd, and Ms. Virginia Wallace (Agnes Scott College), also made use of earlier versions of this text and provided insightful comments.

Neumann's wife, Mary Spink Neumann, provided unflagging encouragement and assistance as an anthropological archaeologist, friend, and partner.

Sanford's wife, Robin Sanford, helped research information and provided support. Richard Sanford reviewed numerous drafts, providing comments from the perspectives of an engineer and an avocational archaeologist, as well as a father. Special thanks to Drs. Garrett Cook and Steve Marqusee for their teaching and inspiration.

Credits

Unless otherwise noted, all photographs are property of T. W. Neumann.

Figures 5.1, 5.5, and 5.6 provided courtesy of R. Jerald Ledbetter and Southeastern Archeological Services, Inc., Athens, Georgia.

Figures 7.1, 7.3, and 7.4 provided courtesy of Paul Brockington and Brockington and Associates, Inc., Norcross, Georgia.

CHAPTER ONE

PROFESSIONAL ARCHAEOLOGY: AN OVERVIEW

Introduction: Purpose and Overview

Archaeology in the United States has recently moved beyond the realm of universities and museums.[1] Today, about 80 percent of people employed as archaeologists work in private industry or as government regulators who often oversee the archaeological work of the private sector (Neumann and Sanford 2001:2–3). What caused this shift from an academic-based field to a government-regulated industry? Why should archaeologists be working outside of university or museum settings?

The answers to these questions rest in a series of historic preservation laws and mandates, beginning with the National Historic Preservation Act (NHPA) of 1966. Compliance with these laws and mandates often requires archaeological studies to be done as part of the construction and development process. The culmination of nearly a century of legislation and court rulings, the NHPA and subsequent laws required that archaeological work be done whenever Federal moneys, lands, or permits are involved in land-alteration projects (termed "undertakings"). For example, before a road could be widened using Federal Highway Administration funds, or before a water treatment plant could be built in a floodplain where a U.S. Army Corps of Engineers 404 permit (issued under the Clean Water Act for dredge and fill activities in waters of the United States) is required, a Federal agency must check to see if

---

[1]Throughout this text, we also use "professional archaeology" to describe the archaeology done outside of the university or museum.

archaeological sites or other cultural resources important to the United States would be lost.

States eventually followed with counterpart legislation. In time, many counties and local municipalities also set up statutes and regulations that require an area to be checked for surface and subsurface cultural remains before construction was done. Archaeology became an integral element in the maintenance and expansion of the physical infrastructure of the United States. This text explores what this profession of archaeology involves.

This first chapter briefly summarizes how what was once primarily a university- and museum-based field came to be an extra-academic profession in the United States.[2] The events of the last 150 years helped mold the relationship among the three archaeology realms—the academic sector, the private sector, and the government/public sector—as well as establish how and why things are done the way they are now.

Chapter 2 contains a brief summary of key environmental and historic preservation laws and how they work on an everyday basis in terms of practiced archaeology. Of necessity, we have glossed over many important aspects of these complex pieces of legislation but do refer the reader to appropriate sources that provide a much fuller treatment. We do include some aspects of contract and bid issues in this chapter, since these derive from compliance requirements.

Chapter 3 treats preparation of project backgrounds for any archaeological study. This is the first "methods" chapter. Well-developed background narratives on the environment and culture history are required parts of the overall archaeological compliance process.

Chapters 4, 5, and 6 discuss archaeological assessment steps in regulatory compliance. We use the commonly recognized terms Phase I, II,

---

[2]The use of the term "professional" in this text follows accepted American Association of University Professor (AAUP) usage, where scientists in higher education are labeled as "faculty" or "academics." Scientists working in the same field in industry or government are labeled "professionals" (e.g., Hamermesh 1996:32). Similar usage of "professional" is found throughout Federal code (e.g., 36 CFR 61 Appendix A) and in national (e.g., Registry of Professional Archaeologists) title and regional professional organizations (e.g., Georgia Council of Professional Archaeologists).

and III.[3] Phase I is a resource identification step that uses field reconnaissance and intensive survey in addition to historic documentation to examine the project area. Phase II (testing and evaluation) and Phase III (full excavation, data recovery, or mitigation) procedures are similar to testing and formal excavation covered in university field and methods courses. Here we focus on how these work in regulatory and corporate contexts. These chapters give a fair amount of attention to documentation, with emphasis on durable "hard copy" records. Similarly, we emphasize the use of common, low-cost, traditional field equipment such as tape and compass. We do this in full awareness of computer technology applications, which can facilitate field, mapping and record-keeping tasks. However, mastery of basic field equipment and techniques will facilitate the use of more technologically advanced equipment and is an essential part of practicing archaeology.

Chapter 7 covers the final stages of the project: laboratory analysis and report production. The first involves processing, analysis, and curatorial issues. The second looks at how to set up and produce an archaeological site report. The report must comply with agency administration of applicable legislation and meet stringent contract requirements.

A Brief History of Extra-Academic and Professional Archaeology

Archaeology performed in response to statutory mandates is variously referred to as "cultural resource management," "contract archaeology," "consulting archaeology," "private-sector archaeology," or "public archaeology." Cultural Resource Management archaeology, or CRM archaeology (the

---

[3]The terms "Phase I," "Phase II," and "Phase III" are used in 35 of the nation's 50 states as labels for the "identification," "evaluation," and "mitigation" or "resolution" stages in the archaeology done in response to the Section 106 Process or in response to its state or local counterparts. The student should know that some archaeologists do not use these terms (e.g., King 1998, 2000). However, archaeologists generally know what is being talked about when the term "Phase I" or whatever is used. The widespread understanding and use of these terms, combined with the implied sense of sequential conditional steps, are what makes these terms so useful and why they are so commonly used.

most common appellation)[4] is the latest stage in the evolving relationship of archaeology and government.[5] The very term summarizes the overall approach formalized by government statutes: Cultural materials represent resources that need to be managed. The perception of cultural materials as resources, and the protocols for their management, has developed along with the growth of archaeology in the United States.

National identity plays a key role in archaeology (e.g., Fagan 1997:8; Kohl and Fawcett 1996). Archaeological remains often are seen as the remains of national ancestors as well as evidence for the presence of a people in a particular territory. Thus, archaeology in Ireland, Israel, Mexico, China, Japan, and many other countries is an exercise in historical and national identity, as well as scientific research. The emergence of cultural resources legislation in the United States, and the distribution of funding for archaeological research, is similar in its original justification and in the reasoning behind relevant laws.

Archaeology started in the United States with the idea that the people who produced the prehistoric mounds and associated artifacts east of the Rockies were culturally related to Euroamericans. Specifically, the prehistoric Mound Builders were seen by some to be the Ten Lost Tribes of Israel, mentioned in Christian and Jewish scriptures, who disappeared with the Babylonian conquest. Thus, the remains of such people would be collaterally related to the Western Intellectual Tradition and therefore worthy of documentation. Because of that possibility, there was a strong cultural interest in learning more about the Mound Builders, who many felt had been overrun and displaced by ancestors of the peoples encountered by Europeans in the fifteenth and sixteenth centuries. Although the Mound Builder Debate effectively ended with the demonstration that the

---

[4]King (1998, 2000) rightly points out that "cultural resources" includes other things besides archaeological sites and argues against using the term "CRM" alone to refer to compliance archaeology.

[5]Perhaps the best history of Americanist archaeology is Willey and Sabloff's (1993) *History of American Archaeology*. We draw on its cultural-historical framework here. Willey and Sabloff are thorough in presenting the factors that, from the perspective of our discussion here, led to modern, professional archaeology. Patterson's 1995 *Toward a Social History of Archaeology* in the United States focused on the social dynamics of the discipline in a manner similar to, but with considerably more detail than, what is presented here. It is an excellent study of how attitudes found in modern archaeology developed, especially toward compliance archaeology.

mounds were made by ancestors of American Indians (Thomas 1894), the fuse of national interest had been lit.

There have been three episodes in public, in the sense of government, involvement in archaeology in the United States. Each resulted in a fundamental change in how archaeology was done.

The first episode was the congressional mandate that the Smithsonian Institution solve the Mound Builder question (Willey and Sabloff 1993:41). The research topic of "Mound Builder Origins" had been formally introduced with the publication of Squier and Davis's *Ancient Monuments of the Mississippi Valley* in 1848. The ensuing debate over the next half-century prompted increasingly formal and precise excavation methods in response to a problem-oriented methodology.

The Mound Builder question was answered with the publication in 1894 of Cyrus Thomas's monumental study in the *Twelfth Annual Report of the Bureau of Ethnology 1890–91*. Along with the answer came a lifting of the congressional mandate on spending, with funds redirected by the Smithsonian's director to archaeological and ethnographic work in the Southwest. There also was a shift from problem-oriented archaeology to a focus on better describing what was being found.

The second major episode involving the Federal government and archaeology began in the 1930s with a series of New Deal programs. The best known of these programs was the Works Progress Administration (WPA), which existed from 1935 to 1943. The WPA was not set up to do archaeology per se, but a great deal of archaeology was done as a part of it. The importance of WPA archaeology rests not only in the massive expansion of our understanding of the nation's archaeology, but also in its impact on how archaeological work, done at the behest of the Federal government, should or should not be handled. It can be argued that the WPA experience was the central stimulus for making sure that modern archaeological research is problem-oriented, results in processed and analyzed collections, and generates a final research report.

Also part of that second episode where archaeology was done as part of a Federal program involved the Missouri River Basin Survey, which was administered through the Smithsonian Institution. The River Basin Survey, which lasted from 1945 to 1969, was a prototype of how professional archaeology now is done. How it was organized and handled was an outgrowth of what had been learned with WPA archaeology.

The third episode of government direct aid came with the National Science Foundation (NSF), which began its support of archaeological research in 1954, combined with nearly two decades of graduate student support through the National Defense Education Act of 1958 (NDEA; the NDEA supported anthropological and culture area studies along with mathematics and science education). The existence of NSF funding for faculty and doctoral research, combined with an expanding post–World War II economy and population, resulted in an enormous expansion of academic archaeology. That expansion also resulted in the cultural resources environment as well as the attitudes toward nonacademic, professional archaeology, much of which was a direct response to the archaeology that came out of the 1930s.

Initial Involvement in Cultural Resources

Aside from the Smithsonian investigation of the Mound Builders, the early role of the government in archaeology was slight. The concept that archaeological and built-environment materials are resources of importance to society emerged gradually as national attention started to focus on houses and battlefields associated with historical figures and events.

In the first major incident of public involvement, the Mount Vernon Ladies' Association of the Union purchased the remaining 550 acres of George Washington's Mount Vernon estate in 1853, including the residence, outbuildings, and tomb, for the purpose of preservation. This was socially important in that members of the upper classes had taken it upon themselves to protect what was seen as an important element in the nation's emergence and identity. The preservation of the Washington estate set a social precedent and, while not statutory, it was politically powerful (see Hosmer 1981:184–185, 525–527).

Court action prevented demolition of Independence Hall in 1876. Again, this was prompted by the social importance of preserving places where nationally important events took place, preservation that held precedence over the private interests of any one individual or small group of individuals.

A third major incident in the emergence of cultural resources legislation was the Supreme Court ruling that prevented a railroad from cutting through the Gettysburg Battlefield; this suit was brought up by veterans in 1896 [*United States v. Gettysburg Electric Railway Co.* 160 U.S. 668].

The Supreme Court approved compensated Federal appropriation of lands for the Gettysburg National Military Park. The result was that the taking of privately owned lands of national historic value could be construed as a valid application of the Federal government's powers of eminent domain.

These three incidents involved two of the ways in which the past is preserved. Buildings represent physical structures where important persons lived or events transpired. Battlefields represent areas where important events occurred, even though the traces of those events may no longer be visible or even present. The third category is areas where only the traces of past activities exist—the popular conception of "archaeological site"—and includes prehistoric archaeological sites, referred to in nineteenth- and early-twentieth-century literature as "antiquities."

Antiquities legislation emerged quite slowly, perhaps because of the cultural distance demonstrated to exist between pre-Columbian populations and the current Euroamerican-dominated population. In 1889, we see the beginnings of site-specific legislation when law was passed to protect the late prehistoric Puebloan ruin, Casa Grande, in Arizona. Concern over other threatened prehistoric sites—especially ruins—in the Southwest, as well the desire to protect Civil War battlefields, led to more encompassing legislation in the form of the Antiquities Act in 1906 (see also Rosenberg 1981, Fowler 1982).

The Antiquities Act of 1906 (34 Stat. 225) provided for the protection of historic or prehistoric remains, "or any object of antiquity," on Federal lands. Further, it established regulations and sanctions regarding disturbance of or damage to those remains, while authorizing the President to designate National Monuments on Federal lands. Conservation-minded President Theodore Roosevelt played a significant role in bringing about this legislation and ensuring significant authority for the Executive Branch. The designation of National Monuments was the first official attempt to achieve a national policy on antiquities as a class.

The next major piece of legislation, the Historic Sites Act of 1935 (49 Stat. 666), created a Federal policy encompassing historic structures, battlefields, and antiquities. It went beyond the Antiquities Act of 1906 and it foreshadowed the National Historic Preservation Act of 1966.

The Historic Sites Act was aimed at preserving objects, buildings, sites, and antiquities of "National significance" by declaring a national policy of preservation "for public use . . . inspiration and benefit of the people of the United States" [Section 1]. This followed from the Chief of the National Park Service having designated "uniqueness" as a determining characteristic of "significance" in 1934. The Act was a direct precursor of the National Historic Preservation Act (discussed in chapter 2). The Historic Sites Act dealt with historic properties as the NHPA would; it established the equivalent of the Advisory Council on Historic Preservation, with a composition similar to the present one. The major differences were affected properties and enforcement: The Act established the National Historic Landmarks program (the precursor to the National Register of Historic Places), but restricted inclusion to Federal properties. The Act also levied fines for violations.

WPA Archaeology and Its Influence on Modern Professional Archaeology

New Deal agencies and programs, such as the Civilian Conservation Corps (CCC) and the Tennessee Valley Authority (TVA), also involved archaeology, but the most extensive program that included archaeology was the Works Progress Administration. "WPA archaeology" has come to be the phrase more often used to describe the period and the associated work, both of which contributed greatly to modern, professional archaeology and the structure of the NHPA.[6] The people who would lobby and structure the archaeological preservation mandates in the 1960s either worked as part of the WPA archaeology program or were trained directly under archaeologists who had been involved in and were reacting to it (see Patterson 1995).

The WPA existed from 1935 through 1943, and it was part of President Franklin D. Roosevelt's New Deal, launched to help work the United States out of the Great Depression. The idea behind programs like the WPA was to get money back into circulation by using public funds to support labor-intensive projects in areas suffering the highest unemployment.

---

[6]See also Patterson 1995. Patterson (p.79) observed that it was "[w]ith WPA archaeology still fresh in their minds" that the Committee on the Recovery of Archaeological Remains was formed in 1944 (Johnson, Haury, and Griffin 1945). A major goal was to improve the quality of archaeological research. The Committee was instrumental in the design and structure of the Missouri Basin Surveys.

Archaeology was a labor-intensive field that could accommodate a sizeable population of unskilled labor.

WPA archaeology represented the first large-scale interaction between the Federal government as sponsor and regulator, and the academic archaeological community. It was a learning experience for both. WPA archaeology was a "make-work" program, the purpose of the program was primarily to employ people. Because of that priority, the archaeology was often perceived—from the vantage of the archaeologists involved—to be of secondary interest to the government (Wauchope 1966:vii).

WPA archaeology had a lasting impact on archaeology in the United States, especially in the Southeast, where projects were most common. The intellectual legacy was extensive and profound, including a gigantic advance in overall knowledge about the nation's prehistory in some regions, a large sample of large-area village and mound excavations, improvements in archaeological methods and techniques, the building of the basic cultural-historical sequences, and the establishment of professional networks and reputations that would last—in direct or, through students, secondary form—well into the early twenty-first century. Some archaeologists of this period, including A. V. Kidder, W. K. Morehead, and W. S. Webb, set standards for professionalism and scientific measurement that still guide modern archaeologists.

There are four aspects of WPA archaeology in particular that raised concern among archaeologists:

(1) a perception that government regulators and administrators impose inappropriate bureaucratic expectations;

(2) the occasionally slovenly work that took place under deadline conditions;

(3) excavation for the sake of excavation and not for solution of research problems; and

(4) the lack of analysis and publication.

The archaeology that emerged in the United States in the 1960s and 1970s did so very much in response to those four aspects. It is useful for appreciating why we do things now the way we do to look closer at these aspects.

Government Regulation versus Academic Independence

> Not the least of our burdens was the enormous amount of work that the government required. Much of it was meaningless: "How many artifacts excavated during the period? How many linear feet of trenches excavated . . .?" . . . it was criminally time-consuming nonsense, imposed on already harried archaeologists who urgently wanted to devote more attention to the research itself. At frequent intervals I had to submit the following reports: major purchase requisition for sponsor, balance sheet, petty cash account, report of sponsor expenditures other than payroll . . ., laboratory time sheets, field party's time sheets, mileage records for each vehicle, equipment inventories, equipment transfer sheets . . ., accident reports, equipment receiving reports, and monthly budget requests for WPA-furnished supplies. [Wauchope 1966:viii]

Excepting the Smithsonian's work in the 1800s on the Mound Builder question, the first major interaction between government-funded and -regulated archaeology and the archaeological community came in the context of WPA archaeology.[7] How that interaction was perceived, and the issues raised, can be sensed from comments made by Robert Wauchope. Wauchope was a young archaeologist at the University of Georgia when called upon to managed WPA archaeology projects. The preface to his 1966 study of north Georgia archaeology helps to demonstrate how things were viewed in the 1930s and how that experience influenced the way things are done today.

Much of WPA archaeology was seen by supervisory archaeologists like Wauchope as involving requirements that took away from time and energy better spent on archaeological research. Managing large public archaeological projects required archaeologists to learn new business skills. For example, Wauchope (quoted above) complained about basic business accounting issues: payroll, time sheets, purchases, care for employees. All of these are essential elements in any managerial situation. Patterson (1995:73) noted how these managerial problems, endemic to WPA archaeology, were associated with a lack of business experience. Many research archaeologists had little time or interest in business issues; archaeology viewed itself as an academic field.

---

[7]Just as in a previous world the term "arm-chair anthropologist" was a pejorative phrase, so too for archaeologists is the phrase "like WPA archaeology."

Such problems were not universal at the time: TVA archaeology came out of the experience quite well under the direction of W. S. Webb. However, the poor image of government expectations fueled two sets of attitudes that continue to the present day:

(1) the idea that strict statutory requirements somehow limited legitimate archaeological research and therefore should, in some cases, be ignored by concerned archaeologists; and

(2) the notion that the literature submitted to and eventually passed by government reviewers was somehow of lesser quality than that literature reviewed by academic archaeologists themselves.

It is easy to see that if one thinks the archaeological process is "watered down" by meeting extraneous demands, then perhaps the reports are suspect, too. Still today, academic archaeologists rarely recognize the research reports produced as part of the compliance archaeology process as "peer reviewed," even though the government review process is done by experienced, doctoral-level archaeologists.[8]

Quality of Work under Deadline Conditions

> This was not a fair dilemma with which to confront archaeologists. We should not have to choose between two evils: either failing to employ the needy and, incidentally, not getting archaeology done at all, or employing too many and getting it done in a slovenly way. The system bred false values. Big efficient operations became the symbols of the successful archaeological director, as some projects employed enormous laboratory staffs to process the hundreds of thousands of artifacts that poured in from several large field parties operating concurrently. [Wauchope 1966:viii]

---

[8]All compliance reports are reviewed by agency archaeologists and by state regulatory archaeologists and must meet those review conditions before the final report is produced. Further, some states and agencies send reports to outside peer reviewers. The reluctance of the academic community to accept professional reports as a legitimate part of the archaeological literature continues to be a source of resentment among practicing professionals, including those working within university-based cultural resources programs.

The second aspect of WPA archaeology that raised—and continues to raise—concern among archaeologists involved deadlines: WPA archaeology had to be done within a limited time. WPA archaeology was performed under conditions and on a schedule that was not of the principal investigator's choosing. This was very different than traditional university field work, where one had the time—and a trained or trainable crew—to do the work.

From the WPA experience came the impression that any archaeological work done under deadline pressure would not only be incomplete, it would be rushed and thus sloppy. Since modern professional archaeology is based on deadlines, this attitude has also been transferred.

Reasons for Excavation: Chosen Research Problem versus Circumstantial Research Problem

The main thing to recall is that although WPA was interested in archaeology, it was more concerned with giving employment to a great many people, and that whenever those two aims clashed it was archaeology that suffered. . . .

Perhaps even worse was the violence we knew our archaeological materials were being subjected to. When several hundred unskilled men, with sparse supervision, dug up artifacts, dropped them into boxes, passed unusual specimens around from hand to hand (and, I might add, from hand to pocket), tied them up and labeled the containers, packed them on trucks and unpacked them at headquarters, washed them, and re-boxed them—all this in what was often a spirit of light-hearted irresponsibility and incomprehension—the chances are that proveniences were garbled, if not deliberately falsified. My confidence in the system was not increased by my chief foreman's jocular tales of how, on previous WPA projects, he had often decided that the day's take in cherts at one site was not impressive enough, and he therefore sent his men, when the boss was away, to fill up their pottery bags at some richer site nearby. [Wauchope 1966:vii]

WPA archaeology presented a new situation to archaeologists: Sites were selected as much because of the local unemployment rate as they were for research potential. This required that the data from the site be wrapped around pre-existing research questions. To use an analogy: Instead of choosing which book to read, the archaeologist was having many of the books handed to him, or at least having the selection sharply limited. A lot of this appeared to be driven, and in some cases was driven, by excavation for the sake of excavation and not for the sake of scientific research. And archeologists were very concerned about that.

Professional archaeology on the surface seems to share some of these features. The site excavated is chosen by circumstances, not by the archaeologist. It looks not unlike what happened with WPA archaeology, and as a result there long has been a concern that the excavation done was more pro forma than actual research. While not true, that concern draws on a memory of WPA archaeology.

WPA archaeology also was restricted in who could be hired to do much of the work, as Wauchope's remarks indicated. The issue of training and qualifications grew in part from this, influencing current regulations on who may or may not do archaeology as part of the compliance process. As a result, the lowest level of education and training acceptable for doing archaeology on behalf of some agencies is a college degree and prior supervised field experience.

Analysis and Publication

> Having published the main factual results of the survey in journal articles, I did not feel under too great a pressure to rush the final report, and it is a good thing, for there were many materials to study, and my duties after leaving Georgia, interrupted still further by World War II, left me little time to devote to them: a few weeks out of every summer vacation, plus evenings during the school year. [Wauchope 1966:ix]

One of the lasting complaints about WPA archaeology that continues to influence modern professional archaeology is the dismal record of analysis and dissemination. Much of the excavated material never was analyzed; even less was ever written up.

There were any number of reasons for this: lack of time, lack of supplemental funding, even lack of interest. In addition, there was little incentive for those who came after to analyze those WPA data. In archaeology as in the rest of anthropology, there has always been the expectation that students generate their own data from their own field work, instead of working on someone else's. Better to excavate a new site, and do so with a better-trained crew and a detailed, chosen research problem, than to use possibly flawed data.

It is from the WPA record of poor project curation, analysis, and reporting that many of the modern professional requirements come. Archaeology done under Federal mandates requires specific curation settings, set out in Federal code. It requires that materials be analyzed. And it requires a final report that has been reviewed by state and Federal archaeologists.

Postwar Formulation of Professional Archaeology

After World War II, the pace of academic life in general and archaeological research in particular quickened. With the postwar academic and industrial expansion came massive projects, especially in the western United States. Along with those projects came increasing support for preparatory archaeological work.

Since it was the first large-scale involvement of archaeology with Federal sponsorship and requirements, WPA archaeology set the tone for such future relationships, not only in terms of successes and failures, but also in terms of specific provisions placed in future legislation and regulations. There were other, large-scale Federal exercises—TVA and the Missouri Basin Project/River Basin Survey—that survived or emerged after the 1930s programs ended. The success of these was due in part to the learning that took place during WPA archaeology, both by the academic archaeologists who provided the service and by government managers.

The Missouri Basin Project

If WPA archaeology set a tone for what to do or not do with large-scale, Federally assisted archaeological work, the Missouri Basin Project (1945 to 1969, toward the end also known as the Smithsonian's "River Basin Survey") helped establish all of the pieces that would emerge in professional archaeology at the national level. This included National Park Service coordination, the subcontracting with nongovernment archaeologists to perform the work, the formation of joint academic-government committees to draft memoranda of agreement and memoranda of understanding, the initial forays into formal legislative lobbying, and formal legislation. In a way, it represented in miniature what would happen 20 years later at the national level. It also helped pave the way for an extra-academic cultural resources industry.

The Missouri Basin Project, like WPA archaeology before it, established many professional reputations while greatly expanding knowledge of the area in which the work was done. However, it also continued to encounter the same kinds of problems that were exposed with the WPA projects: budgetary limits forcing decisions between administrative support and actual field work, reporting rates, and finding acceptance as legitimate by the academic community.

The Missouri Basin Project began in early 1945, even before World War II had ended, with the planning for the postwar development of the Missouri River as a series of reservoirs under the jurisdiction of the U.S. Army Corps of Engineers and the Bureau of Reclamation. During that planning stage, those agencies were contacted by representatives from the Society for American Archaeology, the American Anthropological Association, and the American Council of Learned Societies, with the initial coordination of those societies coming from archaeologists at the Smithsonian (Lehmer 1971:1–7). From those three academic societies would come the Committee for the Recovery of Archaeological Remains (Johnson, Haury, and Griffin 1945), which functioned essentially as an advisory and lobbying group, testifying formally before congressional committees and working informally to provide much-needed information to the public.

The National Park Service (NPS), which already had responsibility for natural and cultural resources within Federal parks (Hosmer 1981:926 *passim*), and the Smithsonian Institution were seen as the natural coordinators of any salvage archaeology that would be necessitated by the proposed reservoir project. Under a 1945 Memorandum of Understanding between the NPS and the Smithsonian Institution, the NPS would provide planning, funding, and administration, especially in dealing with non-Federal agencies actually performing archaeological work (at this time, private-sector archaeology did not exist; "non-Federal agencies" essentially meant museums, historical societies, and university Anthropology departments). For its part, the Smithsonian Institution would serve as an advisor as well as another archaeology provider. In the end, most of the actual field work was done by the Smithsonian Institution.

The Missouri Basin Project was notable for several things: professional archaeologists involved at the outset and at all levels of the organization; use of staff historians and a historical research program; and association with legislation, specifically the Antiquities Act of 1906, the Historic Sites Act of 1935, and, over the last nine years, the Reservoir Salvage Act of 1960 (74 Stat. 220).[9] The Missouri Basin Project generated an efficient site numbering system; it issued more final reports than WPA archaeology, and did so in a timely fashion. However, for archaeology in general, the reporting of results continued to be a problem until the emergence of nonacademic professional archaeology in late 1960s.

Legislation, Expansion of Government, and Academic Growth

Following World War II, three things happened that molded modern archaeology, especially professional archaeology: new legislation taking archaeological resources into account; direct Federal support of archaeological research through the National Science Foundation; and the expansion of higher education.

Important new legislation included the Federal-Aid Highway Act of 1956, which authorized a rather limited salvage archaeology in the context of highway planning and construction, and the Reservoir Salvage Act of 1960, which provided for the salvage of archaeological sites threatened by dams and reservoirs. Together, the Federal-Aid Highway Act and the Reservoir Salvage Act made provisions to recover data from archaeological sites before certain types of Federally sponsored land-alteration activities destroyed them, something now covered by National Historic Preservation Act and eventually expanded by 1974 to include all Federally enabled activities. The Reservoir Salvage Act probably covered the majority of prehistoric archaeological sites that such activities would endanger,

---

[9]Lehmer (1971:17) noted that another contribution of the Missouri Basin Project was formalization of the Plains archaeological term "feature," which was first used in 1938. A feature refers to some artificial yet nonportable aspect of a site, such as a storage pit, trash pit, hearth, structure foundation, and so on. Features are excellent signatures of site depositional integrity, one of the basic criteria for a site's eligibility for listing on the National Register.

simply because prehistoric sites in many parts of the United States often are found on relatively level land within 100 meters of streams and rivers.

One result of World War II was a "social contract" between science and the public. That contract held that, in exchange for research support, science would try to provide benefits to society. To enable research, the National Science Foundation was established in 1950. NSF underwrote everything from student training and dissertation research to research done by established faculty.

The legacy of NSF and other Federal-level funding initiatives was one of expanded research, exploration of new approaches to archaeological field work and analysis, increased training opportunities, and perhaps most important, a requirement on the part of the person doing the field work to have a well-planned and scheduled research project in place *before* going into the field. Combined with the surge in college enrollments in the 1960s (brought on by the baby boom), this resulted not only in a major expansion in higher education, but also a proportionately equal expansion of faculty.

Origins of Modern Professional Archaeology

Beginning in the middle 1960s, a second kind of archaeology, one outside of the academic/museum world, began to emerge in the United States. This came about with the passage of the National Historic Preservation Act of 1966. The NHPA required, through its Section 106, that all land-alteration activities enabled by the Federal government be preceded by a checking of the affected land to make sure that cultural resources—including archaeological sites—eligible for listing on the National Register would not be destroyed. In little more than a decade, starting in 1966 and continuing through 1979, numerous acts, amendments, and executive orders protecting cultural resources—including archaeological sites—were implemented.

The legislation of the 1960s and 1970s accompanied a period of increased national interest in social issues. That interest resulted in a surge in majors in the social sciences, especially anthropology, as well as an interest in archaeology (helped greatly by it being a subfield of anthropology), historic preservation, ecology, the environment, and similar social/environmental activist topics.

With the surge in majors and increasing interest in archaeology, combined with legislation calling for archaeology to be done, it was inevitable that archaeology would expand into the newly emerging arena of the environmental compliance industry.

Current Structure of Archaeology in the United States

Regardless of where it is practiced, anthropological archaeology is concerned with understanding how and why human cultures changed over time. Refinements in field technique, analytical procedures, or even how archaeological research questions are asked all represent means to the end of learning about the why of culture change. Recognition of the importance of the answers to questions about culture change is one of the reasons why archaeological sites in the United States are classified by the government as limited and nonrenewable resources. They are treated in Federal law in much the same way as are other environmental resources (Neumann, Sanford, and Palmer 1992).

Archaeology within the Academic World

The demographic structure and research orientation of archaeology have changed since the passage of the National Historic Preservation Act in 1966. In the middle 1960s, virtually all archaeologists in the United States were found either in universities or in museums. Now, only one out of five archaeologists in the United States work in such settings (Neumann and Sanford 2001:2, 22).

What is that university world like? Who works there?

Archaeology in the United States is a subfield of anthropology. There are around 3,800 people in the United States who make a living as anthropologists working either in universities (about 3,100) or in nongovernment museums (about 700) (Neumann and Sanford 2001:2, 22–25). Of those, something like 1,100 are archaeologists. Geographically, a little over 43 percent of all university archaeologists work outside of the United States, mostly in Mesoamerica. Of those working within the United States, about 40 percent have primary interests in the American Southwest, at least based upon the distribution of recent dissertation topics.

Topically, research interests focus on questions about how past cultures worked, as well as how our studying of those past cultures influences *our* interpretations of how they worked. Thus, issues include examining cultural idiosyncrasies like sexual differences in culturally sanctioned behavior, class structure and how that contaminates our interpretation of culture history, critical archaeology, cognitive archaeology in the sense of cosmological/ideological reconstruction, and how the social dominance hierarchies within the university dictate acceptance of scientific conclusions (see Patterson 1995, Fagan 1997; cf. Gross and Levitt 1994, Fox 1996). Some researchers spread a postmodernist interpretive framework over these interests.

Many university archaeologists no longer have much in the way of direct contact with field archaeology in the United States. Some of this is due to interest; some is due to lack of research funding (which would include institutional support of local field schools). Most of the field research done in the archaeology of the United States occurs outside of the university, either in corporate settings or in government settings.

Archaeology Outside the University

In the United States, about 80 percent of the 5,400 or so archaeologists working as such do so in industry or government (Neumann and Sanford 2001:2). Thirty percent of archaeologists work in government regulatory positions at the Federal or state level; 50 percent work in engineering or historic preservation firms. Based upon where the bulk of archaeologists work and where most of the field work is performed and articles written, archaeology in the United States can be said to be an environmental compliance, extra-academic, government-regulated field.

University and college archaeologists normally are required to have doctorates to hold faculty or research appointments. While a large number of professional archaeologists also have doctorates, there are large numbers of people with master's and bachelor's degrees employed as archaeologists, too. Indeed, not only is it true that half of all anthropologists who make a living as anthropologists are archaeologists working outside of a university setting, it is also true that professional archaeology is one of the few social sciences where a person with a bachelor's degree can get professional employment in his or her major.

We learned about archaeology from that . . . **Answering Student Questions on Employment in Archaeology**

We often receive phone calls from recent anthropology graduates who would like to work in archaeology. What, they ask, is available? Most archaeology positions are found in private industry, with some additional positions available in state or Federal agencies. These are accessible to individuals who have had field, method-and-theory, and laboratory courses, and who have an undergraduate degree. Students with a training focus in North American archaeology are especially qualified; those with exposure to how the Section 106 Process works are prized.

By the way, individuals with master's degrees in anthropological archaeology are very marketable. This is true for other fields like chemistry and biology: People with master's degrees generally will be hired before those with doctorates, more because they are seen to be better team players than because they do not expect to be paid as much. Such a hiring preference may or may not be right, but it is the way the extra-academic employment world works. It has been well documented every year since September 1990 when the "Career" segments in *Science* first started to appear.

We also remind the new graduates that private-sector firms are not in the business of training students to do archaeology: that was the responsibility of their colleges and universities.

We have also found in answering their questions that rarely have students been told what the demographic and workplace structure of the field is, much less where jobs are located and what employers expect of their new hires. One of the reasons we have included that kind of information here is to help answer those commonly asked questions.

We have not seen any figures on just what proportion of those 5,400 or so archaeologists have earned what degree, but an off-the-cuff proportion for people working in the private sector—based on firms we work with along with others listed in the American Anthropological Association's *Guide to Departments*—would be about 25 percent with doctorates, 46 percent with master's, and the balance with bachelor's degrees. The number with bachelor's degrees probably is greater, since a large number work independently, moving from project to project and therefore firm to firm.

Those with doctorates and master's will serve as project directors or principal investigators, depending on the firm. Federal code requires that a person serving as a principal investigator on a Federal Section 106 project have at least a master's degree and substantial supervisory experience. Individuals with master's degrees and gaining experience may be found working as field directors or crew chiefs, as may well-seasoned people with undergraduate degrees. We have found that nearly everyone in charge of a firm's archaeology lab is a person with a master's degree.

In the Federal workplace, roughly 30 percent of archaeologists have either a doctorate or a bachelor's, while the remaining 40 percent have master's degrees.

Better figures than these are hard to come by. For example, Zeder (1997), in a carefully prepared report on the status of archaeology in the United States, was hampered by having her figures restricted to the membership of the Society for American Archaeology (SAA). After noting that limit, Zeder went on to state that many professional archaeologists were missed in her study because they did not belong to SAA. This is particularly true for those people with bachelor's degrees who work for several different firms as part of a "project-hire" population. However, most archaeologists with master's degrees tend to belong to the regional archaeology societies/conferences rather than the national SAA. This is due as much to cost as it is to immediate professional relevance.

Most of the work that the graduating student will do as an archaeologist will be outside of an academic setting, either as a government regulator or as a private-sector archaeologist working because a client is required to satisfy preservation statutes. Although a wide assortment of sites will be experienced, including industrial-scale, monumental architecture sites in urban settings, the vast majority of sites encountered will be small, partially disturbed prehistoric or rural historic sites found as a result of the Section 106 Process. The nascent archaeologist will find the emphasis will be less on choosing a research question and digging a site to answer that question, and more on working out how a site chosen by circumstances can answer pre-existing questions.

Because of this, the practicing archaeologist is very much a general practitioner. The profession calls upon field, analytical, managerial, and theoretical skills required by the full range of possible archaeological sites. It is that variety, combined with being able to do archaeology

TIP: Where and How Positions in Archaeology Are Announced

Positions are announced in many ways. The most convenient for the student are bulletin boards in Anthropology and archaeology departments. Both national and local searches tend to be posted. Often, regional firms will send around notices of positions. Occasionally, such a notice will be in the form of a phone call made to faculty.

Anthropology News, published by the American Anthropological Association (AAA), carries national as well as regional searches. However, most position notices are for faculty positions. The Society for American Archaeology (SAA) publishes a bulletin every two months that has a few position announcements; private-sector positions not mentioned in *Anthropology News* will be here, but the academic announcements usually are duplicated. Announcements in the *SAA Bulletin* for private-sector positions tend to be dated. Both *Anthropology News* and the *SAA Bulletin* maintain Web pages that carry these notices as well (http://www.aaanet.org/careers.htm and http://www.saa.org/careers/).

Major newspapers, such as the *Washington Post*, regularly carry regional position announcements under "archaeology," "cultural resources," "engineering," and/or "environmental." Announcements can be regional or national and are usually private sector in nature. These can be accessed over the Internet.

The Internet itself is frequently used for managerial position announcements. The American Cultural Resources Association (ACRA) provides information and workshops on wages, contracting, and other aspects of consulting archaeology including listings of student and summer jobs (http://www.acra-crm.org). One need not belong to ACRA to subscribe to its list serve, ACRA-L. Archaeology jobs are also listed at http://shovelbums.org, http://www.resumegenie.com/jobs.asp?job=Archaeology, http://www.csuchico.edu/plc/conservationjobs.html, http://www.earthworks-jobs.com/, http://archaeology.miningco.com/cs/employment/, and many other sites that can be found through an Internet search query. HistArch and other listing services exist as well, along with linkages to archaeological societies and related sites. (Arizona State University has taken over maintenance of the well-known ArchNet site, which has links to state societies, field school opportunities, and other resources, and is located at http://archnet.asu.edu/archnet/.)

Announcements for Federal positions are available in the Human Resources section of each agency's Web site, as well as in the nongovernment publication *Federal Jobs Digest* (*FJD*). The NPS maintains a listing of archaeology field work opportunities on the Internet as well (http://www.cr.nps.gov/aad/fieldwk.htm).

State and local governments each have their own advertising patterns; check with the local government, state Department of Labor, or the local public library to get a sense about these. Many states also list positions on their Internet Web sites.

Finally, for those interested in working in private-sector archaeology, remember to look in the phone book: Many archaeology firms or divisions are listed in the Yellow Pages and are approachable even if they do not have a current vacancy.

full-time—along with constant opportunities to work in the field—that make private practice especially attractive.

Chapter Summary

Archaeology in the United States is now done mainly outside of university and museum settings. This work, which engages 80 percent of all people in the country who make a living in archaeology, came about as a result of the NHPA. One part of NHPA, Section 106, requires that any land-alteration activity made possible by the Federal government must be preceded by an effort to see if there is anything present that could be listed on the National Register of Historic Places.

The process that led to American archaeology shifting from an academic field to a profession did not happen all at once, nor did it start with archaeology. It began instead in the mid-nineteenth century with an increasing concern about preserving those things associated with the emergence of the United States. Eventually included in that preservation effort would be archaeological sites, including those associated with prehistoric American Indians.

That preservation effort led to a series of laws protecting the places, buildings, and objects associated with the nation's past, both historic and prehistoric. Those laws, though, applied only to property held in joint trust by the nation: that is, property held by the Federal government.

The Works Progress Administration or WPA represented the first extensive interaction between the Federal government and archaeology. Some of that interaction was good but some had problems. Much of the way in which modern archaeology is done comes from responding to the problems that appeared with WPA archaeology. Indeed, the way in which the NHPA Section 106 governing code is written can be seen as overwhelmingly influenced by that WPA experience. The government-archaeology relationship that came out of the Missouri River Basin Survey, which began in 1945 and continued into 1969, would rank just behind the WPA experience in its influence on professional archaeology. This interaction represented, in miniature, the entirety of what would come to be called the Section 106 Process.

23

After World War II, the nation's universities expanded, in part because of the baby boom, in part because of a fear of being overwhelmed scientifically by the Soviet Union, and in part because of a huge infusion of Federal funding, mainly through the National Science Foundation, for all kinds of scientific research. By the 1960s, the Federal law regarding the physical remains associated with the nation's history and prehistory had been rewritten. The National Historic Preservation Act of 1966, in its Section 106, declared simply that any time a land-alteration/-control project was made possible by the Federal government (that is, made possible by the joint action of the citizens of the United States), then the possible destruction of physical remains that might be considered important to the nation's past had to be taken into account. That is, we as citizens are enabling something to be done; we, as citizens, want to make sure that action is not going to destroy something we want to know more about first. It is our money, or permit, or piece of land; it is also our past: It is reasonable for us as citizens to expect that what is ours will be taken care of beforehand.

Although a number of other historic preservation laws have been enacted since NHPA, it is NHPA's Section 106 that is responsible for the shift in American archaeology from an academic field to a professional field. Currently around 20 percent of all American archaeologists who work as archaeologists do so within a university. In the United States, archaeology is a subfield of anthropology. The archaeology in a university setting often focuses on research outside of the United States; when involving work within the country, it is often in the Southwest. Field work is increasingly limited because research funding is limited.

The other 80 percent of American archaeologists making a living as archaeologists do so outside of a university setting, in the compliance world that emerged to satisfy the requirements of the Section 106 Process. Most of the archaeology now done in the United States is done by professional archaeologists in the myriad of private-sector firms that exist to bring those doing construction with public funds into compliance with the governing historic preservation regulations.

Additional Readings of Interest

American Anthropological Association (AAA). *Guide to Departments*. American Anthropological Association, Washington, D.C. Each year the American Anthropological Association publishes what amounts to a census summary of Anthropology. The *Guide to Departments* is, when a few volumes have been accumulated, the single most insightful source for social dynamics and trends in American anthropology. The *Guide* gives not just names, interests, and degree dates/source for all faculty, it also gives enrollment figures by department, and even lists dissertation titles for each and every doctoral dissertation in Anthropology by the listed departments. Anyone thinking of Anthropology, in its various subdisciplinary forms, as a career should obtain from his or her advisor *Guide*s from the past few years and look at trends and numbers.

Hopke, William E. 1993. *The Encyclopedia of Careers and Vocational Guidance*. Ninth edition. Ferguson Publications, Chicago. There are more recent editions. Normally, Hopke's work is available only in public libraries. Useful reference for anyone thinking of working after graduating from college, although it is spotty in its accuracy.

Kehoe, Alice Beck. 1998. *The Land of Prehistory: A Critical History of American Archaeology*. Routledge, New York. This book provides an interesting perspective on American archaeology by a respected scholar.

Larkin, Robert. 2001. *Fabjob.com Guide to Become an Archaeologist*. http://www.fabjob.com/archaeologist.htm. This electronic book is intended for high school students and others interested in careers in archaeology.

Lehmer, Donald J. 1971. *Introduction to Middle Missouri Archeology*. Anthropological Papers 1. National Park Service. U.S. Department of Interior, Government Printing Office, Washington. Primary summary for the archaeology done as part of the Missouri River Basin Survey.

Patterson, Thomas C. 1995. *Toward a Social History of Archaeology in the United States*. Harcourt Brace College Publishers, Fort Worth. A refreshingly insightful study of the social and class dynamics of academic archaeology.

Willey, Gordon R., and Jeremy A. Sabloff. 1993. *A History of American Archaeology*. Third edition. Freeman, New York. Comprehensive and readable summary of how anthropological archaeology emerged.

Zeder, Melinda A. 1997. *The American Archaeologist: A Profile*. AltaMira Press, Walnut Creek. A summary of statistics regarding the membership of the Society for American Archaeology. Although originally intended as a profile of all archaeologists working in the United States, the study focuses almost entirely upon the 20 percent of archaeologists working in academic settings then projects those figures to the field as a whole.

LAWS, REGULATIONS, AND GUIDELINES

Purpose and Objectives

Archaeological laws, regulations, and guidelines set up processes for defining what is or is not important, including various agency procedures for managing archaeological resources and accessing the information that cultural remains can provide.[1] In general, the purposes of the regulations serve to:

- set forth the criteria for assessing the relative importance of cultural remains (that is, defining *significance*);

- outline the procedures for reviewing assessments;

- delineate the responsible parties involved in making such assessments;

- identify and then define the extent of jurisdiction and responsibility of each party in the evaluation process;

- set forth the criteria for making *a determination of significance*, as well as indicating which party can or cannot make such determinations;

---

[1] For a discussion of cultural resources legislation, see King (1998). For a discussion of the Section 106 Process, see King (2000). The National Park Service (NPS; see http://www.cr.nps.gov/history/train. htm) and the ACHP both offer and sponsor through third-party vendors short courses on the Section 106 Process and its particulars. The National Preservation Institute (http://www.npi.org/sem-106rr. html) and other organizations also offer training.

- set forth the criteria for the archaeological and historic preservation work performed; and

- set forth the criteria for who can perform the archaeological and historic preservation work.

Inherent in this process are assessments for decision making. These assessments include determining what should be saved or not saved, evaluating where the responsibilities of the government agencies begin and end and where the responsibilities of the private corporation receiving the funds or permits begin and end, and determining what is expected as minimal documentation. These judgments are difficult. For example, what should be saved of an archaeological site imperiled by construction? Just how is such a decision made? Who makes it? What criteria are used?

For the entire process to work, those questions and many others have to be worked out. The trick, of course, is not to provide an answer for every situation, but instead to set up a procedure that guarantees the best-balanced answer for every situation. This is what the laws, regulations, and guidelines attempt: They describe a process and the rules for its execution. They also engage stakeholders in the process by giving them authority to participate. The process allows the involved Federal agency, in consultation with other parties, to say if a cultural resource really is important, that is, *to make a determination of eligibility* for listing on the National Register of Historic Places.

The National Register of Historic Places is a listing, maintained and updated by the National Park Service (NPS), of archaeological sites, buildings, and other what are termed "properties" that are seen to be extremely important based upon their association with past people or events, their design, or their scientific-data potential. The National Register was originally set up as a kind of planning document. Having a master list available of important archaeological sites or buildings would then help Federal agencies in planning construction projects or permitting, and that list could be checked well in advance of any action that might damage what the country might like to preserve. Although the Register is maintained at the national level, most of what is listed on it is important only at the state or local level.

It is the *eligibility* for listing on the National Register that serves as the governing criteria in cultural resources work generally and compliance archaeology specifically. This is because even if a property is only considered eligible for such listing—even if it has not been formally listed or even nominated—it is to be treated as if it actually is so listed. Federal code spells out the criteria that must be met to be eligible for listing on the National Register. Much of the archaeological work at the Phase I and Phase II stages involves dealing with the issue of Register eligibility.

One other point here before getting into details: Note that the entire compliance process comes into play only if public funds, permits, or lands are involved in some sort of land-alteration/property-alteration activity. For example, the Federal Section 106 Process will be activated only if the project is made possible by some kind of Federal involvement, be it Federal funding, permitting, or land. If those conditions are not present, then the Section 106 Process does not apply. The same holds at the state or the local level, always assuming that the state or local government have some kind of historic preservation system that works like the Federal Section 106 Process. Unless there are local statutes in place saying otherwise, privately funding construction activity on private land does not automatically mean that archaeological sites are protected. Or phrased another way: The presence of an archaeological site, or a historically important building, does not automatically mean that a construction project or similar land disruption activity will stop.

The Section 106 Process

Several inter-related Federal statutes, along with an assortment of counterpart legislation at the state and local levels, regulate different aspects of archaeology and its performance in the United States. The most important of these is the National Historic Preservation Act of 1966 (NHPA), as amended. It was Section 106, a single paragraph in the NHPA, that made it possible for archaeology to become a compliance industry.

Section 106 of the NHPA in effect requires that a Federal agency that enables—through funding, or a permit, or just access to Federal land—some kind of activity must first take into account the effect that that activity will have on anything present that could be listed on the National Register of Historic Places. The procedure that emerged to deal with this requirement is called "The Section 106 Process," and it applies only to Federally enabled projects.

All of this is done to make sure that cultural remains that the society would like to preserve—or at least document—are not inadvertently lost. Reinforcing that societal interest, the Process involves the public along with aboriginal cultures having a special interest or stake in those cultural remains. And it was that requirement to make sure that properties eligible for the National Register would not be lost that established archaeology as an extra-academic profession in the United States. NHPA serves, to a certain degree, to unify the previous statutes and legislation concerning historic preservation. Of importance to us here, the NHPA

- required that all Federal agencies check to see if actions enabled by their agency would *potentially* threaten properties, including archaeological sites, that could be listed on the National Register of Historic Places;

- required that each governor appoint a State Historic Preservation Officer, who would develop state preservation plans and coordinate historic preservation activities in the particular state or territory;

- established the Advisory Council on Historic Preservation (ACHP or "Council"), which would advise the President and Congress, and on occasion serve an active role in the 106 Process; and

- required each Federal agency to establish procedures for identifying, inventorying, and evaluating the Register eligibility of historic properties.

The Concept of "Significance"

"Significance" is a key concept in the application of Federal law to cultural resource assessments. In the Section 106 Process, "significance" connotes being eligible for listing on the National Register of Historic Places. In 36 CFR 60.4, "the quality of significance" means having "integrity" while also being associated with events, people, or information considered "important." More broadly and in somewhat looser usage, "significance" has come to mean being eligible for listing on the National Register, since a cultural resource eligible for such listing has the "quality of significance."

Category of Property: How Cultural Resources Are Grouped

There are five categories of properties or cultural resources used in determining eligibility for the National Register (*National Register Bulletin #16: Guidelines for Completing National Register of Historic Places Forms*, pp. 41–42): Object, Site, Building, Structure, and District.

Objects are things like monuments, mileposts, statues, fountains, and similar location-specific items whose significance is related both to where they were placed and the purpose they served. Generally, relocated objects, because they have been moved, lose any Register eligibility. However, this would not apply to the objects that are by nature mobile (e.g., vessels like the *Delta Queen*, which is listed on the National Register).

Sites represent locations of significant events, prehistoric or historic occupations or activities, buildings, or structures. The buildings or structures can still be in place, or in ruins, or can survive only as archaeological traces.

Sites can range from the standard archaeological site, inclusive of burial mounds and structure ruins, through battlefields, to rock carvings, petroglyphs, and even locations where historically significant events occurred. Archaeologists (except maybe in the Southwest) tend to think in terms of subsurface remains. The procedural definition of "site" for Section 106 purposes is broader.

Buildings refer to structures that shelter human activities: houses, barns, outhouses, businesses, churches, and similar structures. A "compound" (like a farm compound or a parish compound) is considered to be a "building," provided all structures are essentially unchanged and part of the original group that functioned as a unit. Otherwise, the complex of structures, some of which may be intact and some of which may be absent or substantially altered, are considered a "district," with "contributing elements" (that is, essential parts of the overall district) or "noncontributing elements" (extraneous elements physically present).

Structures refer to elements of the built environment that do not include "buildings." A bridge would be a structure, as would a highway, a railroad tunnel, a Civil War breastwork, an aqueduct, a subway, or a canal, among others.

Districts refer to a collection of "buildings, sites, structures," or even "objects" that all have a unifying theme. These all are concentrated in space and have a continuity in terms of time, aesthetics/style, historical association, or other unifying theme.

Districts may be continuous or discontinuous. In a continuous historic district, everything within the geographic boundaries of the proposed district falls under a unifying principle, such as historic association or architectural style. Discontinuous districts refer to situations where many of the buildings and structures that made up a unified whole still remain, but interspersed are elements that do not belong with that set, such as buildings or other intrusive elements built later or in a style inconsistent with the unifying theme.

Category of Property: How Cultural Resources Are Grouped *(Continued)*

For example, the Oxford Historic District in Oxford, Georgia, is a discontinuous historic district (Figure 2.1). It consists of eight structures, one monument, and a Civil War cemetery located on the campus of Emory University's Oxford College, along with eight residences, the Old Church, a community cemetery, and the Yarbrough Oak, all spread over an area about a mile and a half north to south and a half mile east to west. The structures and buildings are associated with the founding of the Emory College community in the 1830s and 1840s. The church is allowed because of its architecture and because it was a contributing element in the overall community. The community cemetery was part of the original town plan, and also a contributing element.

Figure 2.1. Monument Plaque Describing Oxford, Georgia, Historic District. The area has served as the setting in recent years for movies and television series.

However, there are several buildings and objects located within that 0.75-square-mile area that are not part of the District: the newer campus buildings, for example, or the post–World War II residences. These would be "intrusive elements."

Sites, especially subsurface remains, within the bounds of a district are considered to be a part of the district unless specially *excluded*. This holds even if the sites are currently unknown. This automatic inclusion of subsurface remains as part of the district is important to remember and is one of the reasons for conversing with the SHPO and ACHP in dealing with districts.

The criteria for listing on the National Register of Historic places are listed in 36 CFR 60.4 *criteria for evaluation* [a–d] and *criteria considerations* [a–g]. The 36 CFR 60.4 *criteria for evaluation* [a–d] states that "the quality of significance . . . is present" if a property "has integrity" and also satisfies one of the following:

(a) association with events that have made a significant contribution to the broad patterns of our history; or

(b) association with the lives of persons significant in our past; or

(c) embodiment of distinctive characteristics of a type, period, or method of construction, or represent the work of a master, or that possess high artistic values, or that represent a significant and distinguishable entity whose components may lack individual distinction; or

(d) having yielded, or likely to yield, information important in prehistory or history. [Usually the major reason for prehistoric archaeological sites to qualify.]

"Integrity" is a complex concept linked to significance and the condition of the site (see box; for detailed consideration, see also Neumann and Sanford 2001:34–35). Broadly, it means remaining as physically true as possible to the reasons why (36 CFR 60.4 [a–d]) the property is eligible for listing on the National Register. It also means that the site, structure, or whatever is undisturbed or unaltered relative to currently known examples. For example, a plowed Mississippian site probably would not have sufficient integrity for listing on the National Register, since there are a large number of less disturbed Mississippian sites already known and excavated. However, a plowed Paleoindian site in the eastern United States may well be seen as having sufficient integrity to retain its significance, since examples of such sites, plowed or not, are not common (see also National Park Service 1995a, 1995b).

The 36 CFR 60.4 *criteria considerations* sets forth criteria for what can and cannot be listed. For example, a church as a religious property normally cannot be listed, nor can a cemetery. But such may be eligible if they

Integrity

For a property to be eligible for listing on the National Register, it must have integrity as well as satisfy the criteria of significance listed in 36 CFR 60.4 [a–d]. 36 CFR 60.4 lists seven aspects of integrity: location, design, setting, materials, workmanship, feeling, and association. The best definitions for these are given in the National Park Service's (1995) *How to Apply the National Register Criteria*, which are paraphrased below.

Integrity of location refers to the particular place where an event happened, a building was built, or an object was placed. Archaeologists would think of the term "context" here, and their term would not be too different from how the location functions as an aspect of integrity. When we discussed objects as a type of historic property, and what rendered them potentially eligible for listing on the National Register, it was integrity of location that was most important.

Integrity of design has to do with how true the building, structure, or element is to the original way in which it was conceived then produced.

Integrity of setting involves the match between present conditions and the original *character* of the place. Thus, topography, vegetation, relationships among other features natural or artificial all have to do with setting. Setting is considered particularly important for historic districts and when structures like flood walls or levees are built.

Integrity of materials refers to the match between materials on the property or structure now and the original building materials, or the original deposit materials.

Integrity of feeling involves the ability of the property to capture a sense of period or aesthetics (including things related to historical figures, events, craftsmen, or even potential data) under the criteria of Register eligibility, even if this sense is unrelated to the property's origins. Thus, Eisenhower's house in south-central Pennsylvania may be extensively remodeled from the eighteenth-century farmhouse, but it retains its sense of feeling for the 1950s and the 1960s, which was the period during which the President was associated with it.

Integrity of association holds if "the place where the event or activity occurred . . . is sufficiently intact to convey that relationship to the observer." "Sufficiently intact" becomes subject to documentation, since the verb "convey" implies a lack of objective criteria.

Neither feeling nor association are sufficient by themselves to support eligibility for listing on the National Register.

Integrity and Archaeological Sites

The potential of an archaeological site to yield information important in history or prehistory is the most commonly cited reason for assigning "significance" (36 CFR 60.4). This means that the archaeological deposits must be conducive for yielding such information.

The archaeologist faces two issues. The first is the site's capacity to address research questions. Under ideal conditions, could the site yield information that is important in addressing research questions? There are many ways to determine this, including a review of literature, exploration of where research questions stand relative to the nature of the archaeological site encountered, and examination of the State Historic Preservation Plan (a comprehensive planning document required under NHPA).

The second issue concerns integrity: How intact is the deposit relative to its information potential? An archaeological site represents a three-dimensional information storage matrix. Its capacity to address research questions depends in large measure on how intact—how uncorrupted, to use the computer engineering term—that memory storage system is. This involves, in archaeological parlance, context and association. *Context* is where things were last deposited or left relative to the behavior that caused their leaving; *association* has to do with whether things are found with the other things they were dropped with. For archaeological sites, it is the *context* in which things are found combined with the *associations* among those things that enable questions about the past to be answered. In short, does the stuff belong together or not?

Archaeologists are more concerned with the *patterns* in physical remains than in the remains themselves. Artifacts that are "out of context" normally are so compromised in their ability to yield information that the archaeologist will consider them worthless scientifically. Thus, looting, erosion and other site disturbances can destroy the context and association so vital to information retrieval from a site, rendering the artifacts recovered virtually worthless scientifically. The artifacts lack context and association. For the archaeological site, this means that it lacks integrity.

For archaeological sites, especially those being considered under 36 CFR 60.4 [d], evaluation of integrity will involve location (e.g., stratigraphic context), association (e.g., being able to be dated to, that is associated with, a particular period or culture), material (e.g., preservation of organic artifacts), and design (e.g., a tool kit that remains essentially intact). (See ACHP 1991; NPS 1995a; Parker and King 1995; King 2000.)

have "distinctive characteristics of a type." Properties "that have achieved significance within the past 50 years" are also excluded unless "of exceptional importance" (see 36 CFR Part 65, NHPA Section 110 [f], and 36 CFR 800.10).

If something is eligible for listing or actually is listed on the National Register, it is not automatically protected. In fact, it can still be destroyed. However, an opportunity to collect sufficient information about the structure or site must be made, such that its continued existence is largely redundant, before it is destroyed.[2] Further, such a site may have religious or cultural value that becomes damaged through loss of the site.

The Section 106 Process, and procedures similar to it, were never intended to stop construction or development. Rather, they are meant to provide enough of a pause where cultural resources can be assessed and, if found to be of interest to society at large, recorded in sufficient detail for posterity *before* being compromised. The National Register of Historic Places is specifically intended to serve as a planning document, alerting Federal agencies to the existence of historic properties that may come under their jurisdiction.

The Parties in the Section 106 Process

In addition to the Federal agency enabling the undertaking, the Section 106 Process [36 CFR 800.2 (c)] identifies six sets of "consulting parties" who must be included by the Federal agency in the Section 106 Process. Consulting parties include the State Historic Preservation Officer (SHPO); the Tribal Historic Preservation Officer (THPO) if tribal lands are affected; any Indian tribe or Native Hawai'ian organization that attaches religious or ceremonial importance to a Register-eligible property affected by the undertaking; the local government within whose jurisdiction the undertaking will occur; the applicant for Federal funding or permit that may be setting off the undertaking; and any others with demonstrated legal or economic interest.

Of those, the most important usually will be the SHPO (pronounced "ship-oh"). The SHPO, as much a regulatory office as an officially designated individual, is responsible for implementing national historic preservation programs at the state level. This includes reviewing and keeping a list of Register-eligible properties at the state level. The SHPO in most states actually serves as the apologist for the state's cultural resources. The SHPO will review the reports and recommendations submitted by the practicing archaeologist to the Federal agency with an eye toward what is

---

[2]We use the term "redundant" in the sense of physical existence/information content. We recognize that such a term leaves out certain values of a site, such as importance to descendent cultural communities. The archaeological inventory or investigation must deal with many aspects of value, significance, and integrity to give insight into a decision on redundancy.

TIP: Working with Indian Tribes

As of June 2000, the U.S. Congress had recognized 562 Indian tribes, each with its own treaty with the U.S. government. Consequently, there may be quite a variety of land-use regulation and jurisdictional authority on tribal lands. For example, some tribes have autonomy over their resources and employ a comprehensive set of land-use regulations. Other tribes defer most of the regulatory authority to state or Federal agencies. Thus, planning for any project on Indian land requires careful checking; it also benefits from the cultivation of long-term relationships.

Some tribes do not have Federal recognition but do have state recognition. The environmental protection agencies at the state level may therefore have special agreements with these tribes. Primarily in the West, one finds Tribal Environmental Protection Acts at the state level, based on a Federal initiative.

Indian tribes may participate in the Section 106 Process through the Tribal Historic Preservation Officer, but they may also be involved through tribal councils and other groups. Further, tribal political leaders may have very different agendas than do tribal spiritual leaders. Thus, it is necessary to consider the various constituents and entities within a particular tribe, in addition to the specific regulations governing the tribal lands.

in the best interests of protecting the cultural resources of the state. The SHPO will do the same thing at the state level or even the local level, depending upon how the laws in the given state work. The THPO serves in an analogous role on tribal lands.

It should be noted that the regulations that went into effect in 1999 (and revised by rule on January 11, 2001) make considerable allowance for the input of consulting parties. The Federal agency is charged with involving those parties in the Section 106 Process. However, as with the pre-1999 Section 106 Process, in most cases only two parties—the Federal agency along with one consulting party: The SHPO/THPO—have any real authority in deciding whether or not something is going to be done. This is reflected in the later stages of the Process, where the agency and the SHPO/THPO, or the ACHP as a substitute for one of those, are the only parties allowed to sign off on plans to resolve any adverse effects.

Given the relatively recent (1999 and 2001) changes to the Section 106 regulations contained in 36 CFR Part 800, in which public participation of various cultural groups is encouraged, the increased role of consultations, and the greater accountability of the overall evaluative exercise, the practicing archaeologist should pay close attention to who is a consulting party. It is essential to be aware of the local public's possible involvement in the Section 106 Process. This is especially true in situations where the local government is a consulting party in the Process. In most situations, the archaeologist will be dealing with at least the Federal agency along with the SHPO/THPO and one or two other consulting parties.

The ACHP can enter the process in a couple ways. For example, if the Federal agency and the SHPO/THPO disagree and cannot resolve the disagreement, the ACHP casts the deciding vote. If one of the consulting parties, especially a tribal or native group, disagrees with the agency finding, then they can request the ACHP to step in. Historically, around 3 percent of Section 106 cases have required ACHP review in a given year. Otherwise, the ACHP is a passive party that monitors overall policy. The Keeper of the National Register deals with disputes about actual nominations to the National Register.

Steps along the Way: The Process

36 CFR 800.3–800.5 sets out the following steps for the Section 106 Process (see Figure 2.2.):

1. The agency first needs to determine if there is an undertaking and, if so, if there is any chance it could affect historic properties. If there is no such chance, the Process ends here.

2. If the undertaking has potential to cause effects, then the agency needs to:
   a. identify the appropriate SHPO/THPO and other consulting parties;
   b. develop a plan to involve the public;
   c. review existing information on historic properties [properties eligible for National Register listing] potentially

Revised Section 106 Process and NEPA

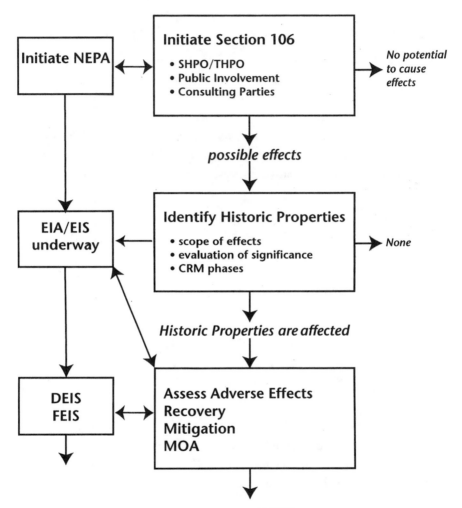

Figure 2.2. Revised Section 106 Process and NEPA.

affected by the undertaking, as well as the likelihood of encountering unknown properties; and

d. consult with the SHPO/THPO on other background information that may be needed.

3. Next, the agency develops the scope of identification efforts needed, which includes identifying the area of potential effects. Indian tribes or Native Hawai'ian organizations are to be contacted about possible properties of "religious or cultural significance," even if those are located off of tribal or native lands.

4. If at this point it seems a good idea to physically check the project area, then the Federal agency in consultation with the SHPO/THPO will "make a reasonable and good faith effort to carry out appropriate identification efforts" to locate historic properties within the area of potential effect [36 CFR 800.4 (b)(1)]. For the practicing archaeologist, this would be part of the Phase I identification process.[3]

5. If cultural resources are identified in Step 4, those properties are to be evaluated by the Federal agency in consultation with the SHPO/THPO, along with any Indian tribe or Native Hawai'ian organization that attaches religious or cultural significance to the resource, to see if they are eligible for listing on the National Register. This corresponds to an archaeological Phase II investigation.

6. If no cultural resources were identified during Step 4, or if the cultural resources identified were not considered eligible for listing on the National Register in Step 5, documentation of those results are given to the SHPO/THPO. The SHPO/THPO has the opportunity to agree or disagree.

7. If cultural resources eligible for listing on the National Register (that is, "historic properties" in Federal terminology) were identified during Step 5, then the effects of the undertaking on the properties will be determined (that is, the Criteria of

---

[3]There are three levels of field investigations, discussed in chapters 4, 5, and 6. For the eastern and most of the midwestern United States, "Phase" terminology is used. In the western United States and in some parts of the Midwest, descriptive terms like "inventory," "survey," "identification," "reconnaissance and intensive survey," "testing," or "evaluation" drawn from the Secretary of the Interior's Guidelines, are used.

Adverse Effect [36 CFR 800.5 (a)] will be applied). The regulations provide procedures to help resolve differences in interpretation between the agency, the SHPO/THPO and other consulting parties [36 CFR 800.6].

There is a critically important point here. The lead agency will make a determination: "Evaluation is completed with a written determination that a property is or is not significant based on provided information" *Federal Register* 48 (190):44724. It is the agency (and *not* the practicing archaeologist working on behalf of the lead agency) that makes a determination. The lead agency will submit a report and conclusions to the SHPO/THPO. The report contains sufficient information for the SHPO/THPO reviewer to assess independently whether the cultural resource does or does not satisfy criteria for listing on the National Register (see also *We learned about archaeology from that* . . . The Transco Incident).

For the practicing archaeologist, one outcome from Step 7 may be a determination that the only way to avoid the adverse effect on the archaeological site is to recover sufficient data from the site to render its physical existence redundant. Avoidance of cultural resources is preferred but it is not always practical. In the context and wording of the statutes, full-scale archaeological excavation of a National Register-eligible site is seen as one way to avoid or mitigate an adverse effect. This would be Phase III data recovery or mitigation.

(Ironically, the archaeological excavation of a site is considered in Federal guidelines to also be an "adverse effect." This underscores not only that any archaeological excavation really is controlled destruction, but also how full-scale data recovery is to be considered only as a final alternative. The irony then is that such archaeological work becomes an adverse effect that offsets another adverse effect.)

The Section 106 Process contains a series of checks and balances. If the archaeologist does inadequate work, this will likely be caught by agency or SHPO/THPO reviewers when the submitted report is examined. If there are disagreements about the determination of adverse effects, the ACHP may be invited to join the consultation upon proper notification [36 CFR 800.5(c) and 800.6(a)(1)]. Even if an agency is tempted to ignore or undervalue the importance of the cultural resources

We learned about archaeology from that . . . The Transco Incident

The "Transco Incident" refers to a $35.5 million settlement reached between the Federal Energy Regulatory Commission (FERC) and the Transco Energy Company (Transco) for cultural resources and pricing violations. Failure to execute the procedures in proper order, regardless of good faith, can result in enormous penalties.

In the late 1980s, Transco, a gas pipeline firm based in Houston, sought permits from the FERC to build a natural gas pipeline from Tampa to Texas. The corridor project was a Federal undertaking subject to Section 106 requirements. FERC, the lead agency, required Transco to see that the actual Section 106 work was done.

Transco contracted an archaeology firm to conduct an assessment on a corridor that went through five states: Florida, Alabama, Mississippi, Louisiana, and Texas. Each state's SHPO reviewed the cultural resources investigation of the proposed pipeline corridor (area of potential effects) through its jurisdiction.

The archaeology firm made determinations of eligibility without consulting with the Alabama SHPO (or with FERC archaeologists). Having made its own determinations, it structured a Phase II program, and again made its decisions. Next, it conducted Phase III studies on some sites, all without consulting with the Alabama SHPO. The firm had flagrantly exceeded its authority. The Alabama SHPO, as defender of the state's cultural resources, filed suit against FERC for failure to comply with NHPA Section 106. FERC turned around and charged Transco with noncompliance with the NHPA.

On May 29, 1991, FERC approved a $35.5 million settlement between Transco and the FERC enforcement section of its Office of General Council. The settlement found that Transco began construction of the pipeline before properly completing National Register eligibility surveys, and that 48 of the 77 Register-eligible sites were lost as a result (Rogers 1991:37).

Of the final settlement, $10 million represented fines associated with marketing and pricing violations unrelated to the historic preservation issues. Another $12 million represented civil penalties ($11 million) and investigation fees associated with the NHPA violations ($1 million). The remaining $13.5 million was paid to Alabama for "remediation and future environmental and cultural resource research and protection" (Rogers 1991:37).

There are several lessons here, but the basic one is this: Professional, Section 106, archaeology is a no-nonsense world. Mistakes, even procedural errors, carry serious consequences. (See Rogers 1991; *New York Times* 31 May 1991.)

in a project area, the SHPO/THPO has intimate knowledge of cultural-historical patterns within the state, and normally will catch such an irregularity. In some states, the SHPO intentionally maintains an adversarial relationship with agencies in order to better execute its role as an apologist for the state's cultural resources.

Additional Factors and Agency Regulations

There are a series of controls on the Section 106 Process to handle individual situations (see also ACHP, 1991, *Treatment of Archeological Properties: A Handbook*). Agencies have developed specific management guidelines and policies to implement Section 106. The 106 regulations themselves contain review and notification deadlines designed to help keep the process moving along. For example, a SHPO/THPO (or the Council if it has entered the process) has 30 days to object to a determination that there are no historic properties or that no adverse effects on historic properties will occur [36 CFR 800.4(d)(1)].

The qualifications of archaeologists are stipulated in 36 CFR 61 and in The Secretary of the Interior's Guidelines [48 FR 44738–44739]. Under some Federal contracts, field workers must have a BA or BS in anthropological archaeology or closely related field. However, Section 106 projects must be led by a principal investigator ("professional archaeologist") who possesses at least an MA or MS in anthropological archaeology or closely related field in addition to significant amounts of supervised field training and experience in North American archaeology.

The expectations, guidelines, and requirements for archaeological field work and reporting are outlined in *Archeology and Historic Preservation; Secretary of the Interior's Standards and Guidelines* [48 FR 44716–44742] and in the Advisory Council on Historic Preservation *Manual of Mitigation Measures (MOMM)*, as well as other documents.

Curatorial standards for Federal archaeological collections are set out in 36 CFR Part 79. These arose from concern over the need to provide continuing professional-quality curation of materials recovered during Federally sponsored projects (see especially Trimble and Meyers 1991).

In essence, the statutes and guidelines for reporting of archaeological data should lead to archaeological documents that would allow someone

Professional Certification

Archaeology is at an interesting point in its development as a field in the United States. Historically an academic and museum field, it has become an "extra-academic," practiced profession. This raises questions of credentialing and certification.

Most fields that involve a commitment of public resources or public well-being to an individual's professional judgment are licensed. Thus, engineers, architects, geologists, nurses, physicians, accountants, land surveyors, beauticians, lawyers, and so on are required by different states to obtain a license.

Archaeology is not a credentialed, certified field. At least not yet. However, the qualifications of archaeologists to do Federally reviewed archaeology are stipulated in 36 CFR 61 and in The Secretary of the Interior's Guidelines [48 FR 44738–44739]. Many states use Federal criteria of qualifications, which equates to eligibility in RPA (Register of Professional Archaeologists, see http://www.rpanet.org), to help potential clients determine if an archaeologist is competent to do professional work. Proto-certification programs have emerged in different states, requiring archaeologists to demonstrate past experience in order to get on a list of archaeologists deemed qualified by the SHPO. The intent is to make sure that the professional archaeologist is familiar with the state's archaeology and therefore is responsive to the needs of the resource.

entirely unfamiliar with the culture history and environment of the project area to make sense of the work that was done. Further, this person should, given the material recovered and the field records (including both notes and photographs), be able to pick up where the original investigator left off, even two centuries from now.

Additional Regulations and Requirements

The Section 106 Process and the National Environmental Policy Act

Nonarchaeologists often confuse the cultural resources work expected under NHPA with requirements that come from the National Environmental Policy Act. This confusion sometimes is even found in more advanced archaeology textbooks, where what is the Section 106 Process is thought to be a part of a larger effort to do Environmental Impact Statements (EISs). Some clarification is in order.

The National Environmental Policy Act of 1969 (NEPA) declares a national policy to protect the environment through evaluating proposed

Federally enabled actions. The environment is defined to include both natural and cultural resources, giving a valid role for aesthetic considerations in evaluating the quality of the environment (e.g., visual resources, settings). NEPA is administered by the Council on Environmental Quality (CEQ), which the Act established. The implementing regulations for NEPA were issued in response to Executive Order 11991 by the CEQ in 1978 as 40 CFR parts 1500–1508, and were binding as of 30 July 1979. The procedures for implementing NEPA relative to NHPA are contained in 36 CFR part 805.

NEPA regulations include guidelines for conducting Environmental Assessments (EA) and preparation of EISs. Essentially, NEPA sets out a process by which potential impacts of a project are subject to public scrutiny. It added fairly comprehensive environmental accountability to the mission of every agency. NEPA complimented the NHPA through encouragement of impact assessment and evaluation of archaeological sites that may have local or regional importance even if there is no direct national significance (Rosenberg 1981:768).

Early EISs often assumed that satisfying NEPA requirements would also satisfy NHPA Section 106 requirements. However, all that a NEPA EIS required was identifying previously known sites within the impact area (Scovill, Gordon, and Anderson 1977:43), a requirement a lot less thorough and rigorous than making a good-faith effort to see if Register-eligible properties were present in a broader area of potential effects, regardless of if they were already known or not. However, there was also a concern that both statutes—NHPA and NEPA—required what we could call cultural resources to be documented and taken into account before a given land-alteration project continued. NHPA had—and has—statutory precedence over NEPA, meaning that its requirements, as set forth in 36 CFR 800, must be satisfied regardless of what happens with NEPA compliance. However, the reality is that one event—a firm's given project—will need to take into account two laws and their codes. The question is how to work this out so all parties come out ahead.

In 1992, amendments to NHPA modified the Section 106 Process so that cultural resources work done under NEPA would mesh better with Section 106 requirements. However, those changes were not entirely effective in smoothing the interplay between satisfaction of Section 106 requirements and the work done as part of NEPA. In 1999 and 2001, the

ACHP revised the Section 106 regulations—36 CFR 800—yet again. While most of the changes involved how consulting parties work within the Process, an important part of the revision clarified NEPA coordination relative to Section 106 requirements. These changes allow satisfaction of historic preservation requirements under NEPA to also meet an agency's obligations for compliance with Section 106, provided the NEPA cultural resources work would satisfy the more rigorous documentation and survey requirements expected for any project that would come under Section 106 jurisdiction.

Set forth in 36 CFR 800.8, the revised code does allow the cultural resources aspect of a NEPA EA or EIS to be substituted for Section 106 documentation, but only if it is done in a manner identical to the Section 106 Process [36 CFR 800.8 (c)(1) and (2)]. Thus, an EA or an EIS can substitute for the specific *steps* of the 106 process, but the process itself cannot be compromised. For example, under NEPA, an agency can designate a list of "categorical exclusions," actions that do not need to go through the NEPA EA/EIS process, but these actions are not automatically exempt from Section 106 and will get reviewed like any other undertaking [36 CFR 800.8(b)].

NEPA has led to a large amount of archaeological work on private property. NEPA has also inspired numerous states to create so-called little NEPAs. Many states ended up using NEPA legislation as a model for handling cultural resources, and the "cultural resources code," as it were, is embedded within the little NEPAs.

Other Legislation, Regulations, and Guidelines

In law, legislation provides authority, regulations set required procedure, and guidelines give the advice and guidance needed to accomplish the intent of the legislation on a day-to-day basis.

With the exception of the legislation aimed directly at American Indian concerns, much Federal historic preservation legislation deals with specific cases that might also be covered under Section 106 of the NHPA. This is recognized in several places within 36 CFR 800 where Federal agencies are urged to coordinate their activities so that the requirements of NHPA's Section 106 and those of the other statutes are not needlessly duplicated. Some of the more important of these acts are listed in Table 2.1.

Table 2.1. Some Other Federal Legislation Governing Historic Preservation and Cultural Resources Archaeology

The Federal-Aid Highway Act of 1968* Section 4(f) requires Secretary of Transportation to take into account the historic significance of sites or public lands affected by a proposed project and includes exploring all feasible and prudent alternatives to highway design and other transportation projects that would otherwise adversely affect those cultural resources.

Coastal Zone Management Act of 1972 (CZMA) Important to protect and manage coastal areas as natural and economic resources, including their aesthetic qualities such as scenic, cultural, and historic values. Evaluate coastal archaeological sites.

Housing and Community Development Act of 1974 Department of Housing and Urban Development may delegate its Section 106 responsibilities to the local government receiving the Community Development Block Grant [36 CFR 800.12(c)].

Archaeological and Historic Preservation Act of 1974 (AHPA)** Requires proper planning and surveying to avoid the loss of archaeological data. Authorizes spending Federal funds up to 1 percent of the overall budget to recover data from sites facing destruction and to conduct surveys in threatened areas.

American Indian Religious Freedom Act of 1978 Federal agencies must preserve religious rights of American Indians with respect to religiously/ceremonially important sites and objects. Provides structure for involvement of American Indians in cultural resources matters—key to complying with Native American Graves Protection and Repatriation Act of 1990.

Archeological Resources Protection Act of 1979 Tennessee Valley Authority, Department of Interior, Department of Agriculture, and Department of Defense required to issue uniform regulations regarding treatment of archaeological resources on Federal and Indian lands, primarily in terms of permitting, ownership, and penalties. The regulations are repeated in the Code of Federal Regulations with a different title for each of the four agencies.

Abandoned Shipwreck Act of 1987 Allows recovery of shipwrecks and underwater sites consistent with the protection of the historical values and environmental integrity. Encourages states to manage underwater cultural resources (e.g., create underwater historic districts and parks).

Native American Graves Protection and Repatriation Act of 1990 (NAGPRA) Improved protection of American Indian graves and cultural materials on Federal and tribal land. Also led to return of funerary and other sacred items from Federal and Federally funded institutions to American Indian groups culturally affiliated with the human remains or artifacts. Affects treatment and disposition of burials and funerary objects encountered through archaeological assessments on tribal and Federal land in compliance with NHPA Section 106 (see box NAGPRA and Cultural Perspectives).

*Section 4(f) analyses, usually carried out in conjunction with NEPA, "are a major preoccupation of DOT agencies" (King 2000:11).

**Originally known as the Moss-Bennett Act. If an agency encounters archaeological resources after a project has been started, it can follow the AHPA and its regulations instead of the Section 106 Process [36 CFR 800.13 (b)(2)].

Nine sets of Federal regulations govern most of the implementation of cultural resources legislation (see King 1998 for details). These detail such things as applying National Register criteria, implementing the procedures required to satisfy NHPA's Section 106, and curating archaeological collections produced as a result of Federally enabled projects. Table 2.2 lists these regulations, with which professional archaeologists particularly—both in government and private practice—need to be familiar.

NAGPRA and Cultural Perspectives

The Native American Graves Protection and Repatriation Act of 1990 (NAGPRA) allows Indian tribes to take back or claim human remains and associated funerary, as well as ritual objects, and to dispose of them in a manner consistent with their culture's current values. When NAGPRA was first seriously considered, many archaeologists were concerned about loss of scientific information. While much concern still exists, it is important to place NAGPRA in a comparative cultural context.

Americans use what is called the Eskimo kinship system for reckoning relationships and applying terms to classify relatives (e.g., Mother, Uncle, Cousin, Sister, Nephew). Generational distance is recognized by adding the term "great" or "grand" to separate generations, such as great-aunt, grandson, great-great-grandfather. The English language measures time with connotations of distance and familiarity. Old things are far away and unfamiliar. Consequently, for an English speaker, someone who died generations ago has been dead a long time; they are "long gone." The language and the kinship terms result in a feeling of distance and lack of immediate relationship in a day-to-day sense.

People think in their languages and define reality based upon how that language organizes and implies relationships within the world. Of course, the speaker thinks that *his or her* world is *the* world, as described by his or her language. Hence the problem: Every culture believes that *it* truly understands reality and the other guy is mistaken and superstitious.

American Indian cultures do not necessarily reckon relationships in the same way as Americans. Other ways, such as the Crow and the Iroquois kinship systems, do not recognize great generational distances. Further, for many Indian languages, time is not a quantity that is, or can be, measured. Rather, time is a quality, like beauty, flowing, pervasive, and experienced. Distance in time is inconceivable. This view of time combined with their kinship system, produces equal feelings of immediate family with a parent who died last year and with a relative who has been dead for centuries.

Appreciating this perspective helps one understand why American Indians, arguing with archaeologists or English speakers in general, will quickly go to the example of "how would you feel about having *your* grandfather exhumed and put into a warehouse for storage or on display in a museum?" For the speaker of that Indian language, this comparison is how the matter is felt and there is no other way that the matter can be expressed. For the native English speaker, the example sounds bizarre, since human remains that are millennia old cannot possibly be those of close relatives. For the English speaker, the example—especially since it is being expressed by the other person in English, who is therefore assumed to be using those cultural ground rules—represents a false analogy and irrelevant argument. And therefore the English-speaking archaeologist or anthropologist, for whom such remains would have only marginal emotional importance, is frustrated that the American Indian uses—and is allowed to use by law—what seem to be illogical or impossible arguments to withhold objects of scientific value.

Guidelines are protocols; they do not have the force of law. However, the Federal regulatory agency is bound by the guidelines to the extent needed to avoid being "arbitrary and capricious," and the guidelines themselves usually address the circumstances by which they may be exceeded or modified. The Section 106 Process uses mainly two sets of guidelines:

- 47 FR 46374 "Guidelines for Exemptions under Section 214 of the National Historic Preservation Act." NHPA Section 214 (16 U.S.C. 470v) authorizes the ACHP, in consultation and concurrence with the Secretary of the Interior, to set out exceptions to the Section 106 Process; 47 FR 46374 provides specific guidance for doing this.

- 48 FR 44716 "Archeology and Historic Preservation: Secretary of the Interior's Standards and Guidelines." See 36 CFR 800.2 (a) (1) and 800.4 (b) (1). After NHPA and 36 CFR 800, this is probably the most important document for the practicing archaeologist to understand.

State Laws, Regulations, and Guidelines

State laws, and the regulations drawn from them, fall into three broad sets: (1) counterpart Section 106 statutes; (2) counterpart NEPA statutes

Table 2.2.   Core Federal Regulations

36 CFR Part 60 "National Register of Historic Places" This sets out the basic rules for the National Register, including what can and cannot be listed. Of import to professional archaeologists is 36 CFR 60.4, which sets out the criteria for evaluating the eligibility of a property for listing on the National Register.

36 CFR Part 61 "Procedures for Approved State and Local Government Historic Preservation Programs" This governs certification of local governments; see also 36 CFR 800.3 (c) (4) and NHPA Section 101 (c) (1).

36 CFR Part 63 "Determinations of Eligibility for Inclusion in the National Register of Historic Places" This is directed toward Federal agencies to help them understand how to go about having determinations of Register eligibility made, and what to do after such determinations are made (see also 36 CFR 800.4 (c)).

36 CFR Part 65 "National Historic Landmarks Program" National Historic Landmarks (NHL) are seen to be extraordinarily important to the nation as a whole (as opposed to just the state or locale) and command appropriate consideration and treatment. NHPA Section 110 (f) sets out the policy for this. The additional requirements as they pertain to Section 106 are given in 36 CFR 800.10.

36 CFR Part 68 "Secretary of the Interior's Standards for the Treatment of Historic Properties" This sets out the standards for treatment of historic properties to be used by the National Park Service and the SHPOs for Federal grant-assisted preservation, rehabilitation. restoration, or reconstruction projects. See also 36 CFR 800.5 (a)(2)(ii).

36 CFR Part 78 "Waiver of Federal Agency Responsibilities under Section 110 of the National Historic Preservation Act" This allows suspension of the Section 106 process in situations of immediate emergencies involving human life and health [36 CFR 800.12].

36 CFR Part 79 "Curation of Federally Owned and Administered Archaeological Collections" This sets out curatorial requirements required of facilities/institutions holding archaeological collections and associated records that have been generated by Federally enabled projects, especially Section 106 projects.

36 CFR Part 800 "Protection of Historic Properties" These are the basic regulations for the Section 106 Process discussed earlier in chapter 2.

43 CFR Part 7 "Protection of Archaeological Resources: Uniform Regulations" These regulations applied to the Department of the Interior; identical regulations exist for the departments of Agriculture and Defense, and the TVA. The regulations deal with the permitting process.

("little NEPAs"); and (3) other, hybrid statutes such as focused burial legislation. Most require that any state-enabled land-alteration/jurisdiction project be examined first for cultural resources. States also maintain a state equivalent of the National Register.

In many states, the SHPO has jurisdiction over actions enabled by state funding or permits or involving state property. Projects trigger a process that may be similar to Section 106 at the Federal level, or a roughly equivalent process similar to NEPA EA/EIS reviews. All states and territories have an EA requirement of some kind or another, depending on where a project is located and the nature of the project. Some states, such as Vermont and Oregon, have a comprehensive environmental assessment requirement built into a permit process for all actions of a certain magnitude. Other states, like Arizona, Delaware, Georgia, Louisiana, Michigan, New Jersey, North Dakota, Pennsylvania, Rhode Island, and Utah, use a state-level EA/EIS process that is not as comprehensive as NEPA.

While procedures may vary by state or commonwealth, the regulations are quite accessible. Most states have the regulations and even permit applications set out on the Internet. Usually, there is also a statewide archaeological society with an Internet home page that includes links to state archaeological laws and assessment procedures. Federal agencies such as the NPS and professional societies such as SAA and RPA also maintain an Internet presence with links. One of the most useful Web sites with connections to various states, Federal agencies, professional and avocational societies, and much more is hosted by the University of Connecticut at http://archnet.uconn.edu. The practicing archaeologist can get much information from the Internet but should also contact the SHPO of the given state for copies and clarification of regulations and procedures.

Municipal and County Regulations

Approximately 10 percent of the nation's 3,066 counties have counterpart Section 106 legislation, at least in a very broad sense of the term "counterpart." Most of this legislation, and its statutory regulations, are set within regulations for the review of proposed development. The issuance of a permit or license for a housing development depends in part on a developer's compliance with the county's equivalent of Section 106.

As at the state level, some of these regulations resemble Section 106, some resemble NEPA. It depends entirely on the legislative history of the local area. Those that follow a Section 106 procedure will have a local archaeologist whose role will be similar to that of a SHPO. The entity undertaking the project (be it private developer or a public agency) will serve in the role of "lead agency."

The ability to monitor and enforce the process varies by locale. Some areas have municipal or county archaeologists who work with the planning

51

commissions. The necessary permits for construction are not released until the archaeologist or equivalent historic preservation officer is satisfied that cultural resource compliance has occurred. In other areas, there may be a historic preservation commission that recommends zoning or permitting actions to the local planning board, but which lacks statutory authority beyond social censure. These are usually found in situations lacking any counterpart historic preservation regulation or having a counterpart to NEPA.

The archaeologist is responsible for finding out what kinds of statuary regulations exist within the business domain of his or her organization. The best place to start is with the SHPO.

Chapter Summary

The legislation that most directly affects professional archaeology is the National Historic Preservation Act (NHPA). The NHPA established the State Historic Preservation Officer (SHPO), who coordinates historic preservation activities within the state. The NHPA established the Advisory Council on Historic Preservation (the ACHP or Council). But most important, through its Section 106, NHPA required that any Federal agency that makes a land-alteration activity possible, be it through funds or permits or just control of Federal land, must first take into account any properties present that could be listed on the National Register of Historic Places. Those properties can be standing buildings; they can also be archaeological sites. Regardless of what they are, if the project is Federally enabled, then the enabling agency is held responsible for seeing to it that such properties are accounted for before work begins.

Section 106 is a paragraph long and broadly written. The regulations for implementing Section 106 are contained in the *Code of Federal Regulations*. Although there are several parts of the code that are involved, two make up the basic elements for how Federal agencies are to comply with Section 106. The first is 36 CFR 800, which outlines how the Process is supposed to be accomplished and who all will be involved. The second is 36 CFR 60, which sets out the rules for listing properties on the National Register.

A particular note here: When a property—a cultural resource as it were—is seen to be eligible for listing on the National Register, it is said to have the *quality of significance* as defined in 36 CFR 60.4. It is from that

that the term "significant" comes when it is used to quickly summarize the importance of an archaeological site. "Significant" is a word that is in common use that also has, in professional practice, a more specific connotation. That more specific connotation is "eligible for listing on the National Register."

The Section 106 Process, presented in 36 CFR 800, requires that Federal agencies, enabling land-alteration or land-control projects, make a good-faith effort to take into account any property that could be listed on the National Register of Historic Places. The Federal agency must first determine if such a project exists. If it does, then that same agency must determine if it would have any chance of damaging a Register-eligible property. If that is the case, then the Federal agency is required to consult with the SHPO, or the tribal equivalent THPO (Tribal Historic Preservation Officer) if tribal lands are involved, and other specified parties about what actions need to be taken to make sure Register-eligible cultural resources will be accounted for.

The first step in the Process is a good-faith effort to see if Register-eligible properties are present. Archaeologically, this normally is called *Phase I survey* or *Phase I identification*. This combines historic background research with field survey to see if archaeological sites might be present.

If sites are present, that required good-faith effort continues with what is known archaeologically as a *Phase II evaluation*. The purpose of Phase II is to get enough information about the archaeological site so that the Federal agency can determine if it is eligible for listing on the National Register. Although the Federal agency makes the initial determination, its decision can be challenged by the SHPO/THPO or by other involved consulting parties. In such disagreements, the ACHP casts the deciding vote.

If it is determined that Register-eligible properties—including archaeological sites—are present, then a series of decisions will be made by the Federal agency in consultation with the SHPO/THPO and others about what the impact of the project will be on those properties, as well as what should be done to offset any impact. Once a course of action has been decided, a Memorandum of Agreement (MOA) is executed between the Federal agency and the SHPO/THPO.

Sometimes the course of action is to have the project redesigned so the Register-eligible cultural resource is not damaged. Often, though, such a change of plan would be impractical, and then the goal is to record as much about the resource as possible before it is lost. For archaeologists, this would be a *Phase III data recovery* or *mitigation*, the purpose being to mitigate the damage from the project by excavating and recording the threatened part of the site.

At the Federal level, the law with precedence in treating cultural resources like archaeological sites is the NHPA. This can result in some confusion, since the National Environmental Policy Act (NEPA) often is cited, even in college level method-and-theory texts, as the law that drives compliance archaeology. The confusion comes because NEPA also takes cultural resources into account in its assessment of the impact of a Federally enabled project on an area. However, the NHPA and the Section 106 mandate must be satisfied by any project that is covered by NEPA, and the most recent revision of 36 CFR 800 addresses this in no uncertain terms.

What of cultural resources adversely affected by non-Federal activities? Many states and local governments have legislation and accompanying regulations to deal with cultural resources that could be lost through construction or similar land alteration activities. Sometimes the law and regulations are similar to the Section 106 Process; sometimes they are similar to NEPA and actually are embedded within the state's equivalent of NEPA (so-called little NEPAs).

One last item: Neither the Section 106 Process nor its local counterparts is intended to stop construction. A site or building eligible for or even listed on the National Register can still be utterly destroyed. Rather, the Process is intended to allow governments, Federal or local, time to evaluate the importance of cultural resources and to plan for handling them. If the resource will be lost, the Process provides a way in which that resource can be recorded so that the loss from its disappearance can be kept at a minimum. The idea is not to stop construction. Rather, the idea is, to use a metaphor, to give us as a nation a chance to see if we want to make note of what is going to get tossed out from the national attic, or even if we all might be better served by holding on to it.

Additional Readings of Interest

Advisory Council on Historic Preservation (ACHP). 1991. *Treatment of Archeological Properties: A Handbook*. National Park Service, U.S. Department of the

Interior, Washington, D.C. Straightforward guide to handling archaeological sites in the broader context of the Section 106 Process.

Hardesty, Donald L., and Barbara J. Little. 2000. *Assessing Site Significance: A Guide for Archaeologists and Historians.* AltaMira Press, Walnut Creek. This book is in the "must have" category for professional archaeologists.

Kanefield, Adina W. 1996. *Federal Historic Preservation Case Law, 1966–1996: Thirty Years of the National Historic Preservation Act.* A Special Report Funded in Part by the United States Army Environmental Center/Advisory Council on Historic Preservation, U.S. Government Printing Office, Washington, D.C. Annotated summaries of important historic preservation cases, particularly as they involved the National Historic Preservation Act. Excellent reference for anyone interested in pursuing a law degree focusing on environmental or historic preservation issues.

King, Thomas F. 1998. *Cultural Resource Laws and Practice: An Introductory Guide.* AltaMira Press, Walnut Creek. Readable primer on historic preservation law assembled by one of the true masters of the field.

King, Thomas F. 2000. *Federal Planning and Historical Places: The Section 106 Process.* AltaMira Press, Walnut Creek. A comprehensive discussion of the Section 106 Process from the planning perspective, including detailed advice on assembling things like Memoranda of Agreement (MOAs).

National Park Service. 1995. *How to Apply the National Register Criteria for Evaluation.* National Register Bulletin 15. National Park Service, Washington, D.C. (http://www.cr.nps.gov/nr/bulletins/nr15_8.html) Excellent instructions on how the criteria of evaluation given in 36 CFR 60.4 work in day-to-day life.

Parker, Patricia L., and Thomas F. King. 1995. *Guidelines for Evaluating and Documenting Traditional Cultural Properties.* National Register Bulletin. National Park Service, Washington, D.C.

CHAPTER THREE
PREPARING THE
PROJECT BACKGROUND

Purpose and Objectives

Once it is decided, be it at the Federal or the state level, that an undertaking exists that could possibly damage cultural resources, the first formal step for the professional archaeologist is to conduct background research. This identification step is a comprehensive assembling of what is already known about the project and the project area. This information draws from history, archaeology, geology, soils, other environmental sciences, and other social and cultural background research. For Section 106 projects, this preparatory or background research is the first step required of the Federal agency [36 CFR 800.4(a)] after there is a determination of an undertaking. The Secretary of Interior's Standards and Guidelines [48 FR 44716–44742] sets forth the standards expected for documentation, in effect using that background to establish clearly the criteria needed for any evaluation of significance.

The background research puts the project and associated archaeological research into the broader context of what is known and why the work is being done. The nature and thoroughness of the project background informs the review agencies of the practicing archaeologist's preparation for the work that was undertaken.

Occasionally, the background research might even be a stand-alone document. This occurs when preservation plans or disturbance studies are done on behalf of agencies. "Preservation Plans" refer to historic preservation plans prepared at the behest of a Federal agency or installation. These tend to be miniature equivalents of state historic preservation plans, and are tied to the specific situation of the installation or agency property for which they are prepared.

Preservation plans contain a set series of information: the physical geography of the Federal property, a cultural history/cultural geography of that same property, a summation of work done to-date, and a relation of the cultural history to the larger State Historic Preservation Plan. The jurisdiction for cultural resources on Federal land still rests in the Section 106 Process with the SHPO, and therefore needs to be placed in the context of the state.

Preservation plans have two major components: (1) the core research questions/historic issues on cultural resources that might be within the project area, and (2) sensitivity determinations for the property. Sensitivity determinations refer to the likelihood that historic or prehistoric cultural remains will be located on/in various landscape types of the property.

Preservation plans include a synopsis of what already is known about historic and prehistoric sites and structures within the agency's jurisdiction. The synopsis addresses the possibility of National Register eligibility for those sites and structures. Potential resources, based upon historic documents, are mentioned. For example, early Spanish forts at Parris Island near Port Royal Sound in South Carolina (on the golf course) could be inferred from very early historic records.

"Disturbance studies" also are planning documents and summarize the past land use of a project area. They differ from preservation plans in that they focus on a given project area and look more at the probability of the project area still containing viable historic or prehistoric cultural remains.

Disturbance studies are more likely to exist in urban or semi-urban environments. However, this kind of work could be for any landscape. Generally, disturbance studies use historic documents—written histories combined with historic maps—to plot out the areas of a proposed undertaking that may or may not be severely disturbed. The threshold for disturbance is not always apparent.

The Camden Yards ball field, in Baltimore Maryland's Inner Harbor area, can serve as an example. We were involved in structuring the general probability that the landscape would be disturbed. Portions of the urban environment had been built over, including Babe Ruth's father's tavern, the 1915 or 1916 one in which Babe Ruth is pictured behind the bar with his brother and his father (see Ward and Burns 1994:160–161). The tavern—built into a row house brownstone—had been torn down in the 1950s and a warehouse built over it (the house footprint actually was under the warehouse's loading dock). Disturbance had not extended deeper than the second above-surface course of bricks of the building. The basement had been filled with rubble. However, the two-seat brick-lined privy remained full of artifacts and other household debris that could address how the family had lived. Using digitized maps as well as a sense of what the probable disturbance for that part of the urban area was, the firm was able to locate and eventually excavate what remained of the structure.

Disturbance studies give a qualitative statement on the likelihood of cultural resources remaining intact within the bounds of the project area. They do, though, include detailed histories and prehistories of that project area that allow for a sense of what *may* still survive within the project bounds.

Related to preservation plans and disturbance studies is the development of predictive models for use in planning. This kind of work, which often combines state site file research with disturbance studies, results in a series of exercises that borders on what we call "actuarial archaeology" (see Neumann, Sanford, and Palmer 1992:122–123). Professional archaeology as a resource management discipline has worked its way into a situation where it is needed for planning. The development community and its associated regulators and planners seek a binary process, a yes or no. The flaws in creating such a process, based only on known information, are obvious. The solution has been to develop predictive models for whether or not an area is likely to contain sites.

For example, portions of Maryland (Kavanagh 1982), Pennsylvania (Hay, Hatch, and Sutton 1987), and West Virginia (Neumann 1992) have used extant site file information to develop quantitative probability models of differing levels of resolution that help identify landscapes likely to contain prehistoric archaeological sites. These are by no means the first or the best such models, but all have in common development in immediate response to cultural resources planning needs. Early attempts were qualitative and consisted of statements in the range of "level land near rivers on the inside of meanders have a good chance of having prehistoric archaeological sites." Later work quantified those physiographic variables, so that in eastern West Virginia it is known that about 95 percent of all prehistoric archaeological sites are on land with a slope, and under 10 percent within 200m of a stream with a flow rate of at least 12 cubic feet per second. Such studies grew out of the need by planners and state agencies to have some sense of just how likely it would be for archaeological sites to survive in a given area.

A good way to develop a risk-based probability statement for cultural resources on the landscape is to first record variables such as soil type, distance of the site from water, stream flow rate, current slope of the land, elevation above sea level, and cultural-historical affiliation. The next step is to do a cluster analysis using numerical classification for each cultural-historical set. It is likely that the sites will sort themselves into subsets. The third step is to work out the averages and other descriptive statistics for sites contained within each cluster.

The last step depends upon the goal of the exercise. Results can be presented as a table, or as a map for a particular area. Soil survey analyses, such as crop suitability or soil type, are not necessarily reliable in making probability statements for prehistoric sites, since the soil types currently found in many places are not the soils that people were facing half a millennia ago. Soil type depends on covering vegetation, sediment accumulation on fields, and the like; soil in a given place can and does change over time in response to those factors.

Exercises like this are becoming increasingly easy with the conversion of site files to GIS (geographic information systems). Currently, the results are given either as qualitative visual maps showing known presence of archaeological sites, along with descriptive statistics, or as data sets. It will be comparatively easy with GIS to go the next two steps in working out a hierarchy of site locations then providing a probability statement for areas on the landscape where sites of given cultural-historic affiliation may be found.

In many western states, the background research is particularly critical when Phase I reconnaissance and intensive surveys do not require subsurface testing. Usually, the background research is part of the larger compliance report, be it Phase I survey, Phase II testing, or Phase III data recovery. The quality of the research background helps the SHPO or similar review agency evaluate the reliability and quality of the archaeological work.

Regulations in most states urge that the historic and prehistoric background research for a project area be finished prior to the field work, but this does not always happen. The nature of some projects might result in the two tasks being done concurrently or in reverse order, particularly for

Phase I projects. This is acceptable if the archaeologist has a sound understanding of the nature of the sites and archaeology of the region. However, for Phase I reconnaissance and survey projects, since their responsibility is identification, it is important to have advance knowledge of what archaeological sites have been recorded for the project area or corridor as well as in the area of potential effects that may extend well beyond the immediate construction zone. Failure to locate previously identified sites during field work will result in reviewers requesting additional testing to see if the boundaries of the site were improperly recorded.

Project History

The project history has two aspects: The history of the undertaking itself and the history of the project area, both in general and in terms of past research efforts.

History of the Undertaking

The history of the undertaking covers the nature of the proposed project, the reasons for the project, and what other options have been explored. Summarizing the history of the undertaking helps the client and the review agency in the event that mitigation or redesign becomes necessary as a result of encountering cultural resources. This enables the archaeological work to be integrated into the overall planning effort.

The information for the history of the undertaking usually comes from the Scope of Work (SOW or Scope) as well as the original RFP (Request for Proposals).[1] This information should include detailed design and project maps showing just how the land will be altered, where buildings and roads will be sited, and similar specific indications of intended actions such as placement of buried utilities or septic fields. The archaeologist needs a detailed project map before the project can be planned and bid, if only to have a sense of scale and of terrain.

Additional information usually is supplied by the client after the project has been awarded to the archaeologist's firm. This can include earlier

---

[1]See Neumann and Sanford 2001, chapter 3 for details on locating contract opportunities, structuring bid proposals, and generally responding to RFPs and other announcements.

project design maps, previous studies conducted on the area (including percolation [perc] test data and similar engineering analyses), and even some historic background material. If the project has been controversial, then local newspapers will have carried stories. That information is available from the associated public library or from the newspaper's files.

A history of the undertaking needs to cover some specific details:

- What is it that is planned and why is it going to be done?

- When was the project conceived and what is the rough time table?

- Who is doing the design work?

- Who will be doing the construction (that is, who is the general contractor)?

- What will be the extent of land alteration, both in terms of area and depth?

- Will the land alteration be construction only, or will there be road grading, tree removal, and other topographic changes?

For Phase III data recovery projects, and for Phase II testing projects that look as if Register-eligible archaeological sites will be threatened, it is important to detail what other design options have been considered for the project and why those options were unacceptable. The reason for this kind of information is to set out why the project was not redesigned to avoid damaging the cultural resources. All of the players—especially the Consulting Parties if this is a Section 106 exercise—need to know what has been covered.[2]

In nearly all cases, the history of the undertaking will be presented in the first chapter of the report. In some Phase II testing and Phase III mitigation reports, the first chapter will contain an abbreviated summary of the undertaking's history and the third chapter (treating the history and prehistory of the region) will contain a detailed synopsis of the undertaking.

---

[2]"Failure to adequately describe the project" is one of the most commonly cited flaws of individual NEPA environmental impact statements (EISs).

History of the Project Area

The second part of a project history involves the history of the project area. This includes what has happened directly within the project area, along with describing any previous archaeological research. This background segment usually requires interviews of landowners, local historians, and area residents. It also includes research done at the state site files, contacting the SHPO/THPO to see if any properties within the project area have been nominated for the National Register, historic research at the local libraries, map research, and working with local Indian tribes and other cultural groups. The history of the project area is presented as parts of the second and/or third chapter of the final report.

The history of the project area addresses basic questions:

- What has been the history of land use of the project area?

- Are archaeological sites recorded for the project area?

- Has anyone ever examined the project area for the presence of archaeological remains?

- Are National Register-eligible properties known to be present within the bounds of the project area?

Interviews

Two sets of individuals are interviewed: community historians and similar individuals who have a knowledge of the area; and local residents and property owners, including representatives of any local tribes or native groups.

Every county and just about every community no matter how small, has at least one community historian and sometimes a local historical society. The role of historian may be an official position. More often, the community historian is a volunteer. These people are the community's equivalent of an elder in the anthropological sense and should be located if at all possible. How does the practicing archaeologist locate the community's historian or historical society? The easiest way is to either go to the information/reference desk of the public library and ask, or to go to the courthouse or town hall and ask. Local historians are

We learned about archaeology from that . . .
Area History and Testing Expectations

A history of a project area helps the practicing archaeologist to set bounds on testing and expectations for testing results. A good example of this is a New York State Department of Transportation (NYS-DOT) project we did in upstate New York.

The seven-mile road corridor project ran between the cities of Lowville and Glenfield, along the eastern base of the Tug Hill Plateau as it sloped toward the Black River valley. This part of New York was settled in the late 1700s, and property arrangements were influenced by French custom: The original fields were long and narrow, at right-angles to the general south-north flow of the river. The road itself was built in the 1930s without regard to where the farm field boundaries were, instead following the toe slope of the Plateau and cutting diagonally across those fields. Prior to that time, travel between Lowville and Glenfield required zig-zagging back and forth since the roads followed the perimeters of the farm fields.

Knowing the road construction date and that much of it was built on fill (it ran mostly on a berm raised just out from the slope proper) allowed us to judge areas of fill, disturbance, and likelihood for the kinds of cultural resources that might be present. For example, there was only a small possibility of early historic sites being directly associated with the road, simply because the road was comparatively new. The possibility is much higher where the older roads were integrated into the 1930s design.

almost always quite willing to assist with oral accounts and in finding additional information.

The local library is one of the most important sources of primary and secondary research information on the history of an area. Librarians are often focal nodes of information about communities, and should be among the first people contacted in the search for leads on the history of the community and the project area (Figure 3.1).

The questions asked of the community's historian should focus on the general history of the project area as well as sources available on that history. Sensitive or controversial projects (e.g., a contested pipeline or a military installation) may make it difficult to get into

Figure 3.1. **Virtually all county seats as well as many other small communities have public libraries, a legacy of Jefferson's vision for the country. These house not only local histories and special collections, but also reference librarians who are very aware of who is doing what historically in the community.**

specific questioning or may require significant diplomacy. Some Federal and state contracts prohibit speaking about the undertaking with unauthorized nonproject personnel in certain situations. If the contract allows, always ask if the historian is aware, personally or through hearsay, of any archaeological sites, historic roadways or other features, or historic structures located in or near the project area. At these times, it is very useful to have a map of the project area relative to the greater community available. But again, *showing such maps—especially planning maps—to nonproject personnel should be done only if the contract so allows and one is authorized to do so.*

The second population to be contacted are the local residents. It is a basic field courtesy to speak with the property owner and with the property resident. This contact is extremely important if there is any intention of crossing the individual's property, and even more important if any subsurface testing is anticipated for that property. The need for interviews of local residents in the vicinity of a project area varies by the situation, although interviews may be required by state or local mandates.

Interviews with property owners and residents can indicate if any cultural resources are known for the project area that may not have been caught by the more formal records of local history or of state site files. People resident on their land have a wealth of knowledge that comes from living there. Many will have information about cultural resources and area history that has never been solicited.[3]

Further, it is a simple matter of courtesy to speak with the people resident on the land that will be tested or examined. The interview is important even if the subject does not have a knowledge of the landscape history or previous land use: They live there, and to enter in to work is to enter into their homes, their territory, their personal space. Proper interviews help the archaeological crew gain the respect of the wider community, with whom the practicing archaeologist and associated crew must interact, sometimes rather intimately, on a daily basis for the duration of the project.

State Site Files Search

The history of the project area includes previous archaeological investigations. This information is available from at least one of two sources: the state site files and the SHPO/THPO. All states and political equivalents maintain a file of previously identified archaeological sites. Those sites normally are given a trinomial site number, consisting of an initial number representing the alphabetic order of the state for the 48 continental states (Alaska is 49 and Hawai'i 50), followed by a two-letter alphabetic abbreviation for the county, then a site number based upon the order in which the site was recorded by the state site files. So, for example, the Paleoindian–Late Archaic site of 44FX1517 is (or was; there are houses on it now) located in Virginia (the 44th state alphabetically), specifically in Fairfax County, and was the 1,517th site recorded in the county.

Not infrequently, sites will also have a colloquial name. For example, site 44FX1517 is also called the Hobo Hill Site. In documentation, the

---

[3]The interview process merits particular attention. In addition to structured interview formats, open-ended questions might also be used. How people respond to questions varies, among other things, by part of the country and by social class relative to the interviewer. For example, in New England and to some extent in southern Appalachia, it is common not to volunteer information unless asked. In rural areas of the upper Midwest, especially in Iowa and Minnesota, as well as in similar settings in Wisconsin and Michigan, a general statement of what is of concern and why you need to know it will likely result in people volunteering information and suggesting other people to contact. In those areas as well as in the South, custom dictates the importance of first chatting about things in general before getting to the point.

site should be referred to by number rather than name. This reduces ambiguity and makes keeping field notes much easier.

State site file searches are relatively easy. The site files are arranged by county. Most SHPO offices have a master state map showing where sites have been identified, or a series of USGS topographic maps upon which the bounds of the site have been penciled in. All that the practicing archaeologist needs to know is where—in map terms—the project area is, then go to the site files and find out if any sites are recorded for that tract of land.

A number of states, such as Maryland and Georgia, have converted their site files to a computer-based GIS (geographic information system). Some states also are making access to that computerized site file available through the Internet, provided specific security protocols are observed. Some states (e.g., New Mexico) charge an access fee to use the site files or charge for computer searches of site files (e.g., Colorado).

The background work done at the state site files results in the following information on every site within about two kilometers of the project area:

- site number and, if present, name;

- location of site;

- horizontal bounds of site;

- depth at which materials were found;

- presence or absence of features;

- cultural historical affiliation;

- when recorded;

- when, if ever, investigated;

- nature of investigation;

- where and in what form research results were published (that is, full citations); and

- National Register status if appropriate.

It is useful to have a photocopy of the USGS map or maps for the vicinity of the project area, and to note where previously recorded sites are located; in some areas of the country, the final compliance report will include a copy of the portions of the USGS map where the project is located. Inclusion of such a map depends greatly on how restricted public access is to site location information in the state; many states quite rightly do not want that kind of information accessible to the general public. On that map segment will be shown the locations and bounds of known archaeological sites. Check with the particular office's protocol: Some site file offices and states do not allow transferring map information.

It is well to note at this point that access to the state's archaeological site files is usually restricted to those with legitimate research needs for the information compiled there. There is a reason for this. Archaeology in the United States is not only a private-sector endeavor, it also is a commercial endeavor. There is a considerable economic substratum dealing in prehistoric and historic artifacts. The individual values for artifacts vary greatly. Prehistoric projectile points average about $40 each in a proportionally small but ready market, although prices range from $2–4 for Savannah River points (a comparatively common 5,000-year-old point found in Atlantic coastal states from New Jersey to Florida; Overstreet 1997:507) to $500–7,000 for Clovis points (found throughout most of the nation and dating from around 12,000–11,000 years ago; Hothem 1999:14). Pottery from the Southwest can sell for mid-range four-figure sums. Bottle collectors and Civil War curio collectors get two- to three-figure sums for things like entire bottles or excellent-condition belt buckles in an eager and accessible market.

The average per capita income in the United States at the turn of this century would be on the order of $26,000 a year, a little less in rural areas. Thus, 10 arrowheads picked up on a Saturday potting a site can, as often as not, be equal to a week's wages.

Most individuals who engage in this activity, labeled variously as "pot hunters" or "looters," have a very good idea of where archaeological sites are located. They tend to ignore legal statutes and may even view legal penalties as "business costs." For such people, anything that can help in locating profitable artifact deposits will be used. And of course site files, with their listing of where all of the known archaeological sites are, and generally what those sites contain, would be a great resource. It is to prevent their use for such looting that state site files have restricted access and why site locations are generally exempt from state "right-to-know" and "open records" laws.

If sites are located within the project area, then obtain copies of all previous reports and journal articles on the site or sites. Full reports may be filed with the site files, with the SHPO or equivalent historic preservation office, or with the state archaeologist's office (which may or may not be an administrative unit separate from the SHPO within the given state).

It is important to note from those reports the depth at which cultural materials were found and exactly what it was that *was* found. This includes whether or not features were present, since these are excellent signs of site integrity as well as sources of contextual information.

Site file information will be presented in two ways in the third chapter of the compliance report. The first way will be as a table and accompanying figure that summarize the known archaeological sites in the vicinity of the project area. The second way will be in brief narrative form for well-researched sites that exemplify regional history or prehistory.

SHPO/THPO (State/Tribal Historic Preservation Office[r])

In most states, the SHPO or equivalent historic preservation office (e.g., on tribal lands, the Tribal Historic Preservation Officer or THPO) will have copies of all compliance reports. The reason for going to the site files first when the files are separate from the SHPO is to know just *what* reports need to be examined for the project area. It is usually wise to have budgeted funds for copying reports that seem relevant to the project. In time, this may not be an issue as states make more and more of the original compliance reports available through the Internet (e.g., Missouri and Georgia). Some reports may also be available for sale.

The SHPO/THPO will also be aware of any properties that are under consideration for nomination to the National Register.

Local History

The research into local history helps to place historic cultural resources in their general historic/cultural context, especially relative to the State Plan. Research can also identify potential resources in the project area.

That historic/cultural context is the evaluative element of 36 CFR 60.4 *criteria for evaluation* in assessing if the site has the quality of significance in National Register terms (see Secretary of Interior, "Standards for Historical Documentation" [48 FR 44728–44729]). This is especially true for criteria [a]–[c] (those dealing with associations with persons, events, or master craftsmanship). All of this must be considered in the context of the State Historic Preservation Plan.

Most local history searches begin with the local historical society or with the local public library. Each will have numerous source materials that might mention the project vicinity. In the eastern and midwestern United States, many counties compiled at least one county history in the 1800s (sometime around the nation's centennial). Often there is a second history written around the 1860s and a third, written around the time of the bicentennial in the late 1970s.

There often are local, specialized histories, as well as special collections in the local library. The library may have a room containing special primary sources on the history of the county and its communities. Another library might have some of the same books in its general circulation collection, making it advisable to check more than one place if a desired document has restricted access.

Local history research occasionally will also include deed research and an examination of the chain of title for the project property. A "chain of title" chronicles legal ownership for the property or parcels within the project area. Usually, a title search is done by a title company prior to any land transfer, although it rarely is more than a cursory check to make sure that the ownership is clear. The archaeologist's interest comes from how the resultant information contributes to the history and genealogy of previous occupants of the project area.

Chains of title normally are more tedious than complex, although it does depend upon the quality of the records involved. The courthouse is the usual repository for title information, although most local municipal offices retain some information in their assessor, permits, or planning departments. The tax map designation or similar bit of locational information is needed. The current owner will have that information as a title abstract (which also may contain links in the chain of title), or it can be obtained from an overview map.

Armed with the location of the parcel, it is only a matter of working back through the previous owners until the records run out. Chain of title is useful for historic purposes in connecting a piece of land with a family or a known individual, thus helping establish association of the property with "important" people (criterion [a] of 36 CFR 60.4 *criteria for evaluation*). Information on the property may even include a summary of the buildings and structures present, and their assessed value, always useful if the buildings and structures are gone.

Map Research and Area Reconstruction

Maps are a major source of historic information in locating previous historic occupations and for understanding potential disturbance in a project area. The locations of structures at specified times can be interpreted from USGS topographic maps, county maps/county history maps, aerial photographs, orthographic projections of communities, Sanborn Fire Insurance maps, and USDA NRCS (Natural Resources Conservation Service, formerly the SCS or Soil Conservation Service) soil maps.

The entire country has been mapped by the U.S. Geological Survey. Map information is generally presented in 7.5' topographic quadrangles ("7.5'" means "7.5 minutes of a degree"; each map covers 7.5' of latitude and 7.5' of longitude). Those maps include cultural features, such as residences, outbuildings, bridges, paths, old rail lines, and countless other features. All maps have a date for when they were compiled. The USGS topographic maps are periodically updated, and thus become powerful sources for the history of an area.

Mapping of the country in this fashion began in the late 1880s around Annapolis, and has continued nonstop. The initial mapping was done as 15' quadrangles (maps that were 15' latitude and 15' longitude on a side, representing the area of four 7.5' quadrangles). Those maps were periodically updated through the 1930s before the system began focusing on 7.5' maps. The 15' map upgrades often neglected to indicate changes in the presence or absence of structures.

A sequence of USGS maps documents with some precision when buildings appeared or disappeared from the cultural landscape. A series of such maps becomes a chronicle of historic development in an area (see box). However, it should be noted that areas of urban expansion no longer show individual structures, but rather a magenta-purple shading indicating a built environment. In coastal areas, draft and print versions of the Coast Survey charts (begun in the 1840s) may also be of use and supplement the USGS maps available.

Historic county maps provide a second major source of information about structures and ownership. Detailed county maps were made in many parts of the country around the same time that many of the county histories were produced in the nineteenth century. These maps are scaled; show the locations of residences, schools, major commercial structures, and some other buildings; and usually give the name of the structure or of the occupant of the residence. Such maps may be bound into published county histories, but more often exist as large, rolled painted-canvas maps meant to be hung. The combination of a map date and names associated with structures make these documents particularly powerful tools in reconstructing the historic landscape. Municipal offices often have one or more such maps and/or nineteenth century orthographic projections—"bird's-eye views"—of the community framed and hanging on the wall. It is fairly easy to photograph these images in place.

A third and, for urban environments, one of the best sources of information are the Sanborn Fire Insurance maps, compiled, published, and updated for many municipalities between the 1880s and the 1930s. These maps, available on microfilm and microfiche as well as original hard copies, are extensive sources of information. The only drawback is that they tend to be limited to the built-up parts of the more populous communities that existed around the turn of the last century.

The Sanborn Fire Insurance maps are color-coded maps of cityscapes, meant to give assessors a sense of fire risk for given areas. The scale is 1 inch to 50 feet, and the maps are usually remarkably detailed. The color coding indicated material from which the buildings and structure were made, and therefore their fire risk. The notations on the maps indicate the number of stories, if business or residence, and very often the name of the family or the business occupying the building at the time the map was made or updated. In addition, the maps often show adjacent structures, including bridges, railroad corridors, roadways, and mill races.

TIP: Setting Up a Map Matrix

In the 1980s, we did several Phase I surveys on behalf of the New York State Department of Transportation (NYS-DOT). The requirements for the Phase I surveys were a little different than those for strictly archaeological Phase I surveys, since we were charged with documenting architectural features along corridor right-of-ways. Highway construction could imperil structures, and it could also change the visual setting in which such a structure existed. If that structure was eligible for listing on the National Register, then that change could materially affect its eligibility and would constitute an adverse effect. To have a sense of what buildings had been present how long (and to know where historic sites might be), survey requirements included historic map documentation of all structures known to have existed in the project area.

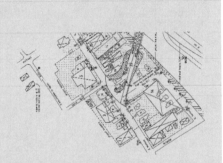

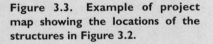

Figure 3.2. Example of a summary map figure used in a New York State Department of Transportation cultural resources survey in the 1980s.

Figure 3.3. Example of project map showing the locations of the structures in Figure 3.2.

We did this using a matrix, where the left-hand column listed the structures while the other columns were headed with the date and name of the map examined. The cells were filled in with the presence or absence (or rebuilding) of the feature in question. The result was a compact reference of where structures exist or existed, as well as when they were known to have been present.

Copies of the original maps were included in the report. Also present was a master line-drawing of the project area showing locations of previous structures, each keyed to the matrix.

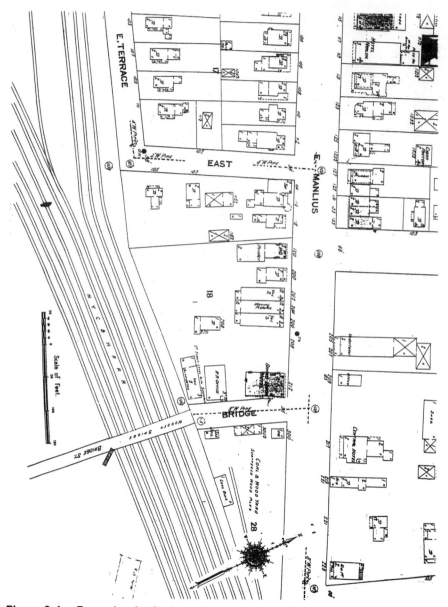

Figure 3.4. Example of a Sanborn Fire Insurance Map. Copyright 1911, The Sanborn Map Company, The Sanborn Library, LLC. All Rights Reserved. Further reproductions are prohibited without written permission from The Sanborn Library, LLC.

Field work done in an urban setting should make use of the Sanborn Fire Insurance maps. The information from the maps can be digitized then scaled, allowing the maps to be overlaid and used in conjunction with a map matrix. Such data can be a powerful cultural resources planning tool for a project area.

A fourth source of map information are county soil survey books. Around half of the 3,066 counties in the United States have had a soil survey done by the old USDA Soil Conservation Service (now part of USDA NRCS), with the soils classified and the extent of those classified soil bodies mapped. This information is presented in an $8\frac{1}{2} \times 11$-inch softbound booklet, at the back of which will be a series of aerial photographs with the bounds of the soil bodies lined in. The year of the aerial photographs will be given (often in the 1960s). The images are sufficiently clear to see structures, buildings, roads, and adjacent land uses. This information can help in reconstructing the landscape history, and can provide useful information about the expected nature of the soils.

Environmental Background and Soil Survey

All cultural resource assessments summarize the physical geography and ecology of the project area and its immediate vicinity. This constitutes the second chapter of the compliance report. The purpose of the environmental background is threefold:

(1) to recount how the ecological system has changed over time so that the prehistoric background and any prehistoric sites may be put into their proper environmental-resource context, along with historic sites;

(2) to document how conditions exist now; set out what the baseline ecological systems in which the project area is located are, so that variations from these may be appreciated when the field work and landscape conditions are discussed in the submitted report; and

(3) to describe the expected soil/geological conditions.

We learned about archaeology from that . . . Maps and Insights into Community History: The Bridge Replacement in East Syracuse

An area that has been mapped frequently and in detail over the years provides not just a chronicle of who lived where or what buildings were around, but also insight into local community life. One such instance was a bridge-replacement project we did for the New York State Department of Transportation (NYS-DOT) in the Village of East Syracuse.

East Syracuse grew up adjacent to a rail yard, expanding from a main street area that first formed along the north side of the tracks, then continued on the south side. Until 1927, vehicles would cross the tracks at grade. In that year, though, a new steel truss bridge was finished, which had enormous earthen ramps at either end that raised the bridge 22 feet to clear the rail lines. By 1987, the bridge needed to be replaced. We did the Phase I survey.

Thirteen maps, from 1859 to 1987, documented the changing streetscape of the areas north and south of the rail lines. The streets were on a grid. A few streets extended over the tracks as grade crossings into the 1920s. Those streets had comparatively few houses, all of which, judging from the Sanborn maps, were small and comparatively inexpensive. However, the new bridge did not go along those streets. Instead, it was placed diagonally relative to the street-grid and tracks in such a way that three of the most expensive residences were destroyed. The grade crossings were closed off, and the bridge became the only way to get across the tracks.

This was intriguing. Sanborn maps often tell what buildings were used for, and it was interesting that the three structures taken out by the north ramp of the bridge consisted of a large house with a semi-detached building shown as a "saloon" on the 1911 map but as a "dwelling" on the 1925 map, and an adjacent building listed in 1911 and 1925 as a "store."

We wondered about the project decision made in 1927, at the height of Prohibition. The placement of the bridge did not fit existing streets and caused removal of several expensive buildings. The condition of the 1927 NYS-DOT design map itself further piqued our interest: An attempt had been made to erase a good deal of the design part of the drawing. Equally interesting was the major map error on the south side that showed a building directly in the way of the ramp, suggesting that residents both north and south of the proposed bridge location would be equally compromised. However, that house actually was about 100 feet farther east than it was shown on the map. When the map was enhanced, we found that the building had been drawn in the middle of a pre-existing and active four-way street intersection. Was the building drawn there to show the project was the ideal compromise?

Perhaps the three removed structures had represented a "speak easy," or were related to illicit trade in liquor. Something went awry and the bridge project was used to eliminate the structures, thus settling the matter.

The environmental background provides a temporal-environmental setting for any cultural remains encountered for the project area. This tells the conditions that affected past cultures. For example, different climatic regimes necessitated different adaptive techniques and behaviors and may well be reflected in the artifacts as well as regional site distribution. The background also provides a current-situation account of the condition of the physical deposit.

Some archaeological reports, especially compliance reports, portray the ecological system as it *might* develop in the absence of human interference. This does not make much sense because people must be present for this entire exercise to have any meaning, and the presence of people alters ecological systems in fundamental ways (e.g., Neumann 1985, 1989a, 1995; Russell 1997; Krech 1999; Redman 1999). Environmental background information to be collected includes the vegetation and animal community that might be expected in the absence of a resident industrial-agricultural population, along with the nature of the plant-animal community that really is there, or at least has been present in recent history. The first is rather easy and actually will be a summary page or two in most county soil survey books. The second generally has to be constructed from a variety of sources involving landscape ecology and cultural ecology.[4]

---

[4]It probably would be thematically more proper to put any paleoenvironmental and paleoecological studies in the environmental background section. However, we have always placed such synopses in with the prehistoric or historic background narratives. This is because the paleoecological conditions represent the setting within which and to which the past cultures adapted, and it has always seemed to us a better idea to place the discussion of any past physical world side-by-side with a discussion of the culture and especially the technology that was a response to that world.

Soils are equally as important; a failure to understand the basics will seriously jeopardize the work being done. The county soil survey indicates what soils and related conditions to expect in the project area. The soil survey maps give a sense of the extent to which the ground cover may have changed.

Historic Background Narrative

The historic background narrative is an abbreviated history of the region and the immediate vicinity of the project area. It identifies and describes the events and people that were important in the history of the region within which the project is located (including those related to aboriginal peoples), then relates those people and events to the State Historic Preservation Plan. The people and events form part of the consideration in assigning "significance" to sites. The State Plan indicates what is important in this regard. Thus, the archaeologist must address the context of the project to the State Plan and to the overall history. In doing research, considerable effort may be needed to make sure that references to the project area, and areas near the project area, are adequately handled in the research and in the resulting project report. Consideration of nearby past events and people helps to confirm in the review agency's mind that the archaeologist has been thorough.

The historic background uses the following sources:

- local and county histories, both primary and secondary sources;

- official archives and records in municipal and government buildings;

- map research;

- site file information; and

- oral histories from the local community.

In addition to the research themes identified in the State Historic Preservation Plan, the historic background narrative addresses previously identified archaeological sites and historic buildings/structures in or near the project area.

All information on sites, buildings, or structures within the project area needs to be included. The archaeologist must not overlook these types of built-environment resources. If an architectural historian is not normally part of the background research work, the SHPO/THPO may need to be consulted about the likely presence of such cultural resources.

An understanding of how the land was used by historic peoples is helpful. Much can be gleaned from the obvious use of land in large, clearly important ways, such as timbering, mining, or farming. But some uses are more subtle: backyard gardens, wells, outbuildings, paths, and the like. The field of *landscape archaeology* examines not just great formal gardens with known designers and histories, but also the daily domestic gardens and yard use so common for most of the history of the country (see Kelso and Most, ed. 1990; Yamin and Metheny, ed. 1996; examples of method through interpretation and reconstruction are found in A. Noël Hume 1974 and I. Noël Hume 1974; for bibliography, see Firth 1985).[5]

TIP: Civil War Battlefields

Immediately after the Civil War, the U.S. Army Corps of Engineers published a massive compilation of all of the battlefield maps used or made during the conflict. A facsimile of the map portion of the publication has been republished and is a treasure-trove for cultural resources purposes. In many cases, the detail is surprising, and more to the point, the maps are scaled. Used in the field in conjunction with various summaries of ordinance (e.g., Coates and Thomas 1990; Thomas 1985), it is possible to plot with great resolution the troop movements over the battlefield for the duration of the engagement. The battlefield maps are useful both for documenting historic structures and other features of the landscape, just as they are for later working out the dynamics of battlefield engagements, a challenging and rewarding exercise in cultural resources work. (See Davis, Perry, and Kirkley 1983; Thomas 1985; Coates and Thomas 1990.)

---

[5]It is all too easy for archaeologists to undervalue this recent history. Interestingly, much of the fairly immediate past seems to drop from the cultural memory, leaving seemingly mysterious structures such as root cellars to be misinterpreted as ancient Viking houses; bore holes for splitting boulders as ancient Viking ship-docking sites; tobacco cleavers as ancient Viking battle axes; and neatly stacked field stones by immigrant farmers from southwest Ireland as ancient aboriginal burial cairns.

Prehistoric Background Narrative

Like the historic background narrative, the prehistoric background narrative does two things at once. It addresses the local prehistory as it relates to the overall trends in the prehistory of the region, and it does so with reference to the State Historic Preservation Plan. The prehistoric background is assembled differently from the historic background narrative. The process requires familiarity with the often disparate sources on prehistoric archaeology for the area. That information is located in a variety of sources:

- national summaries of prehistory that also mention the region where the project area is located;

- regional summaries that include the project area;

- local summaries of prehistory that include the project area;

- individual site reports, primarily previous compliance reports, filed with the SHPO or equivalent agency;

- national, regional, or local journal series containing articles treating different facets of the prehistory; and

- the state site files.

The prehistoric background has somewhat less detail in terms of specifics compared with historic backgrounds, but it covers a much greater time range and involves substantially more extensive background reading and research. This is why many firms, if they can afford it, have both prehistorians and historians/historical archaeologists on staff. Both can work in either area, but it makes life so much simpler and more pleasant if the chores can be divided.

The preparatory work for the prehistoric background narrative involves reading the pertinent monographs and journal articles. Most of the relevant information is located in four places:

- the state site files;

- the compliance reports filed with the SHPO or the THPO;

- the conference papers delivered at the regional conferences; and

- the research articles published in the regional journals.

Local and regional studies become the primary sources of information.[6] The prehistoric background narrative is put together with an eye toward three things:

(1) the overall chronology or prehistoric sequence (for example, Paleoindian-Archaic-Woodland-Contact);

(2) the State Historic Preservation Plan; and

(3) what is known and has been excavated within the immediate region/vicinity of the project area.

The intention behind the prehistoric background narrative is a bit different than that for the historic background narrative. With the historic background narrative, the idea is to have some sense of what had happened in or near the project area; the issue is less on the deposit or what the deposit might contain (not always, but often enough). With the prehistoric background narrative, there is also the issue of what objects are likely to be found in deposits, the conditions under which the deposits exist (including depth and nature of contents), and how those relate to the overall prehistory of the region.

Historic background narratives are more a matter of knowing what transpired and how deposits may fill in gaps in knowledge. Prehistoric background narratives are as concerned about the structure of the deposits and their likely contents as they are with what all of that stuff might mean.

---

[6]This is why professional archaeologists often choose a regional archaeology conference over a national one: It provides more information of immediate need. This cost-benefit issue is another main reason why private-sector attendance at the annual SAA meetings is proportionally low compared to that of the academic sector. National conferences cost three to four times as much to attend as regional conferences. In addition, few businesses can justify having a large number of employees absent for the time that a national conference takes.

Chapter Summary

The background research is an exercise in establishing context. The background research is meant to gather together what is already known about the project area, specifically its history, prehistory, geology, soils, and basic ecology. It is the first step in that good-faith effort stipulated by 36 CFR 800 of identifying properties—cultural resources—that could be listed on the National Register of Historic Places. It is also the first step in putting the project area into a physical and cultural context of soils, animals, and plants, and of prehistoric and historic peoples. All of that information is needed so that the physical structure of any archaeological site can be correctly understood. It is also needed so that any question of Register eligibility based on association with events, people, on exemplifying master craftsmanship, or on research potential can be judged for encountered cultural resources, in this case archaeological sites.

Background research is needed for all professional archaeological projects, Phase I, Phase II, or Phase III. That background research includes checking the state's site files to see if any sites have been identified in the project area, checking with the SHPO/THPO to see if any properties are listed or considered eligible for listing on the National Register, and checking with both the site files and the SHPO/THPO for any previous compliance reports that may have been filed. Most of the primary research information on an area's history and prehistory will be found in previous compliance reports. The search for information and previous accounts of the project area includes written community histories found in public libraries; historic maps (especially the Sanborn Fire Insurance maps for older urban areas); soil survey books; and at times more detailed archival research, including photographs, tax records, and land titles. All of this will be in addition to examination of research journals, monographs, and scholarly books written about the area/region and associated history and prehistory.

There is a field component to background research. Some involves interviews with local people. A lot will include doing basic background research into the vegetation present in the project area and the nature of soil development under that vegetation. Much of the field aspect of the background work will be done during the period when the Phase I survey work is done.

Additional Readings of Interest

Barber, Russell J. 1994. *Doing Historical Archaeology: Exercises Using Documentary, Oral, and Material Evidence.* Prentice Hall, Englewood Cliffs, NJ. This manual contains activities and exercises that develop skills useful in conducting background research and preliminary field investigations.

Handbook of North American Indians. William C. Sturtevant, general editor. Smithsonian Institution, Washington, D.C. A projected 20-volume project, with the first volumes produced in 1978 (*Volume 8. California;* and *Volume 15. Northeast*), the *Handbook* is encyclopedic in its coverage of prehistoric and historic American Indians throughout North America north of Mexico. The *Handbook* is a basic source with which all professionals should be familiar. As of this writing (fall 2000), the volumes on the Arctic, Subarctic, Northwest Coast, California, Southwest (two volumes), Great Basin, and Northeast are in print.

Hubka, Thomas C. 1984. *Big House, Little House, Back House, Barn: The Connected Farm Buildings of New England.* University Press of New England, Hanover. A wonderful exercise in historic architecture and land use. Hubka's work provides a model for understanding how historic farm compounds were assembled by New England farmers. Since much of the West, especially the Pacific Northwest, was settled by people with the same architectural proclivities, the book has a somewhat broader appeal than might first be thought.

McAlester, Virginia, and Lee McAlester. 1984. *A Field Guide to American Houses.* Knopf, New York. A thorough, well-illustrated, and comprehensive presentation of American residential house styles. Anyone doing architectural history in the context of a Phase I background survey would benefit from this excellent volume.

Sloane, Eric. 1954. *American Barns & Covered Bridges.* Harper and Row, New York.

Sloane, Eric. 1955. *Our Vanishing Landscape.* Harper and Row, New York.

Sloane, Eric, 1956. *American Yesterday.* Harper and Row, New York. [Published together as Sloane, Eric. 1982. *Eric Sloane's America.* Promontory Press, New York.]

Sloane wrote a large number of books focusing on the vanishing American historic life, of which these are a tantalizing sampling. The books treat the landscape, the passing technology, and a world—literally—of other things that are now entirely forgotten. Throughout all of his volumes are detailed line-drawings that teach as much as illustrate. Most compliance archaeology involves historic sites; reading through Sloane helps immeasurably in getting a sense of the world that produced those sites.

CHAPTER FOUR
THE PHASE I PROCESS: IDENTIFICATION OF POSSIBLE HISTORIC PROPERTIES

Identification of Possible Historic Properties

P hase I refers to the identification of archaeological resources through reconnaissance and intensive survey mentioned in the Secretary of Interior's *Standards for Identification* [48 FR 44720–44721].[1] The Phase I survey represents "a reasonable and good faith effort to identify historic properties that may be affected by the undertaking" [36 CFR 800.4 (b)]. In practical terms, this means that the purpose of the Phase I survey is to see if archaeological resources are present within the surveyed area ("reconnaissance survey" or "inventory"). If archaeological resources are present, the Phase I survey also seeks to get some sense of the horizontal extent of those resources and, to a lesser extent, the vertical extent as well as the cultural affiliation and integrity of the deposit ("intensive survey"). This information helps review agencies decide if there might be a *chance* that the sites are "historic properties," that is, eligible for listing on the National Register. If that seems possible, the Phase II testing and evaluation process will be started.

The Phase I identification addresses the following:

- Are there artifacts or some kind of cultural materials present within the project area?

---

[1]"Phase I" is the term used in most parts of the eastern and midwestern United States; "reconnaissance survey" and/or "intensive survey" (or, in Colorado and Wyoming, "Class III Cultural Resources Inventory") are the terms used instead of "Phase I" in many parts of the western United States. We use "Phase I" here because it is widely used and understood, and it implies a conditional step in a sequential evaluation process.

- If there are artifacts present, are they contained in an archaeological deposit that should be called a site, if it has not been so labeled already?

- What is the horizontal and, to a much lesser degree, vertical extent of the archaeological deposit?

- What is the general cultural affiliation of the archaeological materials?

- What is the likelihood of depositional integrity?

It is hard to over-emphasize the importance of the work done for a Phase I survey. The results of the Phase I survey provide the starting point for all subsequent archaeological resource management decisions. The Phase I information resolves whether there is any chance at all that the project area contains archaeological remains that satisfy criteria for listing on the National Register of Historic Places (36 CFR 60.4 [a–d]). Although the Phase I work is meant to be identification or survey work, it often serves as a kind of site evaluation step by suggesting what can be excluded. In situations where subsurface investigations are done, the Phase I survey often can give enough information to tell if the integrity of the deposit has been compromised enough so that it could not be listed on the National Register. If further examination (Phase II testing) is needed, the testing program will be based upon the Phase I results.

Project Structure and Pre-Field Preparation

Phase I projects are far more common than are Phase II or III projects. Although most are small, Phase I projects often provide the bulk of income for a firm.[2] However, there is a lot of competition for Phase I projects, and to be competitive, they need to be budgeted tightly with very little margin for error. Success depends upon good pre-field planning and preparation.

---

[2]For a detailed discussion of corporate archaeology, cash-flow, and structure, see Neumann and Sanford 2001.

Most firms and other organizations that conduct archaeological assessments have a standard procedure for Phase I investigations. Prior to entering the field, basic preparation includes:

- obtaining a map with project boundaries or corridor clearly marked;

- knowing what sites, especially National Register–eligible sites and properties, have been recorded within or near the project area;

- contacting landowners to ensure that permission and proper legal clearance have been received to conduct the field work;

- contacting "Dig Safe" and local utilities to ensure that subsurface cables, gas lines, water mains, and similar items are marked or are absent from the project area if subsurface testing will be done;

- knowing the allocation of labor;

- planning and scheduling personnel tasks for office, laboratory, and field;

- arranging logistics, including billeting, provisioning, and transport when needed;

- making sure that equipment is available for the needs of the project; and

- planning the actual testing or surface survey pattern.

Site and Regional Documentation

State site files are checked to see if any archaeological sites already have been recorded in the project area and within the general vicinity. This check may already have begun if the archaeologist conducted the background research in preparing a bid on the contract to do the project.

The site information required for a Phase I project includes everything touched on or crossed by the project (or within the area of

PENNSYLVANIA ARCHAEOLOGICAL SITE SURVEY

PENNSYLVANIA HISTORICAL AND MUSEUM COMMISSION

SITE NAME __USPS/ Latshaw_____ SITE NUMBER _____
CULTURAL PERIOD(S) __Historic -- Late Victorian to Early Modern_____
TYPE OF SITE _Farmstead___ PUBLISHED REFERENCES _None_____

COUNTY _Montgomery_____ TWP. _____ NEAREST TOWN _Royersford____
OWNER _U.S. Postal Service_____ ADDRESS _Philadelphia, PA 19197_
TENANT _NA_____ ADDRESS __NA_____

MAP REFERENCE: MEASURE IN CENTIMETERS FROM THE BOTTOM PRINTED EDGE UPWARD, AND
THE RIGHT PRINTED EDGE ACROSS

7.5 QUAD NAME _Phoenixville_____ EDITION _1983_ UP _33_ ACROSS _12___
U.T.M. COORDINATES: ZONE _18_ NORTHING _4449400_____ EASTING _454465___
PHYSIOGRAPHIC PROVINCE _Lancaster -- Frederick Lowlands_ MAP ELEVATION _200 ft_
TOPOGRAPHIC SETTING _Level to Gently Sloping_____

SLOPE DIRECTION AND DEGREE _N-NE_ 4%_____ CULTIVATION _None____
SOIL TYPE _RaA Raritan Silt Loam_____
BEDROCK _Brunswick Shale and Fine-grained Sandstone_
IMMEDIATE VEGETATION _Lawn --_
NEAREST WATER _Unnamed Low-_
(NATURE AND DISTANCE)
2ND NEAREST WATER _Mingo Cree_
(NATURE AND DISTANCE)
TESTED (X) __X__ EXCAVATED _
STRATIFIED (X) YES _____ NO _
FEATURES _None_
COLLECTION LOCATIONS _None_
INFORMANTS _Mr. Leon Levine_
CRITERIA FOR NATIONAL REGIST.
Does not satisfy criteria for
POSSIBILITY OF DESTRUCTION _Wi_
SUBMITTED BY _Dr. Thomas W. Ne_
CITY _Frederick_
S.P.A. CHAPTER AFFILIATION __No_
P.A.S.S. REMARKS

SKETCH MAP OF SITE (WITH SOME POINT OF REFERENCE: HOUSE, ROAD, ETC., WHICH CAN BE
RELATED TO THE 7.5 MIN. U.S.G.S. MAP, INCLUDING A SCALE AND APPROXIMATE ACREAGE).
NUMBER OF SQUARE FEET ___20,182 ft.__

LIST SPECIFIC CULTURAL COMPONENTS AND THEIR PRIMARY IDENTIFYING ARTIFACTS.

Mixed Historic Assemblage, Including:
Transfer printed whiteware
Yellow ware
Redware
Blue tinted glass
Wire nails
Vinyl
Rubber
Plastic

SKETCHES (WITH SCALE) OF MAJOR OR REPRESENTATIVE PROJECTILE POINT SHAPES.

NA

LITHIC MATERIAL BY PERCENTAGE.

NA

Figure 4.1.   Site File Form with Map Information. All site forms in the state site files provide information on where the site is located and include a map of some kind.

potential effects for Section 106 undertakings) and everything within a given distance, usually 2.0 km or 1.6 km (one mile) of the project boundaries. This information may be presented in the final report as a map showing the location of the project area or corridor relative to known sites and as a tabulated list of sites.

Contacts, Public Relations

Prior to starting field work, two types of local contact may be needed: landowners and utilities. These can be quite extensive, as in the case of highway or pipeline corridors, where there may be many hundreds of individual property holders. Some states, such as Georgia, require that written permission be obtained from the landowner and submitted to the SHPO prior to the start of field work, even if it is the landowner requesting the Phase I survey.

Publicity sometimes is augmented by public notice, such as the local newspaper, announcing that such work is starting. However, small, private projects usually require no notice. In other cases, a concentrated public relations effort may be appropriate and there may be a public education component to the project. Further (and this is particularly true for western and southern states), the project may involve lands culturally important to Indian tribes or other aboriginal peoples; an effort must be made in such situations to involve the parties concerned. Generally, though, publicity is not an issue for Phase I projects.

If subsurface work is anticipated in urban or suburban areas, local utilities must be contacted. They, or a designated central clearinghouse, will identify buried cables, water lines, and gas lines. It is risky at best to rely on the landowner's knowledge to verify existence and location of buried utility easements and infrastructure. In some states, the law requires checking first before any kind of digging is done.[3]

There are other underground risks that the public utilities might not have on record. There may be buried private utilities—water pipes, power cords, intercom lines—linking various structures and houses on

---

[3]Many people are unaware that such requirements exist. If a buried utility search is to be done, the property owners and residents need to be informed, especially if it will involve any kind of physical alteration to their property.

We learned about archaeology from that . . . The Scared Mom

Every field worker should carry personal identification. The field supervisor should have a copy of the contract, right-of-entry letter, or the Phase I (or Phase II or III) archaeological permit if in a state that requires such. There are very good reasons for this, for example . . .

In a small village near the Canadian border, we headed up the road after an unsuccessful attempt to interview a landowner adjacent to a state highway project near a prison. Our knocks went unanswered, although we saw a small shadow flitting about behind the curtains. We decided that the person must be overly shy about strangers. Not wishing to cause alarm, we left and went back to the field vehicle. Soon after starting to drive off, we suddenly found we were being followed, and then practically forced off of the road by a stranger . . . male, at least six-foot-three and about 300 pounds.

We were glad we were observing our rule about working in pairs, but we were still a little concerned. The man came over to our car door and demanded some identification. Apparently, the hamlet lacked an official police force and had simply delegated such tasks to the largest person in town. It was just our luck that the person who would not answer the door—that small flitting shadow behind the curtains— was this guy's mother. It took some convincing to get him to believe that we were not burglars casing his mother's house. We had our personal identification, but nothing official from the DOT. Finally, though, he accepted our story after we unfurled the 12-foot-long highway realignment project map and showed that we could explain it.

Always be prepared to explain and verify the reasons for your presence.

the property. Some older houses in areas east of the Mississippi have antiquated storm-water or grey-water buried drainage systems that are still operational but are unmapped and separate from the more obvious septic system. Recent housing developments should have base maps that show the locations of private and quasi-private utilities, including septic systems, on file with the permitting agency at the county courthouse or equivalent.

Labor Estimates

Labor estimates are made at the time the bid is submitted to the client.[4] A Phase I project has five budget categories: start-up; field work; analysis; draft report preparation and submission; and final report delivery and turn-over. Each category has three elements: the level or pay grade of the assigned personnel, the number of hours needed to complete a given task, and the hourly pay rate for task workers. The differences between companies among those three options is what makes the bid process so variable.

"Start-up" refers to the labor estimates needed to logistically prepare for field work. This includes arranging for field vehicles, equipment, accommodations, locations of surface reconnaissance or shovel-test transects, and backhoe placement and operation. Other preparatory expenses are associated with the background investigation, including research and obtaining maps, reports, and interviews.

Labor estimates vary by the scale of the project and the expectations of the reviewing agency (usually the SHPO/THPO). Experience may lead to some rules of thumb for allocating labor time. For example, in the forested eastern United States a 20-hectare project requiring shovel testing in a mixed pasture-woodlot may take about 8 person-hours to prepare a site-specific testing program and to set out equipment. Background historic research may range from 8 to over 40 person-hours, depending on the distance between the main office and each source, the presence or absence of previously known sites, prior project area background preparation, and the extent of associated background history.

Field data collection for Phase I projects usually fits into three categories: shovel testing; ground-surface reconnaissance, which involves areas with good surface visibility and is common in western and southwestern states; and heavy equipment work, used both in urban settings and in

---

[4]Effective labor estimates are the product of experience. However, there are various sources that can help, such as the U.S. Department of Labor and professional associations. For example, ACRA (American Cultural Resources Association) often posts information on its Web site and in its newsletter on fee structures and on labor estimates (http://www.acra-crm.org). For details on structuring competitive bids on public-sector and private-sector contracts, see also Neumann and Sanford 2001.

areas with substantial overburden. Labor estimates can be complex and are figured on a project-by-project basis since they depend in large measure on SHPO or local agency testing protocols and the nature of the terrain. Some firms use a "fixed" per-acre (or per hectare) Phase I rate for "normal" or expected field conditions.

Shovel-test costs are made on the basis of the estimated number of test units and the amount of time expected to complete them. Controlled surface collection time is estimated on the basis of the terrain and size of the project area. "Open-ground" surface reconnaissance, as in western states or in more exposed areas of Plains states, depends upon coordination of available maps with GPS positioning of survey crews. Urban Phase I subsurface field work also is a case-by-case matter.

"Analysis" labor estimates vary by region. Compared to computing most field testing estimates, there are even fewer rules of thumb for estimating labor needs for analysis, since the amount of laboratory processing labor will vary by SHPO or equivalent regulatory office protocols (including labeling and records requirements), by the normal artifact yield for sites in the region, and by in-house laboratory procedures. Our experience in the eastern and midwestern United States can give some sense of scale: Most Phase I projects require about 1 hour of analysis time for a laboratory technician for every 4 to 5 hours of total field time, plus 1 hour of laboratory supervisor time for every 16 hours of field time. Any additional sample analysis and testing costs should be added.

Labor estimates for "Report Preparation and Delivery" take into account the actual writing, the production, any special illustrations and figures, and delivery or presentation of the report. The "final" report is a physical hard copy, even if the draft report was approved without need for revision and was submitted electronically.

Budgets and labor estimates for the Phase I project—like Phase II testing and Phase III data recovery projects—include allowances for revising and reproducing the draft report. The amounts of time and costs associated with this last part of the Phase I project usually are about the same as the labor time and costs for the initial, start-up phase of the project.

Staffing Needs

Phase I projects require both nonfield and field support. In larger firms, different people may be used for those staffing needs; in smaller firms, many of the same people will do both. Having a wide assortment of skills in addition to those associated with basic archaeology is important both to the employee and to the firm. This also applies to the state and Federal government workplace, where agency personnel fill a variety of roles.

Staffing needs include:

- *Secretarial:* Preparation of correspondence; coordination of project communications; maintenance of office records including travel vouchers, work orders, and payroll; and scheduling;

- *Project management:* Coordination and assignment of project personnel, preparation and monitoring of the project budget, execution of the research design, personnel management, logistical management, writing of the report, client and agency relations;

- *Field labor:* All aspects of standard field work as well as equipment assembly and maintenance;

- *Laboratory labor:* All tasks from the cleaning of artifacts through their identification and tabulation to coding into a master data base, conservation tasks as needed, preparation for turn-over to a permanent curatorial facility;

- *Graphics;* and

- *Cultural backgrounds:* Background research into the history and prehistory of the project vicinity, which includes site file searches, maps, and research on the history of the project vicinity.

Staffing needs are met either by assigning in-house personnel or by hiring outside personnel to assist in-house personnel. Temporary outside help, referred to as "project-hires," is drawn from a professional migrant population that shifts from one project to the next in a manner very similar to that found in the construction industry. Project-hires usually are only needed for the field work portion of a project, and then only if the scale of the project is such that it cannot be completed using permanent employees of the firm.

Much of the information about the day-to-day activities in archaeology in the United States is communicated through the project-hire community. They know which firms are fair and equitable, and which are not. The labor force must meet applicable Federal or state standards for education and work experience. In many cases, the lowest level of expertise for field operations will be a person with a college background in anthropological archaeology; it is not unusual for Federal contracts to specify that field workers have a completed college degree along with a year or two of supervised field experience.

Field Logistics: Housing, Per Diem, Transport

Most Phase I projects are done within a couple-hour round trip of the main office. In situations where the project is at too great a distance to commute, issues of housing and per diem come up. "Per diem" refers to money allocated to field workers to reimburse room and board costs while in the field.[5]

Housing arrangements vary by the firm. Some firms arrange housing beforehand, others leave it to the employees.

Transportation to the project area on a per diem project usually is the responsibility of project-hires. For permanent employees, the firm provides transportation, or reimburses transportation costs to and from the project area. Once at the staging area for the per diem project, the firm is responsible for getting crew to and from the actual site of field work.

Equipment and Supply Needs

Some firms issue to each crew member most of the equipment listed in Table 4.1; other firms expect crew members to supply equipment. The crew chief or field supervisor will also have the equipment listed in Table 4.2.

Depending on the area and terrain, it may be important to have an extra set of vehicle keys, a good road map, and a shared plan for emergencies. Federal contracts require a developed safety plan with a designated safety officer. Often, it is assumed that the crew had first aid training, including CPR, or that at least one person is certified in emergency

---

[5]Per diem is a critical topic and represents substantial cash-flow along with IRS tax issues. While beyond the scope of this text, anyone looking to work in professional archaeology might benefit from our discussion of this in Neumann and Sanford 2001:121–122.

Table 4.1. Equipment Required by Each Crew Member for Phase I Subsurface Survey

- range-finder compass
- two colors of flagging tape
- bags
- indelible ink marker
- retractable metric hand tape (3-m, locking)
- shovel-testing or surface survey field note forms
- pencil
- clipboard (shielded metal)
- trowel
- root cutters or folding knife
- round-nose shovel or a square shovel with sharpened edge
- small screen (mesh size varies by state, site, and field conditions)
- simple hand-held calculator
- hard hat if working on a construction site or highway corridor
- safety vest if working along a highway or other high-profile area

Table 4.2. Equipment Carried by Crew Chief or Field Supervisor

- Munsell soil color book
- project map or copy showing planned shovel-test or collection area locations
- first aid kit (if far from the field vehicle)
- hand-held GPS unit
- cell phone (as needed)
- cameras (not always needed for Phase I; however, some states require soil profile or general landscape photographs); sometimes black and white film and color slide film are used in two cameras, sometimes a digital camera is used.

responses. This is a requirement for Federal contracts. OSHA (Occupational Safety and Health Administration) regulations address these issues.

Setting Up

After the project has been awarded, and a budget and schedule are in place, the Phase I project must be set up. "Set-up" refers to all of the preparatory steps undertaken to make sure that the project is done properly and within time and budget limits. Part of this will involve securing maps of the project as planned/conceived as well as of the project area; part of this will involve planning out how the land will be checked, especially if subsurface examination ("shovel testing") will be done.

Project Maps

Project maps are both design drawings and planning tools, and may be thought of as equivalent to the rough plans for how the project will be done. These maps, necessary for permitting approval if not construction, are usually submitted for courtesy or mandatory review to a local planning board. Such maps eventually form the basis for the plans that will be used to actually do the project itself. The scale of such a planning map is at 1 inch to 50 ft, 1 inch to 100 ft, or 1 inch to 200 ft, and typically shows what will be done as part of the construction project. Such maps have landscape features shown, as well as other survey marks.

As planning tools, project maps attempt to capture current information. However, they may contain errors and the archaeologist's field measurements may contradict the information on the project map supplied by the client. While archaeologists also make mistakes, in our experience the majority of project maps supplied to us by clients have had

---

TIP: Project Map Terminology

What is a *preliminary project map*? Government agencies use specific terminology for the type of map and what stage it represents in the planning process for an undertaking. The terminology varies quite a bit by agency, and there are no universal definitions.

The category of map is generally determined by the least-precise data recorded. Thus, if the map is concerned with possible route corridor selection, the terrain may be mapped fairly accurately, yet the map will be labeled something like *Preliminary planning—not for construction*. Negotiation may help in obtaining a project map with the types of information needed for the archaeology if the designers see providing this information as helpful to a particular route or design. A proper Phase I archaeological survey requires only enough finalization of design to properly identify the project area, anticipate disturbances and their nature, and locate cultural and natural features.

errors of varying degrees, such as mistakes in distances or feature locations. The proper procedure is to verify one's field measurements as
closely as possible, make notes, inform the client where important, and
continue.

Subsurface Survey: Planning Shovel-Test Transects

In the western and southwestern parts of the country where surface
visibility is good, aggradation is rare, and soils are inactive, subsurface testing rarely is done—except in depositional settings—as part of Phase I.[6]
However, for most of the country, Phase I site identification will involve
some form of subsurface testing. The most common method by far is
shovel testing.

Shovel tests are widely spaced, often rather small tests that are, as the
name suggests, little more than a few shovels-full of fill removed to a
depth of maybe 40 cm (size and shape of shovel tests varies by state). Unit
and transect spacing varies by state/jurisdiction, project area conditions,
and probability of subsurface remains being present. Many states, such
as Maryland, typically recommend as a default a 20 × 20 meter grid of
30-cm diameter, 40-cm deep shovel tests. During the setting-up stage of
the Phase I project, it is useful to figure out where in the field those shovel
tests will be done.

Shovel tests are set out in parallel, usually straight-line transects, with
the shovel tests placed at intervals determined by review agency protocol
and by budget. Typical shovel-test planning involves setting up a gridlike
pattern on the project map before testing begins. This normally is done by
hand using an engineer's rule to work out scale, a set of dividers (like used
for navigation) to make evenly spaced marks on the map, and a protractor
to work out what the compass bearings will be when the lines drawn on

---

[6]Ten states currently (2000) require little if any subsurface testing during Phase I or
an equivalent inventory/survey: Arizona, North Dakota, California, Oregon, Hawai'i,
South Dakota, Nebraska, Utah, Nevada, and Wyoming. Another eight states currently
have discretionary subsurface testing protocols: Idaho, Missouri, Kansas, New Mexico,
Massachusetts, North Carolina, Mississippi, and Wisconsin. The remaining states require shovel testing to be done in some kind of interval fashion, or require such testing
when certain terrain conditions apply, such as when surface visibility is below a certain
percentage or on a case-by-case basis.

the map are brought to operational reality in the field. The transects themselves are then penciled onto the project map. Setting things up like this before getting into the field not only makes the project move along more smoothly, it also helps the person directing the field part of Phase I to know just how many shovel-test units will be needed and, by extrapolation, how long the field time should last.

Something that might be noted when Phase I transects are ruled out on paper: The project map may already have north set out as a true—as opposed to magnetic—bearing. It is tricky, and not really more efficient, to try to figure out from the project map the true bearing of the base line or of the transects set at right angles to it. It is better to wait, enter the field, then simply use uncorrected, magnetic bearings, using large-scale landscape features that the land surveyors already have recorded. These features will be more accurately placed than the archaeologist could do using a hand compass or a GPS instrument.

Phase I shovel testing assumes that archaeological debris will be spread about in a sheet, referred to as "sheet litter." The individual shovel tests are meant to puncture that sheet and document the horizontal extent of any site present. The shovel tests represent individual points from which a coarse image of the site can be discerned. The denser the points,

Figure 4.2.   Setting Up Phase I Shovel-Test Transects on a Project Map.

the better the resolution and definition of the image. This illustrates the advantages of a formal grid pattern as opposed to a haphazardly distributed series of shovel tests.

An implicit assumption about archaeological sites in planning a testing pattern is that cultural materials are distributed within a site as continuous sheet litter. There might be areas of high artifact concentrations and of low concentrations, but the transitions from one to the other are assumed to be gradational, not discontinuous. Another assumption is that there is a threshold density for sites that would met the data potential criterion in 36 CFR 60.4. One artifact recovered from a 30-cm diameter, 40-cm deep shovel test (cylindrical volume: 0.028 m^3; parabolic volume: 0.019 m^3) represents an artifact density of 52.6 artifacts per cubic meter. Finally, it is assumed that there is a threshold area for sites that would meet the data potential criterion in 36 CFR 60.4. The largest circular area that can be missed by a grid of points is $\frac{1}{2}\pi$ times the distance squared between shovel-test intervals. For example, a 20-m testing interval could conceivably miss a site of around 628 square meters (about the size of a modest suburban residential lot).

If the boundaries of the project are not clearly marked, it becomes even more important to mark and plan the transects (or "traverses" in the west, where there is no "cutting" of the soil) so that adequate shovel testing and/or visual inspection will occur. Existing roads and other landscape features can help in orienting the grid. All Phase I exercises must

TIP: Cautions on Using Compasses

Although GPS (global positioning system) instruments are increasingly used for Phase I positioning, the standard hand-held, range-finder compass remains the most common piece of positioning equipment. Compasses are inexpensive and dependable; the commonly used range-finder type forces the field worker to sight on a physical object in the distance and walk to it, rather than depend upon a screen reading. However, compass users should be aware that any electromagnetic fields in the vicinity of the compass can alter readings. That is, power lines, transformers, and microwave transmitters can affect the compass needle and therefore the direction in which the person is walking off for a transect. Always remember to look around—especially up where those power lines may be—before choosing references and bearings.

be set up as if someone else will have to come back in and relocate the shovel tests.

The set-up for field work should include a health and safety "tailgate" meeting to review and prepare for potential hazards. Personnel should be familiar with procedures ranging from treatment for snake bites to urban traffic control, depending on the circumstances of the project area.

Field

Although Phase I is termed "shovel testing," "inventory," "reconnaissance survey," or even misleadingly "cultural resources inventory,"[7] much is done during this stage of the field work. The order in which the work is done does not matter too much since everything is completed quickly. Most non-Federal Phase I surveys involve comparatively small areas and can be done within a week. Surveys over large tracts, such as pipelines, Federal forests, or military installations, take considerably longer.

Three sets of data are retrieved during field work: vegetational, pedological, and archaeological. The first two, which chronicle depositional integrity, will indicate if the third has any meaning in terms of the National Register criteria.

Landscape History: Vegetational and Pedological Data

Landscape history is derived from two data sets: vegetation and soils. Together, these data can answer most initial questions about past land use and therefore the likelihood that the project area lacks near-surface depositional integrity. The vegetation, especially tree cover, records the sequence

---

[7]The term "inventory" is misleading because the purpose of any kind of Phase I identification exercise is not to "inventory"—that is, locate all existing—cultural resources, be they archaeological sites or standing buildings. Rather, the purpose is to make a "good faith effort" to see if properties eligible for listing on the National Register might be present. This may seem trivial; it really is not. The student will come across, time and again, archaeologists and historic preservation people who should know better thinking that the intent of the Phase I identification process is to "find sites" or to "locate all of the sites" in a given area. That is not the idea at all. Thus, Phase I is not an inventory—stuff will probably get missed. Rather, Phase I is, along with the background work we talked about in chapter 3, part of the good-faith effort required to see if Register-eligible properties might be present.

of land-use events over the last 100 years or so; the actual time depends upon the part of the country. The soil augments the interpretation of the vegetation and serves as a bridge to understanding the impact of past land-use activities on the archaeological deposit, if such is present.

Land-Use History Based on Vegetation

Almost no forested area in the eastern/midwestern United States and few in the western United States escaped lumbering activities sometime in the last 200 years (see Neumann 1985, 1989b, 1994, 1995; Neumann and Sanford 1987; Sanford and Neumann 1987; Russell 1997). East of the Mississippi there are few stands of trees present that are older than 100–150 years; most are less than 50 years old. Nearly all of the landscape represents vegetation communities that have emerged subsequent to land clearance. The original land clearance could have been from lumbering, cultivation, pasture, charcoal production, or even military encampments like those east of Manassas Junction in Virginia. Subsequent human activity often included cycles of use that resulted in land disturbance.

The vegetation community present at the time of the Phase I survey represents what has succeeded over the landscape after the last landscape modification took place (Figure 4.3.). Some of the plants present come from locally available seed sources; others from intentional plantings, as in the case of the even-aged stands of longleaf and loblolly pines in the Georgia Piedmont, planted for erosion control. Understanding the plants and their origins helps reconstruct landscape history and can indicate depositional integrity.

The easiest way to reconstruct the land-use history is to document vegetation succession for the project area, particularly the tree cover if such is present (Neumann and Sanford 1987). Tree demographics can be used as a rapid method to document vegetation succession if a few assumptions are made. The field work itself consists of noting the *diameter at breast height* (dbh; about 1.2 m from the ground surface) of the tree, the kind of tree (genus and, if useful or possible, species), and the form of the tree (open-growth or closed-canopy growth). It is necessary only to record those diameters in 10-cm increments.

Information is collected on all trees within a given radius, say 3 m, of the shovel-test unit or some regular point along a transect (Figure 4.4). "All," in this case, means those numerous little saplings just as much as the

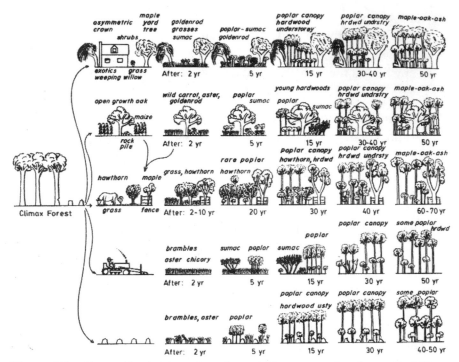

Figure 4.3. Generalized categories of vegetation succession for central New York (after Neumann and Sanford 1987:121). Similar sequences have been developed for other local environmental settings (Neumann 1989a, 1989b; Neumann, Sanford, and Warms 1993; Neumann and Williams 1990, 1991; Sanford et al. 1994; and Sanford, Neumann, and Salmon 1997). Succession is a somewhat loose concept that has been criticized for its deterministic nature (e.g., Drury and Nisbet 1973; Russell 1997), but for archaeologists working in localized environmental settings, it remains a convenient tool for a generalized sense of landscape history.

larger trees. This is a point sample, similar to how foresters survey a stand of timber. The advantage of tying the tree and vegetation data to the shovel-testing regime is that it allows the investigator to discern changes in past land-use activities *within* the project area. Many Phase I exercises involve project areas larger than 20 hectares; often, those project areas once were farms where some of the land was pasture and some of the land was cropped. If vegetation can be linked to a shovel-test grid, the local cultural geography and attendant land disturbance may be reconstructed.

Trees can be sorted by diameter class; usually 10-cm dbh increments is sufficient resolution (Figure 4.5). Under many circumstances, one can assume that the age of a tree, in years, is roughly the same as its diameter

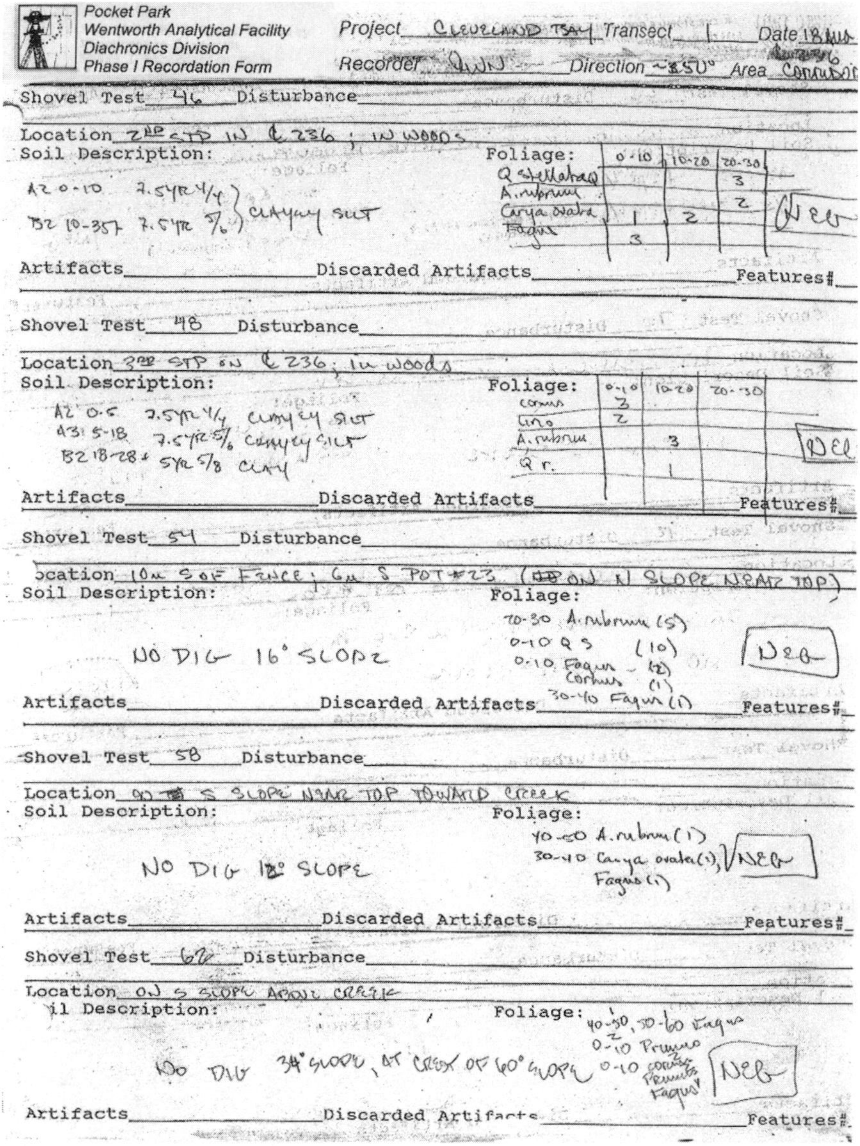

Pocket Park
Wentworth Analytical Facility
Diachronics Division
Phase I Recordation Form

Project CLEVELAND TSAY Transect 1 Date 18 AUG
Recorder Direction ~350° Area CORRIDOR

Shovel Test 46 Disturbance
Location 2ND STP IN ¢ 236; IN WOODS
Soil Description:
A2 0-10 7.5YR 4/4 } CLAYEY SILT
B2 10-35+ 7.5YR 5/6 }

Foliage:	0-10	10-20	20-30
Q stellata			
A. rubrum			3
Carya ovata	1	2	2
Fagus	3		

NEG

Artifacts Discarded Artifacts Features#

Shovel Test 48 Disturbance
Location 3RD STP ON ¢ 236; In woods
Soil Description:
A2 0-5 7.5YR 4/4 CLAYEY SILT
A3 5-18 7.5YR 5/6 CLAYEY SILT
B2 18-28+ 5YR 5/8 CLAY

Foliage:	0-10	10-20	20-30
Cornus	3		
Lino	2		
A. rubrum		3	
Q r.		1	

NEG

Artifacts Discarded Artifacts Features#

Shovel Test 54 Disturbance
Location 10m S OF FENCE; 6m S POT #23 (ON N SLOPE NEAR TOP)
Soil Description:
NO DIG 16° SLOPE
Foliage:
20-30 A. rubrum (5)
0-10 Q S (10)
0-10 Fagus (2)
Cornus (1)
30-40 Fagus (1)
NEG

Artifacts Discarded Artifacts Features#

Shovel Test 58 Disturbance
Location ON S SLOPE NEAR TOP TOWARD CREEK
Soil Description:
NO DIG 18° SLOPE
Foliage:
40-50 A. rubrum (1)
30-40 Carya ovata (1), Fagus (1)
NEG

Artifacts Discarded Artifacts Features#

Shovel Test 62 Disturbance
Location ON S SLOPE ABOVE CREEK
Soil Description:
NO DIG 34° SLOPE, AT CREST OF 60° SLOPE
Foliage:
40-50, 50-60 Fagus
0-10 Prunus
0-10 Cornus, Prunus, Fagus
NEG

Artifacts Discarded Artifacts Features#

Figure 4.4. Example of shovel-test record form with information entered on tree types and size classes observed within 3-m of the particular shovel test.

in centimeters. In some cases, this rule does not hold. Fast-growing, high water table trees like cottonwood, sycamore, tuliptree, and willow tend to be half as old as their diameter in centimeters. Trees that emerged under closed-canopy conditions, like oak or holly or dogwood in a forested track, may be half again to twice as old as their diameter in centimeters. Wherever possible, stumps and other cuts—even limb cuts—should be used to estimate growth rate relative to age rate, since that "centimeter-a-year" rule is an approximation that varies by part of the country, tree species, and growing conditions.

Also recorded are growth characteristics and patterns. For example, the trees will be open- or closed-canopy in their growth habit. Trees that emerged along fence lines when the land was open and under cultivation will be open-growth, with spreading limbs relatively low on the bole. The age of those trees gives an estimate on the age of the fence line; the age of the surrounding woodlot community gives an estimate on when the field was abandoned. Since the diameter of the trees is strongly correlated with the age of the trees, the diagram can be used to estimate dates of changes in the woodlot community structure (Figure 4.6).

Plotting out the above information in matrix form is the first step. The next step is assessing what that information means and using the summary of the data as a vehicle to support the Phase I conclusions. This essentially is a seriation chart, where the tree genera are like ceramic types

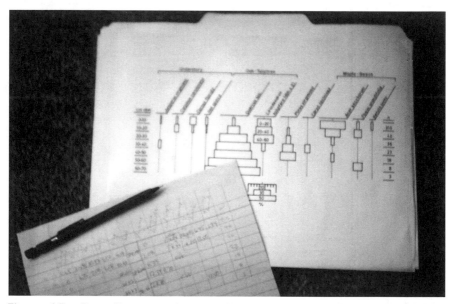

Figure 4.5. Recording tree demographics then assessing how land use has changed requires first that the field data be converted to percentages then graphed. This is a seriation exercise.

Fig. 13. Residential yard cut from abandoned pasture. Isolated trees are live oak; specimen in left foreground around 20 cm dbh. Pasture associates include prickly pear and, along right margin, Ashe juniper growing in a straight line.

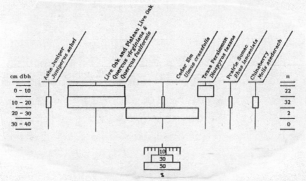

Fig. 14. Demographic profile of trees on a residential lot developed from abandoned pasture. The elms in this sample probably were closer to 20 years old than to 30 years old; the pasture probably was taken out of use in the 1970s. Most of the junipers originally present were removed; residents in this part of Texas prefer oaks over junipers, and the latter usually are removed. In a natural, emerging stand, the number of trees decrease exponentially as the diameter increases. Here, the fact that the largest number of trees is in the 10-20 cm dbh range suggest selection against the saplings that would otherwise be present.

Figure 4.6. Presentation of Field Data. The figure shows how the final product relates to what was originally seen in the field. The data here came from a residential lot in south Texas, where the largest trees were 20–30-cm dbh cedar elms (Ulmus crassifolia). These were joined a decade or so later by various live oaks (Quercus virginiana and Q. fusiformis) along with a mix of secondary species. In this case and using the rule-of-thumb where a tree is about as old in years at its diameter is in centimeters, the field data would be consistent with the land being taken out of use and the residential development being started between 20–30 years ago. In point of fact, the land was developed into a residential community 24 years earlier.

and the changes in their frequency often reflect changes in the use of the land. Different vegetation communities, especially forest communities, are associated with different uses of the land (e.g., Watts 1975, Wessels 1997; for an extensive, albeit dated, list of sources, see Firth 1985). Many parts of the United States have handbooks and manuals on local plants and on local land-use history. From this point, it is only a matter of tying the field data into the known landscape ecology to provide some sense of how the land was used in the past, and if any kind of disturbance—say plowing—had occurred.

Land-Use History and the Soil Profile

An application of soil development principles helps confirm the land-use history, first worked out with the vegetation survey, in those parts of the country where Phase I involves shovel testing. The soils information is often needed to justify arguments about a lack of depositional integrity in the project area.

Just as most of the land east of the Mississippi has been cut over, much of that land also was once plowed. It should not be assumed that the land, because it looks untillable today, had not been plowed in the past. The reason lots of land no longer is farmed today is because people learned in the past, through the failure of farms, that it could not be used. For example, the Root River basin in southeastern Minnesota is filled with abandoned farmsteads left from people in the 1870s–1920s who plowed the 40°–60° slopes, only to have the hillsides wash into the bottomlands. Many small stream valleys in the eastern and midwestern United States have over (sometimes an order of magnitude over) one to two meters of sediment deposited within the last 120 years as a product of those erosion-prone farming practices. Thus, the land surface seen now may not be the aboriginal surface, and the lack of evidence at shallow depths is misleading.

An understanding of how soil horizons and boundaries change will aid in interpretation. Forest soils generally have A horizons only 10 cm thick or so. Historic plowing of ten was as deep as 35 cm (14 inches) before the 1930s; most plowing generally is 20–30 cm deep (8–12 inches). However, while the plowzone or Ap horizon is a visible in the soil profile for several years after plowing ends, its visibility and technically its existence as a soil horizon will eventually disappear. The transition from a farm field soil profile with its clear Ap horizon to a forest soil profile can occur within 30–40 years of the field being abandoned and allowed to become overgrown.

It should be noted at this point that there are two soil horizon description systems used by archaeologists in the literature. One represents a system that began well before 1938 and continued through 1981 (Rice and Alexander 1938:889; see also Soil Survey Division Staff 1951, 1975; Olson 1976). The second is a modification of that system that was set out in 1981 (Soil Survey Division Staff 1981:4-39–4-50; see also Foss, Miller, and Segovia 1985:5–7). The basic aspects of these two systems are compared in Table 4.3.

In the pre-1981 system, the initial Arabic numeral following the horizon letter referred to a particular characteristic of such a horizon. The second Arabic numeral, if one was used, had ordinal meaning. In the 1981 system, Arabic numerals exist for purposes of order only. Subordinate distinctions in horizons, previously designated by numerals, are now represented by one of 22 lowercase letters (Soil Science Survey Division Staff 1981:4-43–4-47). The only major horizon designation commonly encountered or needed by archaeologists that did not change was "Ap," which still means a plowed horizon or "plowzone."

The majority of county soil survey books use the pre-1981 system, primarily because the data were assembled well before the 1981 changes. Much of the archaeological literature and most of the engineering reports

Table 4.3. Comparison of Pre-1981 and Post-1981 Basic Soil Horizon Designations

Pre-1981 Designation		1981 Designation	Meaning
	——surface——		
A1		A	Humus near/at the surface
A2	"topsoil"	E	
A3		AB	Transitional boundary, more like an A than a B
B1		BA	Transitional boundary, more like a B than an A
B2	"subsoil"	B	
B3		BC	Transition from B to unconsolidated material that may or might not be the parent of the B

treated by the practicing archaeologist will also use the pre-1981 system. Recently trained archaeologists know and use the current descriptive system. However, the practicing archaeologist should be fluent in both systems and be clear about which system is being used.

One other point: Soil horizons are not, in themselves, strata. That is, the color of the soil may change as one goes deeper, but that represents the changes through the soil in the concentrations of things like organics. The soil profile for any one soil is a developmental continuum, and excepting for Ap horizons (which *are* strata in the strict sense of the term), is best removed by the archaeologist in arbitrary levels and not by homogeneity of soil color/horizon.

Soils are active, dynamic, three-dimensional ecological systems. Knowing the dynamic nature of soils helps to appreciate the movement of artifacts within the soil.[8]

The movement of artifacts within an active soil is much the same as if the soil itself was behaving like a very thick fluid. The thickness or viscosity of that fluid varies by physical and chemical properties as well as by how biologically active the soil itself is; that is, how many ants and worms and so on are present within the soil.

Because they vary both in texture and biological activity, each soil horizon may be thought of as having a different viscosity. The A or E horizon is more fluid than the B horizon; a plowzone—the Ap horizon— is more fluid than a pasture soil. For this reason, one will observe in the field that artifacts will tend to "bunch up" at an E/B horizon [A/B horizon] interface or Ap/B horizon interface.

There is another issue here: Because artifacts sink, and because prehistoric sites existed in an area long before plowing was present, finding artifacts below the Ap horizon in the B horizon is no indication that one is dealing with a second, undisturbed component. Rather, it is just as likely that the top of the deposit has been clipped and churned by plowing, while the lower end of the vertical spread of artifacts, slowly sinking over the centuries, has managed to settle below plowing depth and remain undisturbed. Whether or not a sub-Ap horizon assemblage represents a separate occu-

---

[8]For additional references as well as a detailed discussion of soil fluidity as it applies to archaeological deposits and the sinking of artifacts through soil horizons or cultural sediments, see Neumann, 1993. The mathematics for flotation-sized particle movement are given in Neumann, 1978.

pation can be tested statistically. If such a spread of artifacts between a plowzone and subplowzone is found in the field, then that vertical distribution must be tested statistically before the Phase I report is submitted.

Field Methods

Three general categories of field methods are used during Phase I investigations: (1) shovel testing or test-pitting; (2) ground-surface examination; and/or (3) heavy equipment testing. Shovel testing is the most common in the eastern United States and in settings with restricted ground-surface visibility. Heavy equipment testing, usually using a backhoe, is generally used in urban areas as well as in situations warranting deeper testing through sediments, as in a floodplain.

Ground-surface examination with no subsurface testing and often no artifact collecting is common in many areas of the western and southwestern United States where the ground surface is visible.[9] Very often in these areas as well, the values of the Indian cultures discourage testing or artifact collecting. This may mean greater attention must be paid to background research, but it can also reduce the cost of the survey because there is no collection to curate.

Archaeological surface reconnaissance has been discussed often in the literature (see Fish and Kowaleski, ed. 1990; Renfrew and Bahn 2000; Sharer and Ashmore 1993:186–192, 196–201, 237; Feder 1997:54–55), with topics ranging from field procedures to regional sampling. Archaeology involving large structures and urban or built-up settings also has been discussed, although perhaps not as often in terms of using heavy equipment in urban areas (see Renfrew and Bahn 2000; Sharer and Ashmore 1993:25–276; Hester 1997:73–77).

---

[9]Not surprisingly, there is a strong correlation between the extent to which a state is forested and the expectation that shovel testing will be done as part of Phase I. Based on standard forest/vegetation maps and individual state protocols, there is a very strong positive correlation between forest cover and shovel testing as a default requirement ($r = +0.85$, df: 39; $p \ll 0.001$ that there is no correlation).

There is a second issue of which the student needs to be aware. Soils are dynamic three-dimensional matrices that function as very, VERY viscous fluids. Artifacts placed on their surfaces will, given enough time, sink through them. Soils in arid or semi-arid areas not only are soils now, they may have been much more active in the past. Thus, while the current protocols do not require—or sometimes actively prohibit—Phase I subsurface testing, this does not necessarily mean that all prehistoric artifacts will still be visible on the surface.

We learned about archaeology from that . . . Subplowzone Components and Sinking Artifacts

An urban floodplain project in West Virginia illustrates the importance of knowing how artifacts move around in an active soil. The Phase I work had been done by another firm and we were providing Phase II testing.

Most of the area around the small town was under cultivation. Several fields contained prehistoric artifacts, and a series of new sites had been identified for the overall project area. The Phase I report noted that many had undisturbed, subplowzone archaeological components in addition to archaeological materials contained within the plowzones themselves.

Obviously, artifacts found in the plowzone could have come from any place between the surface and the maximum plowing depth. It is also reasonable to assume that any material found below the plowzone is in an undisturbed context. However, it is not safe to assume that the artifacts themselves originated in the undisturbed subsoil, nor that they would therefore represent a separate and undisturbed component.

Many SHPOs specify excavation through the Ap horizon into *culturally sterile* subsoil, meaning fill that does not contain artifacts or features. The hidden assumption in that specification is that prehistoric artifacts, between the time they were deposited and the time the site was plowed, did not move down through the soil to a depth below where the plow eventually cut. Further, it assumes that the artifacts could not have moved from the plowzone into the subsoil after plowing commenced. Both assumptions are wrong.

In the situation of the small town and the myriad of prehistoric sites with undisturbed components, it proved relatively easy to demonstrate statistically that the artifacts that came from immediately below the Ap horizon actually had originated from the assemblage still located within the Ap horizon. This was done by subdividing the artifacts into functional classes and raw material classes, then running a chi-squared statistic between the Ap and the upper B horizon populations. In all cases, it was found that there was no reason to consider the two to be independent sets. This was something that really should have been done as part of the Phase I investigation, *before* it was argued that the subplowzone material represented a separate, undisturbed component.

The point to remember here is that active soils behave a lot like very thick fluids as far as artifacts are concerned. Generally, artifacts will keep sinking through those "fluids." Just because artifacts are found in unplowed contexts below the plowzone does not automatically mean that the artifacts are in situ. Prehistoric artifacts have had a great deal of time to shift before plowing commenced. Before a recommendation is made that the artifact population is independent (a separate component) from that found in the plowzone, the supposition must be tested statistically. In the case at hand, only one component was present. The artifacts recovered from the B horizon actually were not located in their original vertical positions.

Shovel testing is rarely discussed in the literature with the same attention given to more traditional archaeological methods, yet it is the primary procedure for collecting field data during Phase I surveys in the majority of states. A shovel test is a limited subsurface excavation that provides information on the presence or absence of artifacts while doing minimal damage to a site and requiring minimal labor. It emulates the effects of a plow and historically is derived from that and the associated data retrieval that would come from surface collecting a plowed field. Usually, a shovel test is a circular excavation about 30 cm in diameter and about 40 cm deep, although this can vary by state or agency protocols. Shovel tests are normally dug along straight-line transects at some pre-set interval, such as 15 m, 20 m, or 30 m.

Many states have established default protocols for shovel testing. These specify the size and form of the shovel test, the kind of screening to be done, the default shovel-test and transect intervals, and the maximum slope on which testing must be done. In some states, such as Arkansas, Louisiana, and Kentucky, it has been acceptable to shovel-sort the fill; in most other states where screening is expected, fill must be screened through ¼-inch (0.635 cm) mesh, although in Idaho and Montana, ⅛-inch (0.318 cm) mesh is required, while in Maryland ½-inch (1.270 cm) mesh may be used on industrial sites. To put this into some perspective, we have found that shovel sorting alone will recover approximately 20 percent of what would be recovered with a ¼-inch screen (Neumann and Sanford 1985).

Supplemental testing, or second-pass testing, should be done after the main transects are completed. This involves testing between shovel tests with artifacts ("positive shovel tests") and shovel tests without artifacts ("negative shovel tests") around the perimeter of the artifact spread represented by any cluster of "positive" shovel tests. The purpose is to refine the edges of a possible archaeological site.

Figure 4.7. Standard Phase I shovel-testing equipment, which includes round-nose shovel, small screen, compass, trowel, clipboard with shovel-test forms, flagging tape or pins for marking where shovel tests were dug, and back pack.

Figure 4.8. Excavation of typical 30-cm-across, 40-cm-deep shovel-test unit.

Figure 4.9. Finished shovel-test unit. The fill will be screened, while soil horizon characteristics, including texture, color, and horizon thickness, will be recorded.

Field Notes and Records

Field notes should be kept in a three-ring, D-ring binder. Round-ring binders should be avoided since the back pages get torn due to the shape of the rings and how the pages move—or do not—as the binder is set flat and opened. Again, this may seem like a rather trivial remark, but it is not. This is one of those things that no one bothers telling students about until it is too late: Using round-ring binders results in pages tearing out where the holes are punched and field notes being lost.

We learned about archaeology from that . . . **False Positives:**
Manure Spreaders and Phantom Sites

Artifacts do not always indicate a site, even if they are spread over a large area in great density or concentrated in clusters. Consider the following.

A once-cultivated field was slated for residential development. During the 1800s, a little community grew up in its vicinity and, until the 1960s, a local kiln had operated on a parcel next to it. The setting suggested a high probability for prehistoric and historic archaeological remains; local code required a Phase I survey.

Phase I shovel testing revealed a light scattering of historic artifacts—bottle and plate glass and common nineteenth-century ceramics—over the entire project area, along with a few prehistoric artifacts and three heavier concentrations of historic artifacts. The plowzone contained heavy concentrations of historic artifacts dating from 1880 to 1925. The dates corresponded to the landscape history indicated by the vegetation of the now over-grown field.

The artifact assemblage and distribution had some interesting characteristics. Each of the three heavy, localized concentrations were near a corner of the farm field: one near a road, another near where the kiln property was, and a third opposite the original, still standing, farm house. Statistical comparison of frequency and type among the three showed that each had the same ratio of bottle glass to ceramics to bone to plate glass to lamp glass. Further, while an assortment of common and occasionally expensive ceramics was present, there was no repetition in ceramic type.

There were no soil discontinuities. There was a 25–30 cm Ap horizon over a C horizon. There were no apparent foundations and almost no evidence of other architecture-related artifacts such as bricks, foundation stones, or mortar.

The possibility of unknown historic sites, coupled with the background history and artifact inventory, led the agency reviewer to request additional testing around the artifact concentrations to locate any structures. However, the most likely source of the artifacts and their occasional concentrations was a manure spreader. Although additional testing was done, this explanation was eventually accepted.

A manure spreader was (and remains) standard farm equipment. On farms with livestock, barns would be cleaned out and the manure tossed into the spreader. Periodically, the contents would be spread over the fields. However, the manure spreader also received kitchen scraps and waste, and occasional small bits of household trash and debris. In many ways, the manure spreader served as the dumpster for the whole farm.

> ### *We learned about archaeology from that* . . . False Positives:
> ### Manure Spreaders and Phantom Sites *(Continued)*
>
> The agency reviewer was right in that the debris was the signature of a residence. However, it had been carried into the field and spread over it. The concentrations represented starting, crossing, and excess dumping points for the spreader. The similarities in artifact assemblage represented the blurring together, over about 50 years, of the common kinds of household accidents that individually would be distinct: a broken window pane, a shattered plate, remnants of a Sunday roast, empty medicine bottles.
>
> This incident illustrates the importance of understanding the behaviors that took place on the land when it was in use, as well as the signatures of such behavior.

Phase I field notes have four categories of information:

- general project information, maps, scope of work;

- the general field notes kept by the field supervisor;

- the specific shovel-test field notes kept by the crew and the supervisor; and

- the field specimen sheets (bag inventory).

Each of the above categories have sections within the notebook. Not always, but often the field notebook will become the project notebook. It will be the core reference for completion of the project and will include most of the project documentation that will be turned over to the client at the end of the project.

Included within the project notebook should be the SOW (scope of work), draft figures for the final report, and other bookkeeping and project management items—tables, figures, list of tables, list of figures, contact sheets, other maps, and pretty much anything else made out of paper that has even a passing bearing on the project. These will be added into the notebook after the project has come out of the field.

Table 4.4 presents the core information that should be included in the field notes, arranged in the recommended order. These notes will be kept by the project manager or field supervisor; the project manager is

Table 4.4. Basic Structure of Phase I Field Notes

The following presents the core information that should be included in the field notes, arranged in the recommended order. The information in the field notebook has the strength of primary evidence if any issue involving the field work comes to trial. The notebook is a "discoverable document" in a legal proceeding, which is why it is important that students understand how to set one of these up.

Section 1. General Project Information

- SOW (Scope of Work)

- Logistics, including work orders from management and hour allocations for the tasks concerned:
  For the purposes of the field notes, the logistics should identify how many person-hours have been allocated to the particular project, based upon specific tasks.

- Project maps and figures:
  Reduced versions of project area maps, including those showing shovel-test locations and transects, are put in this subsection. Often the scope of work will have project area drawings; copies should be included in this section. Additional maps in this part of the field notes include a photocopy of the appropriate section of the relevant USGS 7.5 minute quadrangle, along with a copy of the distance scale. A photocopy of the appropriate sheet from the county soil survey may be included.

- Right-of-entry materials:
  The project manager should have in this part of the notebook copies of returned and signed right-of-entry letters; whenever possible, whoever is in the field should make certain that the landowner is contacted again just prior to entry onto the property.

- Records of interviews and communications:
  Any kind of discussion that occurs between project personnel and people commenting on the project should have a written summary that is put in this section of the notebook.

Section 2. General Field Notes
The narrative part of the field notes ties things together by giving an idea of what transpired. In addition, the narrative section of the field notes contains a detailed description of the landscape as encountered in the field. This description includes trees, groundcover, soils, water bodies, exposed rock, gullies, and fences and other cultural features.

Section 3. Specific Field Records

- Individual shovel-test records, arranged by transect; or individual surface collection area records

- Feature inventory

- Photograph records

Section 4. Bag Inventory/Field Specimen Sheets

responsible for the field notes, even if those notes are kept by the field supervisor. We include this in part because we have often found students, interns, and even new hires to be at a loss about how to set all of this up. However, it is also included, including the remark on D-ring binders, because the field notes from Phase I—or from any research project—represent primary evidence in court. Professional archaeology is like any other compliance or contracting profession: There are parties with other interests and agendas; there are contracts that may not be honored. The field notes from projects become important pieces of evidence in legal proceedings.

Post-Field

Phase I surveys are the bread-and-butter of most archaeological firms. To be cost-effective, many things need to be done at the same time. This does not impinge on quality but it does require attention to logistics. After the field work is completed, the following steps are initiated:

- the artifacts, along with a copy of the bag inventory, go to the lab for processing and analysis;

- draft figures for the report are prepared;

- site forms are prepared as quickly as possible and submitted to the state for a site number; and

- the body of the report, such as the general opening, cultural and environmental background, and similar sections, is drafted.

Level of Analyses Expected

The Phase I exercise is not a sustained, interpretive analysis of the archaeology or the history of the project area. Rather, Phase I is the field part of a good-faith identification exercise to see if there is anything present that may warrant closer examination. The Phase I report, then, provides sufficient information to agency reviewers so that they can decide if archaeological sites might be present that *might* be eligible for listing on the National Register.

The principal interpretative analysis takes place within the report and addresses issues required to assess the eligibility of a site for listing on the National Register, as specified in 36 CFR 60.4. These issues are the integrity of any archaeological deposit, and the deposit's association (e.g., with

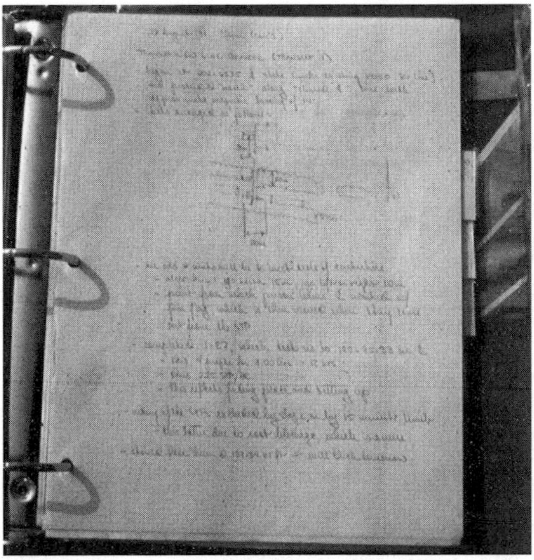

Figure 4.10.   Example of Phase I field notes.

important person, event, design), or potential of the deposit to contribute information to the study of history or prehistory (i.e., "data potential").

The information collected during the Phase I survey may be capable of dealing with some evaluation questions. For example, the information may be sufficient for the lead agency to determine that a site does not merit listing on the National Register and requires no further testing because it lacks integrity and is less than 50 years old.

Generally, artifact analysis is limited to identification, typological classification, frequency count, and distribution across the site or project area. For example, South's (1977) activity-set approach merely requires classification of the historic assemblage into like sets and consideration of how those artifacts are distributed over the project area.

Unlike historic artifact classification, some of the prehistoric artifacts require examination under low magnification to correctly assign function. For example, a dissecting microscope helps separate the microliths in an assemblage from the unused flakes. However, anything beyond simple recognition is over-doing it; if the site is that important, more will be evident during the Phase II testing. Thus, counts, depths, soil horizon, and rough classification are all that are needed for the Phase I. The purpose is merely to figure out what is there and roughly how much is present.

Addressing Basic Phase I Issues

The vast majority of Phase I projects do not contain archaeological sites that satisfy 36 CFR 60.4 criteria for listing on the National Register. In many cases, archaeological materials are present, but are sporadic, common, undiagnostic, or contained within disturbed matrices.

A case for whether or not more testing (Phase II evaluation) is recommended is based on apparent integrity of the deposit, the nature of the apparent artifact assemblage relative to what is already known archaeologically, and statistical tests for patterning.

General Structure of Report

The general structure of archaeological compliance reports is given in chapter 7. The Phase I report is a form of analysis, just as the work in the laboratory—if it was needed—was a form of analysis. In the "Results" section, evidence is given and then interpreted to give reasons why the review agency and the SHPO should or should not continue with a Phase II investigation.

Site Forms

After coming in from the field, and while artifacts are processed in the laboratory, site forms should be completed. If a site was previously recorded for part or all of the project area, then submit an updated site form to the state. A new site form is required if unrecorded sites were encountered.

Review agencies prefer or require that the site number be used in the final report. This means getting the site form filed as soon as possible. A few states also ask that the collections be labeled with the site number. The turn-around time for getting a site number varies by state and by work load; the archaeologist should know how long it usually takes for the particular state in question.

Dealing with site forms raises two issues: (1) determining if what was present was a site; and (2) mechanics for amending, updating, or completing, then submitting, site forms.

Although 36 CFR Part 63 (IV, A, 2) defines a site as any "location of prehistoric or historic occupation or activity" (see chapter 2), there is no firm definition of what this actually constitutes. After all, this is hardly a precise definition. However, Phase I surveys are intended to see if sites are present that might satisfy criteria for listing on the National Register of Historic Places. This means that a consistent, operational definition is needed. For example, does one shovel test having five artifacts in it mean a site? Two adjacent shovel tests with two artifacts each?

The decision should be consistent with the needs and opinions of the state. Some states have explicit definitions of what constitutes a site (e.g., Alabama and Louisiana). More often, the state leaves this to the judgment of the archaeologist. One approach we have used is:

(1) If a feature is found, even in one shovel test, call the area a site;

(2) If at least three shovel tests within an interval of 20 meters have more than two artifacts each, call the area a site.

Calling the deposit or spread of artifacts a site does not mean that it is significant in National Register terms. It is merely a way of keeping track of clusters of debris over the landscape. It allows the practicing archaeologist to decide if site forms should be submitted. If the state disagrees with the archaeologist's definition or threshold, then the state can provide operational criteria.

Many states now require that a completed site form be submitted and be in their possession before a site number is given. The practicing archaeologist should have blank site forms on-hand. Getting the forms, if such already is not present, is easy: Just call the state review agency or visit its Internet Web site.

Chapter Summary

The Phase I Process is the first step in archaeological compliance work. It represents the first part of the "good-faith effort" required of Federal agencies to identify possible historic properties (possible cultural resources eligible for listing on the National Register). That first part is to see if cultural resources—in the case here, archaeological sites—are present. The second part, called Phase II, will be to see if those sites are eligible for listing on the National Register.

In practice, Phase I is essentially a site survey or site reconnaissance exercise. The idea is not to locate every site, that is, do a site inventory of an area. Rather, the idea is to make a reasonable attempt to see if historic or prehistoric sites are present. This means that in addition to checking the state site files to see if sites already are known for the area, the professional archaeologist also must physically check to see if sites are present that have yet to be recorded.

The most common archaeological compliance project is a Phase I survey. Phase I surveys provide a significant part of a firm's cash flow. As with all aspects of professional archaeology, attention must be given to correctly estimating the labor required for the project, locating suitable staff if such are not already employed by the firm, and providing field logistical support. Although to stay in business the firm must turn a profit, it cannot do the work in such a way that it fails to pass peer review by the lead agency archaeologists or by the SHPO/THPO archaeologists. A common misunderstanding is that professional archaeologists will sacrifice basic research quality to increase profit. That is incorrect. If the Phase I work does not pass review, it will have to be continued or redone until it does. Failure to do good Phase I work can result in delays for the archaeologist's client, cost-overruns for the archaeologist's own firm, and sufficient negative publicity within the client's business community that future work is doubtful. All of those mean a very short business life indeed.

Phase I projects include background research on the project area. This research examines what has been done to-date, archaeologically, in the project area, as well as what is generally known about the history and prehistory of the region in which the project is located. Another aspect of the background research is to arrive at a general understanding of the area's ecology (including the various soil types). And finally, the background research can include interviews with local people about the project area. When tribal or other aboriginal lands are involved, Federal code requires that tribal or native organizations be consulted.

Phase I field work consists broadly of two parts: assessment of landscape history using vegetation and soil indicators, and archaeological survey. The type, growth habit, and location of vegetation over the project area provides information about how the land has been used in the past and at times when that use took place. This is important for knowing if there has been any land disturbance that would compromise any archaeological sites that might be present. Soils information can also indicate disturbance, particularly if plowing has been done in the recent past.

The Phase I archaeological field component differs across the country depending upon vegetation cover. In those states with extensive vegetation cover, Phase I includes some form of subsurface testing, generically referred to as shovel testing. This is a limited test excavation that is widely spaced over the project area. This is the default procedure in most states. In states with large areas of sparse vegetation or exposed ground surface, surface collecting and reconnaissance are done instead of subsurface excavation. This is the default procedure in most western states. However, both procedures are meant to be good-faith efforts that go beyond just looking in the site files to see if archaeological sites (or, for that matter, any undocumented cultural resources) are present.

After the field work is completed, any archaeological data collected will be analyzed. Those data will be combined with the background information and vegetation/soils data then submitted as a detailed technical monograph to the government agency held responsible for the compliance work. The initial draft of that report will be reviewed by agency archaeologists (and sometimes by SHPO/THPO archaeologists), revised as needed, then resubmitted as a final report.

The report serves as the eyes for both the government agency and for the SHPO/THPO. The professional archaeologist will make recommendations in the report about whether any archaeological sites should be further tested to see if they are eligible for the National Register, or if any sites encountered could for reasons like extensive disturbance not be eligible for the National Register. Those are recommendations only; the government agency will make the final decision, and that decision will need to be agreed to by the SHPO/THPO, or (if there is disagreement and the Phase I is part of a Section 106 project) by the Advisory Council on Historic Preservation.

If more information is needed about the Register eligibility of any archaeological sites present, one recommendation in the report may be for further testing. That testing, which is part of the Phase II Process, is discussed in chapter 5.

Additional Readings of Interest

Brady, Nyle C., and Ray R. Weil. 1998. *The Nature and Properties of Soils*. Twelfth edition. Prentice Hall, Upper Saddle River, NJ. Comprehensive introduction to soils that also serves well as a shelf reference.

Chesterman, Charles W. 1979. *The Audubon Society Field Guide to North American Rocks and Minerals*. Knopf, New York. Well illustrated and organized field manual of service in identifying lithic raw material.

Feder, Kenneth L. 1997. Chapter 4. Site survey. Pp. 41–68 in *Field Methods in Archaeology*, by Thomas R. Hester, Harry J. Shafer, and Kenneth L. Feder. Seventh edition. Mayfield, Mountain View, CA. Clear, serviceable introduction to the range of site survey methods.

Firth, Ian J. W. 1985. *Cultural Landscape Bibliography*. National Park Service/Southeast Region office. U.S. Government Printing Office, Washington, D.C. As the title states, a bibliography of sources on cultural landscapes. The advantage of the Firth work is that it covers sources from before the mid-1980s, thus avoiding the frequent older-than-10-years-source-cutoffs that occur with Internet-based literature searches.

Foss, J. E., F. P. Miller, and A. V. Segovia. 1985. *Field Guide to Soil Profile Description and Mapping*. Second edition. Soil Resources International, Moorhead, MN. Excellent and readable introduction to field description of soils, written for the practicing archaeologist by individuals who have worked long and in the field with professional archaeologists.

Neumann, Thomas W., and Robert M. Sanford. 1987. The use of vegetation successional stages in cultural resource assessments. *American Archaeology* 6:119–127. The first reading-the-landscape paper written by archaeologists for use by archaeologists, especially those doing Phase I surveys.

Sanford, Robert M., Don Huffer, Nina Huffer, Tom Neumann, Giovanna Peebles, Mary Butera, Ginger Anderson, and Dave Lacy. 1994. *Stonewalls and Cellarholes: A Guide for Landowners on Historic Features and Landscapes in Vermont's Forests*. Vermont Department of Forest, Parks, and Recreation, Waterbury, VT. General guide to cultural landscape evidence written for the lay reader.

Watts, May Theilgaard. 1975. *Reading the Landscape of America*. Revised and expanded edition. Collier, New York. Charming and engaging collection of Watts's papers treating how landscape use has changed in the United States. Watts not only provided excellent drawings, she took pains to make sure that it was clear how outbuildings, gardens, and landscape plantings changed over the years. A volume that one pulls down again and again simply for the joy of wandering through the world portrayed; rather like E. B. White meets cultural geography.

THE PHASE II PROCESS: TESTING AND EVALUATION

Testing and Evaluation

The purpose of Phase II testing and evaluation is to see if archaeological sites identified during the Phase I survey satisfy criteria for listing on the National Register of Historic Places (36 CFR 60.4). From the perspective of archaeology, the site will *both* (1) be associated with important persons or events; exemplify the craftsmanship of a master or design of a period or craft; or contribute to the understanding of the period or culture represented; and (2) have depositional integrity. Phase II testing seeks answers to the following:

- Is the site associated with nationally, regionally, or locally important persons or events?

- Does the site exemplify or chronicle the work of a renowned craftsman, or a particular form of landscaping, construction, or "building"?

- Does the site contain information that can contribute to the knowledge of the associated period or culture?

- What are the spatial and temporal limits of the site?

- Does the site have integrity, usually in the sense of depositional integrity?

- If there is a question about depositional integrity, does the site have deposits that are equal or more intact than others known for the same kind of site?

Phase II testing is an evaluative step. Following from the Secretary of Interior's Guidelines for Evaluation [48 FR 44723], the results of a Phase II are meant to provide the review agencies with enough information to determine whether or not the site could be listed on the National Register, as well as the physical extent of that site. Phase II is concerned with the nature of the site itself, as well as how that site might relate—functionally and temporally—to other sites in the region. The process can also yield substantive data in its own right, even if the site itself turns out to be ineligible for listing on the National Register.

If Phase II involves excavation, only enough of the site is dug to enable a recommendation to be made. The excavations may be small test units, exposing no more than 0.2–0.5 percent of the site area. They may be done as larger area tests, exposing more of the site but not as deeply. Or, the site may be intentionally plowed for purposes of the Phase II, a controlled surface collection done, and a small portion of that plowzone stripped to expose and map features. On rare occasions, backhoe trenches will be dug, primarily to see if there are any deeply buried occupation layers. The idea of Phase II field work is to get just enough information to assess National Register eligibility.

Deciding how to do the testing depends on a host of factors, including the suspected nature of the site and protocols in the given states, funds available, and agreements between the SHPO/THPO and the agency or client. Phase II refines or clarifies impressions of depositional integrity, cultural affiliation, vertical extent of the cultural deposit, and site function that came from the Phase I survey work.

Phase II testing is similar to site testing in field manuals and archaeology texts. However, it differs in three ways:

(1) There will exist a previous study, equivalent to a Phase I survey, indicating the general horizontal bounds of the site and general artifact distribution;

(2) There will be a predetermined number of test units of a predetermined size to be excavated; and

(3) The goals of the testing are to resolve any questions of if the site is eligible for listing on the National Register.

The main difference between academic and professional testing is the need by the latter to address specific questions relating to National Register eligibility or other regulatory requirements.

The depth of test units varies by several factors, including state requirements, agency protocols, nature of the deposit, and nature of the project and its possible effects. For example, 1×1–m units seldom can be excavated deeper than 1.0 m, simply because of the limitations imposed by the length of the shovel handle, which bangs into the unit walls when drawn back to remove fill. However, digging much deeper than 30 cm may be pointless if the site involves the backyard of a historic structure, since what will be of concern or interest may be the layout of garden beds and walkways and the past presence of wells and outbuildings. The U.S. Army Corps of Engineers (COE), in some districts, requests testing to 2.0 m below the surface, which requires at least one horizontal dimension of the unit to be around 2 m for excavation by shovel. Beginning at 4.0–5.0 ft (1.2 m–1.5 m), depending upon jurisdiction, state safety and OSHA (Occupational Safety and Health Administration) regulations require some kind of shoring of the walls; these are spelled out for example in the U.S. Army Corps of Engineers's *Safety and Health Requirements Manual (1996)*. Proper anticipation of this requirement means designing the units to accommodate shoring hardware. Environmental conditions such as soil type and moisture content also affect shoring and may be factored into the applicable regulations.[1]

The Phase II testing is the first opportunity to study the structure of an archaeological deposit because a sizable profile or window on that deposit is opened. Archaeologists dig to answer questions: If the site is so limited and fragile that testing removes most or all of the deposit (called "testing out-of-existence"), then a good argument probably could be made that it did not possess the quality of significance as defined in 36 CFR 60.4, simply because data potential was so limited (but of course that would depend upon the situation). In most instances, to be National

---

[1]The COE maintains an Internet presence for its safety and occupational health office, a convenient source of information for field planning as of May 2000, being http://www.hq.usace.army.mil/ceso/cesopub.htm. For a discussion of shoring and related safety issues, see also Neumann and Sanford 2001:189.

Register eligible connotes that site data are sufficiently robust and redundant to withstand Phase II testing.

Project Structure and Pre-Field Preparation

Phase II testing is initiated in response to one of two situations:

- A Phase I survey has identified an archaeological site of sufficient size, character, or depositional integrity that further examination was needed to see if it could be listed on the National Register; or

- The site already was known and perhaps listed or considered eligible for listing on the National Register. Usually, the Phase II in this case is to obtain further details on the nature of the deposit in preparation for Phase III data recovery.

In the vast majority of the cases, the site was first encountered during a Phase I survey. Consequently, data and results from that Phase I report are critical to structuring the Phase II testing effort. Recommendations in the Phase I report may have helped structure the SOW for the Phase II. In any case, these recommendations should be carefully considered in planning the Phase II approach.

Research and Sampling Strategies

Phase II testing is somewhat similar to much of the cultural historical archaeology done in the United States prior to the 1960s, although the reasoning behind it is much different. While both investigate the range of materials in the site, how abundant those materials are, what their cultural and temporal affiliations are, and how intact the deposit is, the similarity ends there.

The Phase II sampling strategy normally builds upon that of the Phase I and must address its limitations. In the eastern and midwestern United States, Phase I subsurface sampling normally examines the first 40 cm below the surface, depending upon the jurisdiction and protocol. The Phase I field work may have been a surface collection of a plowed field; it often will be the results from a shovel-testing regime. In the western

United States, subsurface testing during Phase I probably was not done. The presence of a site would have been indicated by artifacts or land features visible on the surface.

Surface survey and shovel testing are often sufficient to delimit the horizontal extent of shallow archaeological sites in nonaggrading settings. However, areas with well-developed soils (meaning deep solums) may have prehistoric materials that have now sunk too deep to be found with shovel or plow.

Sites in aggrading settings, being deep, are difficult to reach with shovels. These settings usually involve floodplains, although locations susceptible to colluviation—slope wash—also qualify. The only ways to find out if deeper cultural materials exist is to dig trenches or use some form of remote sensing. If remote sensing is used, it may need to be accompanied by some kind of excavation for physical verification.

If the Phase I investigations encountered archaeological materials, the Phase II test units should focus on those areas having higher-than-average artifact concentrations or culture indicators. It is necessary to get a sound idea of the potential range of artifacts in the site while disturbing as little of the site as possible. Further, areas of high artifact concentrations often are associated with heavily used areas of an archaeological site and are more likely to contain features.

Features—those nonportable human alterations of the site fabric—show site depositional integrity while also serving as data repositories. Features have very high behavioral-information contents. Clues may suggest the presence of features. For example, the habitation areas of open-air prehistoric sites often are indicated by fire-cracked rock. If Phase I testing indicated a confined area of fire-cracked rock, then it makes sense to test the area, since there may be associated evidence of prehistoric dwellings.

Historic sites have a greater range of feature indicators. For example, signs of structures include remains associated with buildings, such as daub, plaster, nails, mortared brick, tiles, roofing nails or slate fragments, and plate/window glass (however, see chapter 4 *We learned about archaeology from that . . .* False Positives: Manure Spreaders and Phantom Sites).

Site and Regional Documentation

The Phase II process, like Phase I, requires review of previous archaeological information. This includes examining the state site files and, as with Phase I, constructing a list of sites and site features located within a given distance of the Phase II site. This examination provides information about what the Phase II deposit may be like while also revealing what is already known, archaeologically, about the area.

The decision about Register eligibility is, to a degree, a comparative decision in the sense of what already is known and what sites already exist. If the site is being considered in terms of Register eligibility because of its ability to contribute new knowledge, it may be that it really does not or cannot do that. This is one reason for checking the site files. That comparative "what already is known," though, will be on a state-by-state basis just as it will be on a site-type-by-site-type basis. Part of the purpose of the background research is to get some sense of what is or is not known already (see also chapter 3).

Contacts, Public Relations/Education

Phase II testing can be extensive and disruptive: While some people may not mind a 1×1-m unit being placed in their yard, they can be uneasy when they actually see the size of the associated backdirt pile. That unease, and the friction that may come with it, can be offset to some degree by good public relations.

Good public relations are important for another reason. In addition to making interactions with the local residents go smoother, the public is supposed to be apprised about what is going on: The Section 106 Process specifically requires public involvement [36 CFR 800.2(d)(1), 800.3(e), and 800.6(a)(4)]. It is the lead agency's responsibility to attend to that.

Contacting landowners becomes a three-step process for Phase II:

- actually contacting and speaking face-to-face with both the landowner and/or resident;

- providing a clear explanation about what will be done, the extent of disruption, and how long that condition will last; and

- describing what will be done to restore the land back to its original condition and, if needed, compensate for damages.

Usually, the client has already obtained written permission from the landowners (called "rights-of-entry forms") to allow archaeological work to be done. The archaeologist should have copies of those completed forms, as well as the names of owners and locations of property.

Landowners and residents should be asked about any archaeological collections that they may have from the site area, or any previous knowledge that they may have about land use. Artifact collections from their property should be examined. Part of this is because of the information value of that collection. Part is because of good public relations: If the people have bothered to gather and curate those artifacts, then those artifacts are important to the people themselves.

Landowners and residents should be asked about past buildings, gardens, flood deposits and other land-altering activities, locations of sewer lines, septic field lines and tanks, and field tile systems, among other local details. Excepting more rural areas, subsurface infrastructure like water and gas lines should have been marked by the utility company or some utility-locating clearinghouse. Phase II testing has a lot greater chance of damaging buried utilities than Phase I survey work.

As in Phase I, utility locations should be identified in the more built-up areas. The clearinghouse then contacts the various utilities, and crews mark the locations of any underground service lines in the project area (for example, in Pennsylvania, call the *Pennsylvania One Call System, Inc.*). Other states may have similar requirements; it is the professional archaeologist's responsibility to check about this. Most states have buried-utilities clearinghouses to call; in many, the law requires that such clearinghouses be contacted and the land cleared before any kind of excavation is done. Be aware that such services cannot always be relied on for precise locations and may not always have records of water lines, fiberoptic cables, and other buried service utilities.

Crop damage and loss of agricultural use may require compensation. Pasture situations will require reassuring the farmer that the test units will be fenced off. The last thing anyone wants is for the crew to arrive in the morning to find that a prime dairy cow had somehow fallen into the test unit late the previous afternoon.

Finally, the owner or resident needs to be aware of the time of day that the field crew will show up, where they will park, and generally when they will leave. Photographs from previous tested and restored Phase II sites may help reduce the qualms people might have about how the area will look after the testing crews leave.

Labor Estimates and Planning

Phase II testing projects have the same five broad budget categories found for Phase I projects. The Phase II may well require an extended field stay far from the home office, and arrangements may be needed for where the crew will stay.

A variety of factors influence field work labor estimates:

- the requirements for mapping;

- terrain;

- the number of test units or size of the field to be collected;

- how deep the test units are to be dug;

- how heavy the soil and what the screen size requirement is;

- the type of site and the abundance and type of artifacts on or in the site;

- density and nature of any features that may be present; and

- weather.[2]

Labor estimates for mapping depend upon the characteristics of the site, the kind of equipment used, and field conditions. Two people can secure around 90 readings in a day in an open setting with an optical transit. Using a "total station" instrument usually cuts the time needed in half.

A fair estimate of labor for standard test units where the fill is screened through ¼-inch (0.635 cm) mesh is 1.3 to 2.0 person-days per cubic meter. This estimate varies depending upon the nature of the soil (dried clayey soils, for example, may well triple the amount of time needed), site, and weather conditions.

---

[2]Archaeologists work under almost all field conditions. Many firms continue working through subzero (Fahrenheit) conditions, either thawing the ground on an as-needed basis or keeping it thawed with some kind of unit-specific shelter. Extreme heat hampers field work in part because of the associated heat stress and partly because the ground is baked and difficult to dig or screen. Shelters also protect sites while allowing continued work during periodic or light rain. Sustained heavy rain is probably the one condition most likely to end the day's field work.

Labor estimates for controlled surface collections depend upon the collection method used, field conditions, and the abundance of artifacts. Most of the labor involved will be either in setting out control points for the collection, or in picking stuff up from the surface. We have found that a controlled surface collection using a 20 × 20–m grid requires about a person-day of labor for every 0.25 ha, but a lot of that has to do with establishing that control grid. Again, though, estimates vary by region, site type, capability of the field workers, and other factors.

Labor estimates for "Analyses" vary by region, type of site, and SOW and SHPO or equivalent agency requirements for labeling, curating, and specialized analyses. Generally, a good estimate to start with allows an hour of analysis time for every 2.0–3.0 hours of field time. The actual number is going to vary by a number of factors, but this should give some sense of scale.

The budget usually has three pay grades assigned to the analysis step: project manager, laboratory director, and laboratory technician. Small firms often have field technicians doubling up as lab technicians. For anticipated high-yield sites, considerable time may be spent cleaning, labeling, and cataloguing artifacts, and this needs to be considered in preparing the budget.[3]

Phase II may also require analytical specialists who have their own time scales and estimates. Those figures are worked into the budget either as a line-item cost estimate or converted for the sake of the bid into an hourly rate.

The analysis step is meant to provide all of the basic measurements and descriptions of artifacts and of the deposit. This includes a full range of descriptive measurements; low-magnification examination of prehistoric flakes for microliths and pottery for temper identification, for example; use-wear analyses; typological classification of diagnostics, including

---

[3]It depends upon the agency, the SHPO or THPO, the eventual curatorial facility, and the firm's practices, but often all diagnostic artifacts will be labeled individually, while some percentage of nondiagnostics will be labeled for each unit-level artifact class. For example, all projectile points from a prehistoric deposit would get labeled, but perhaps only 1 in 10 of the unmodified flakes would be labeled. Those will be mixed in with the unlabeled flakes in the bag used to curate the material, along with an identifier on acid-free paper.

all of the subtle variations in colored glass and glazed ceramics found in collections of historic artifacts; and even flotation processing if the SOW so requested.

By the time analysis is finished, the artifacts should be labeled, bagged, and inventoried with all measurements, weights, counts, and typological decisions made. The artifacts should be in acid-free containers ready for turn-over to a curatorial facility.

The fourth step in the Phase II project is the preparation of a draft report. The amount of time needed for this varies greatly by the nature and scale of the project. Writing the report includes the data analyses themselves, meaning the assessment, interpretation, and syllogistic application of the analytical data. Any statistical tests will be done by the project manager at this point.

Artifact photographs, especially of diagnostics, will be placed in the report. Most firms allow the graphics department three person-hours per illustration, less if it is a photograph. Some firms maintain a permanent desk-top publishing person, assigned either to graphics or to a general administrative staff, who will merge texts and illustrations and assemble the document. Other firms leave this process up to the project manager and the office staff.

The final step in the Phase II project is production of the final report then turn-over of materials. The review agencies will have commented on the draft report, and those comments must be addressed in the final report. Sometimes these are cosmetic, sometimes extensive. Only experience can give insight into estimating accurate times for getting the final report accepted.

Closing out the project includes submission of the final version of the report to the agency as well as to the SHPO/THPO and the other consulting parties, then the turn-over of the collections, field records, and laboratory records to an appropriate curatorial facility. Note, however, that in most states, the artifacts are the property of the client and/or the landowner, as is the case under Section 106 [see 36 CFR 79.3(a)(1)]. In most cases, the rule of thumb is that whoever owns the land owns the artifacts recovered from the land.

Staffing Needs

Most firms have the in-house staffing capability of supplying the core needs for a Phase II project. A small company or partnership will have a few people doing all the tasks. In a larger firm, those people will include:

- *project managers*, who will have the responsibility of overseeing all aspects of the project from its inception until turn-over and who will be responsible for coordinating all field, analytical, and report tasks;

- *laboratory staff*, managed by the laboratory director and responsible for each firm's project needs and for the management of all material products of the project;

- *field labor*, including both field supervisors as well as basic technicians, who will be responsible for the extraction of the information contained within the archaeological deposit;

- *graphics*, usually this is an additional skill held by one or more of the professional staff;

- *secretarial and administrative*, who will be responsible for co-ordinating the production of the Phase II report as well as for all of the managerial paperwork approved by the project manager.

Nonfield support personnel (usually permanent employees) assist with the start-up of the project, do the laboratory analyses, prepare collections for curation and turn-over, create figures and illustrations, and produce the report.

Specialists may be needed for three basic sets of information:

- structure and interpretation either of the soils or of the sediment of the site;

- detailed analyses, such as hydration analyses, ethnobotanical analyses, faunal analyses, or high-magnification use-wear analysis of a prehistoric lithic applications industry or ceramics; and

- advanced statistical analyses pertaining to site depositional integrity and presence/absence of components.

Some firms reproduce the specialist's contribution as an appendix; others incorporate the results into the appropriate analysis section. The specialist might even be a co-author of the report.[4]

Most firms maintain a core population of permanent employees in sufficient numbers for most Phase I surveys but insufficient for larger Phase II testing projects. If a project needing additional people is coming up, the archaeologist usually will call colleagues in other firms to see if they have people who may soon come free because a project is about to end. These represent "project-hires," and they will work in the field for the duration of that part of the project. Sometimes, when there is a critical labor shortage relative to time, local colleges may be contacted, but that is not common.

Field Logistics: Housing, Per Diem, Transport

Some firms make advance arrangements for housing. In these situations, the firm covers the cost of the lodging, and may deduct a corresponding amount from the overall per diem of each crew member. In other situations, the crew—who may consist mostly of project-hires—find their own places to live. The per diem is meant to cover room and board; the Internal Revenue Service has established expected per diem rates for localities. Federal projects are expected to adhere to those rates as minimums, often as a precondition of contract award.[5]

Transportation costs and arrangements depend upon the firm. Project-hires use a staging area or arrive at the work site on their own. Some firms expect employees to use their vehicles but will reimburse mileage. The firm may rent vehicles if the project is a lengthy one.

---

[4]Although not clearly spelled out in archaeology, the listing of who is an author is a matter of professional ethics in most fields as well as in Federal service. In Federal service (and therefore presumably Federal contracts) as well as in the medical and science fields, authorship credit is to be based only on substantial contributions to (a) conception and design, or analysis and interpretation of the data; (b) drafting the article or revising it critically for important intellectual content; and on (c) final approval of the version to be published. All three of these conditions must be met. Participation solely in the acquisition of funding or the collection of data does not justify authorship; nor does editing, the general supervision of the research group, or being the head of the division or firm that produces the report.

[5]For a more detailed discussion about per diem and tax obligations, see Neumann and Sanford 2001:121–122.

Equipment and Supply Needs

The equipment for a Phase II project is the same as that of any archaeological excavation. Any number of standard textbooks supply lists of needed equipment, and the reader is directed to those sources. Nearly all firms supply the basic field equipment needed for the Phase II project. This includes the excavation tools, the screens and/or sorting tables, the bags and indelible markers, and the record-keeping materials.

More expensive, less often used equipment may be rented. This is especially true for survey equipment, but also applies to water pumps, trench shoring materials, and other seldom-needed or expensive-to-maintain items.

Setting Up

Setting up the Phase II testing operation requires attention to logistical needs, equipment needs, and field needs. Field needs include mapping and deciding where testing will be done. That testing may be done using actual test units, in which case decisions need to be made about where to dig. Or the testing may be done by plowing with limited plowzone removal, in which case the land will need to be prepared.

Phase II testing usually requires a formal site map. The client may have provided a topographic map of the project area and this may be just fine. Archaeological maps serve both to keep track of where things were found and units dug; and to allow others in the future to come back and relocate where earlier work was done. Often, though, the project maps supplied by clients are insufficient for archaeological needs since the mapping resolution is too coarse. This is going to be very much of a case-by-case matter, but the archaeologist will need to have a map of the site that satisfies archaeological research needs.

Phase II mapping may require placing a permanent datum, or it may make use of a frequently mapped permanent feature as a datum. The idea of a datum is to have some mapped feature that others in the future can relocate and use to figure out where the archaeological work was done. Whatever does that probably will be just fine for the needs of a Phase II project.

The Phase II map also needs to show, if at all possible, any previous site explorations, especially any Phase I subsurface work. This means that Phase I mapping referents need to be identified. Flagging tape may mark shovel-test locations, for example. Or previous transects may be located using a GPS unit along with compass bearings and the original Phase I project map.

Some firms save time and money in the Phase I by only marking shovel tests that yield artifacts or features. In this case, preparing for the Phase II requires recreating the original shovel test pattern or grid. Fortunately, most Phase I shovel test regimes are properly spaced within a meter (which is better than the ability of GPS receivers even after the Selective Availability restriction was lifted in May 2000).

Previous field locations of Phase I sample is important because part of Phase II is meant to get a better idea of the contents and structure of the site. This often is best accomplished by digging in areas with high artifact concentrations, since it often will be in those areas that features or portions of features survive. The presence of archaeological features like hearths and trash pits may indicate that the site is comparatively undisturbed and therefore may have a great deal of data potential.

Field

There are three elements that need attention in the field part of the Phase II testing project. The first will be verifying landscape history based on current vegetation and the soil profile. The second will be the archaeological field work itself. The third will be the field notes and records.

Landscape History: Vegetational and Pedological Data

The Phase I report should have provided a detailed account of vegetation in the project area, land-use history based upon that vegetation, and discussion of the soils within the project area. This information should be verified or updated for Phase II. Land-use history based on current vegetation is critical. The importance of understanding soil development—and distinguishing soils from sediments—cannot be over emphasized. Past land use, especially agricultural activities that could have disturbed the site, will be evident in the soil profile. Phase II testing also requires that the soil horizons be recorded for each test unit.

We learned about archaeology from that . . . Using Landscape History to Understand Phase II Results: The Case of Heather Heights

The Heather Heights project began with a Phase I in a Maryland woodlot. Many Late Archaic (about 4,000 years old) artifacts were recovered from an apparently undisturbed context. The SHPO recommended Phase II testing, and we came in to help with the analysis.

Most of the Phase II artifacts came from within 30 cm of the surface, but the frequency of artifacts decreased exponentially below that. Given that no Ap horizon was noted, the surface slope was conducive to sheet erosion, and the artifact frequency peaked near the surface, we concluded that the deposit was "plow-truncated" and too disturbed to be considered eligible for listing on the National Register. However, the SHPO, armed with the Phase I report, the impressive amount of artifacts from the Phase II, the absence of field evidence for a plowzone, and the rarity of undisturbed Late Archaic sites in this part of the country, argued otherwise. The SHPO recommended Phase III data recovery.

The Phase I survey described the tree cover and soils but had not addressed land-use history. The Phase I report suggested that the site was in an undisturbed woodlot, which everyone equated with undisturbed land. The lack of an apparent Ap horizon in the Phase I and Phase II field work reinforced this interpretation.

We reviewed the Phase I field notes, looking at the nature of the tree cover. The woodlot contained 30–40-cm dbh oaks and hickories. Since oaks can live 600 years and hickories 300 years, the woodlot was far from a climax forest. Since there were no large trees or stumps present, the woodlot likely began during World War II or a little after.

We also reexamined the Phase I and Phase II notes on the soil profile. The soil profile was not that of a forest soil, which has a thin A horizon over the B horizon. At this site, there was a series of transitional soil horizons that, added to the extant A horizon, would be close to the depth of a plowzone. It helped to know that 30–40 years of continuous forest cover will erase most visible evidence of an Ap horizon. The age of the trees, and the depth and character of the horizon transition suggested that the site had been plowed, with the plowing having ended sometime around World War II.

The final proof of historic age involved a discussion of soil mechanics—artifacts sink through active soils—combined with a simple series of statistical tests. Those tests demonstrated that all of the material encountered in the B horizon had originated in what had been an Ap horizon.

Field Methods

Phase II testing usually involves one of two approaches: (1) excavation of test units or blocks; or (2) controlled surface collection and plowzone removal.

Excavation of Test Units or of Blocks

Phase II subsurface testing often corresponds to the type of test-unit excavation taught in field schools. Test units normally will be 1 × 1 m, 1 × 2 m, or 2 × 2 m depending on project needs and the structure of the site. Units, especially on prehistoric sites, normally will be taken to 30 cm below the last level containing cultural materials, or until C horizon material is encountered. The phrase often used is "30 cm into culturally sterile soil." The actual final depth depends upon the nature of the site as well as the testing policies of the SHPO and agency. This will be specified in the SOW.

Fill will be removed by arbitrary levels within natural levels then screened, as is normally the case in most formal archaeological excavations. Although it depends on the area, site, and SOW, usually the Ap horizon will be removed as one level, with arbitrary levels used thereafter. As a caution, note that except for the Ap horizon, soil horizons are not, in themselves, natural levels or strata. Unless circumstances require otherwise, all unit depth measurements should be taken relative to the original land surface, with the unit floor being at the same depth at each of the four corners as well as in the midsections of the unit walls. That is, the plane of the unit floor should be parallel with the original land surface of the unit or with the natural surface exposed through which the unit has now gone.

In some situations, Phase II testing will involve large, shallowly excavated areas or blocks, rather than deeper units with somewhat smaller areas of exposed surface. This often is the best way to approach deposits around historic structures.

Much archaeological information on a historic-period property is in the past landscaping and building foundations, and that information is contained in the first 30 cm or so of the deposit. Rarely does one actually recover lots of artifacts or patterned artifacts from the yards of historic residences (wells and privies are exceptions). It makes little sense to open a small "excavation window" like a 1 × 1–m or 1 × 2–m unit, then go deep into a landscape where most of the material and associated features will be closer to the surface. Landscape archaeology provides a better option.

Landscape archaeology focuses on the cultural layout of the landscape, most often in terms of gardens, compounds, and similar landscaping and outbuilding exercises (e.g., Kelso and Most, ed., 1990; Yamin and Metheny, ed., 1996). Remember that archaeology is concerned ultimately with understanding how people lived in the past, and thus needs to look

Figure 5.1. Example of shallow Phase II test units defining garden features in the yard of a historic residence. Photo courtesy of R. Jerald Ledbetter and Southeastern Archeological Services, Inc.

at the patterning of the world that people left behind. For many historic sites, that patterning will not be artifacts only, but also the features in the landscape.

Some projects assign a number and/or letter to each excavation unit; others use grid coordinates. If both are available, it is best to use both, especially when labeling artifact bags. Where grid coordinates are used, all coordinate numbers should be given, not the coordinates of just one stake. For example, a 1 × 1–m unit placed roughly 50 m north and 20 m east of the datum should be labeled on the bag and in the field notes as N50-51/E20-21. Use of all coordinates helps eliminates confusion, since the choice of stake used to identify a unit varies across the country as well as over time.

Controlled Surface Collection and Plowzone Removal

The other common Phase II procedure is a controlled surface collection. In parts of the country where ground-surface visibility is good and soil or sediment accumulation is not an issue, a site can be surface-collected as soon as the control system is established. In parts of the country where ground visibility is not good, or where there is or has

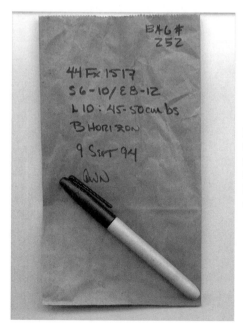

Figure 5.2. Example of a labeled artifact bag. The "field specimen" bag number has been added to the upper right-hand corner. All bags are to be labeled sequentially, with the labeling done each day.

been an active soil, Phase II procedure may call for plowing then harrowing the site, followed by selective plowzone removal. This is done only if there is evidence of previous plowing, and only if it is reasonably possible to do. In most cases, the field itself will be plowed, harrowed, mapped, gridded off, then collected. A portion of the plowzone may then be removed, based upon the results of that surface collection. In these situations, the archaeologist is seeing where cultural materials are concentrated and if any features—trash pits, hearths, post holes, foundation markings—survive beneath the plowzone.

If the plowzone is to be removed, mechanical means usually are used. Although the plowzone does contain archaeological information, stripping might still be better, justified on the basis of the overall needs of the project and consideration of the information to be gained by the stripping.

Most sites plowed for a controlled surface collection have a history of having been plowed. Thus, the artifacts already are out of horizontal and vertical position. If one thinks of artifacts as pixels in an image, then plowing has blurred that image. Pulling back the plowzone to see what, if any, features may have been associated with—or even been a source for—those artifacts becomes an exercise in documenting site depositional integrity and a first step in assessing the behavioral-information potential of the site. The SOW will indicate if any features are to be recovered, but normally when this is done for Phase II, features are only mapped and documented.

Most Phase II exercises of this kind will require that the stripped area be backfilled. It may be over a year before anyone returns to the site. Locating those reburied features will be difficult enough even with sound field notes. Therefore, mapping must be detailed and precise.

Nature of Field Recordation

Field recordation for Phase II excavation units is more parsimonious than in academic excavations. For example, unit floors usually are not photographed and usually are cut cleanly enough with a flat-nose shovel so that troweling is not needed. Unit walls will be cut by shovel, not by trowel; at this stage, what is important is that the walls are flat and plumb. Only one wall will eventually be troweled, but that will not be done until it is time to draw and photograph the unit profile. Measured field drawings will be done of

Figure 5.3. Panoramic view of project area. Panoramic views are made by over-lapping photographs and give a much better sense of the landscape than do photographs with wide-angle lenses, since the perimeter of the image is not distorted. The overlap is intentionally made apparent here to illustrate the process.

features in unit floors, of the features themselves when excavated, and of a wall profile. With respect to photographs: Representative or typical unit wall profiles will be done for each unit. And all features of course will be photographed.[6] There will also be a series of general-area photographs showing the lay of the land and perhaps the nature of the field work.

Traditionally, field photographs involved film cameras, although this is changing as electronic cameras with digitally recorded images become affordable and the image resolution increases. Note, though, that digital cameras give a false sense of clarity. Their initial images are coarse-grained compared to camera film. The image is made "clearer" by interpolating what image should exist between the pixels by using the surrounding bit of image as the base for fractals. The fractal is then used to fill in the blanks. It still makes better sense to use film cameras in the field.

When taking field photographs, a menu board should be used for detail photographs, but not for general views of the project area. Unless

---

[6]The area to be photographed should be clean and tidy. Any extraneous leaves and debris should be removed from around the surface; roots in profile walls should be clipped. Rightly or wrongly, the subconscious assessment of the quality of the work done will be based in part upon how neat and tidy the unit photographs are. Many of the unit profile photographs will be presented in the Phase II report, and unlike the profile drawings (which will be redrawn at the office), the photographs taken in the field will be used in the final product. While it is possible with digitizers to edit those pictures, it is best to get it right the first time, in the field.

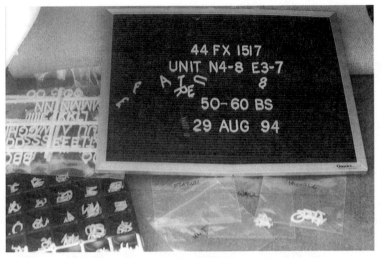

Figure 5.4. Photo menu board, along with pre-sorted words.

specified in the contract or in the pertinent state regulatory guidelines, choose either black-and-white or color. Color film is less expensive and easier to process, and gives better definition for most needs; usually an ASA 200 film will work just fine. However, color images and film negatives are not stable; the colors will deteriorate in a few decades. Black-and-white developing is now, though, virtually impossible to find outside of large metropolitan areas. It is possible to generate black-and-white images from color prints using computer printers. Note, however, that ink-jet images are not stable; if computer conversion is done for printing, use a laser printer. Both computer-based printed images, though, have the same image-density problem inherent in digital camera images.

Digital images present an archiving problem as well. The disks on which digital images are stored have storage-integrity half-lives of 2 years (for magnetic disks) to 10 years (for optical media like CD-R and CD-RW). They have the archival stability of a cracked raw egg sitting on a damp Atlanta lawn in August, albeit without the aesthetic promise. By comparison, color film negatives retain color integrity for about 20 years under household conditions, and longer if kept refrigerated.

TIP: Small Backhoes and Stripping Plowzone

Phase II and Phase III compliance projects may require using heavy earth-moving equipment. In areas where plowing is common, selective stripping of the plowzone may be done. Machinery should be selected based on size, type, and cost.

Some equipment may need modification. The most common piece of equipment used by an archaeologist will be a backhoe. "Backhoe," for an archaeologist, is the comparatively small, scorpionlike device that has a bucket end-loader at one end and a 60-cm-wide bucket on a 4-m arm at the other. "Backhoe," in the construction industry, ranges from those small Bobcat™-like things that fit on the end of a pickup truck to the large, track-tread machines used to dig foundations and move ore out of strip mines. The machine that is desired is termed on the West Coast a "backhoe-loader," the kind of backhoe, with tires, one would use to put in a sewer line.

Figure 5.5. Small backhoes often are used to dig deeper test units, strip areas, and even help backfill. Rental usually is by the day or half-day, depending upon the area, with the cost including both the equipment and the operator. The kind pictured here is most common; the bucket arm will reach 14 ft (a little over 4 meters). Bucket width usually is 60 cm. Photo courtesy of R. Jerald Ledbetter and Southeastern Archeological Services, Inc.

Most backhoe buckets are toothed. When used, the teeth gouge a series of parallel grooves 2-inches deep. To avoid that damage to the site, a steel plate or clean-up blade can be spot-welded to the teeth of the backhoe bucket. This is easier than removing the teeth. Doing this in effect converts the machine to the equivalent of a Gradall™, but at one-third the rental cost and with considerably greater maneuverability. One has this set up by first explaining to the equipment owners what is needed, then asking them to spot-weld a plate or change-out the teeth. They will be more than willing to do so if it can be done within reason. Construction people are very practical, and equally intrigued by the archaeology. They will both help out with what is needed and will advise in how to best use their equipment to achieve your goals. Solicit their comments, then listen to them.

Figure 5.6.   As crew members shovel-scrape, they are expected to recognized feature stains or patterns, then to place pin flags in those stains. After the area has been stripped, crew members will return to the pin flags, clean up the area, photograph it, and map in the feature. Photo courtesy of R. Jerald Ledbetter and Southeastern Archeological Services, Inc.

People are fascinated by archaeology, and it is not unusual for a firm to give the task of working with the archaeologist to the senior equipment operator. The capacity of the operators we have worked with to use a backhoe with a clean-up blade is remarkable. We have seen them shave a centimeter from a 3-m strip.

The backhoe operator will remove most of the plowzone, perhaps all but a centimeter. The field crew will use flat-nose or cut-nose shovels to scrape away the remaining plowzone and define features, should they exist.

Field Notes and Records

The field notes for the Phase II testing exercise should be kept in a three-ring, D-ring loose-leaf binder. Phase II field notes consist of the following:

- general project information, including maps and SOW;

- general field notes as kept by the field supervisor;

- specific unit and unit-level notes kept by each test-unit crew;

- feature records; and

- other records, inventories, and logs.

Each of those information sets will be a general subsection within the field note binder. At the end of the project, the binder will have proprietary corporate information removed and the rest of the information copied. Eventually, the original notes will be turned over to the client, or a suitable curatorial facility, along with photographs, artifact collections, and a copy of the Phase II report.

The Phase II notebook will end up containing draft figures and tables to be used in the final report, progress reports, management summaries, and anything written on paper that has a bearing on the project. For larger projects, the Phase II notes may include other binders devoted to photographs, slides, and drawn figures, and perhaps even tables. The notebook will be accompanied by a site map showing the locations of test units, controlled-surface-collection areas, and other relevant items. Usually, a photo-reduced version will be placed in the binder.

Each test unit has a specific series of field notes particular to it and is maintained by the crew members assigned to that unit. Those records usually consist of standardized forms that the crew members fill out, often consisting of a cover sheet or form for each level. The forms will indicate site number, date, unit number, unit coordinates, level number, level depth, soil color/texture, associated features, notable artifacts, photograph numbers, elevation, and recorders.

If controlled surface collections are done, forms should be used for each of the collection areas. The form should include the collector's impression of where large concentrations of artifacts were located.

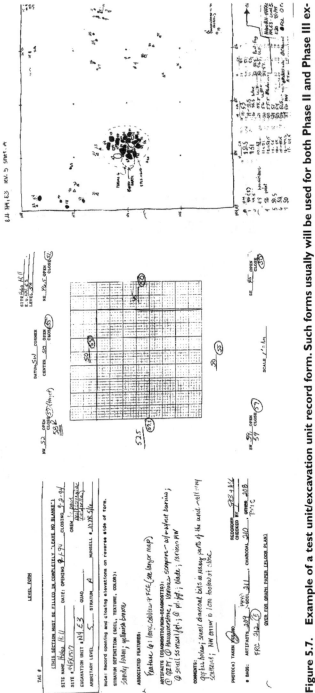

Figure 5.7. Example of a test unit/excavation unit record form. Such forms usually will be used for both Phase II and Phase III excavation. Here, the reverse side of the form is gridded for providing a scaled map of the unit floor. Store-bought graph paper serves as continuation sheets.

FEATURE FORM

SITE NAME (NUMBER) Hboo Hill 44FX1517   FEATURE NUMBER 5

DEFINITION (GENERAL SHAPE AND APPEARANCE) Post mold w/heavy charcoal inclusion

SCREENED? N   MESH SIZE   QUADS SAVED FOR FLOT Bag 189 for Flot.

E.U. S5W7   LEVEL 13C   STRATUM

DEPTH OF TOP BELOW E.U. DATUM 102cm   BELOW SITE DATUM

DEPTH OF BOTTOM BELOW E.U. DATUM 114cm   BELOW SITE DATUM

MAX. LENGTH ca 15cm   DIRECTION roughly circular MAX. WIDTH   DIRECTION

MAX. VERTICAL THICKNESS OR DEPTH ~12cm

ASSOCIATION WITH OTHER FEATURES None

NATURE OF FILL Dark brown fill with heavy charcoal inclusion

LINING Bisection pit depth - 117cm

See excavation map for plan
Profile on back

SECONDARY FEATURES

ASSOCIATED ARTIFACTS

INTERPRETIVE COMMENTS - Appears to be a post mold - the mold
tapers at the bottom not to a point but rounded

PHOTOGRAPHS: COLOR BB   (BW) L.More

DRAW HORIZONTAL AND VERTICAL PLAN AND PROFILE

EXCAVATED BY BB   DATES 8/25 THRU 8/26

RECORDED BY BB   DATE 8/26

BAGS: ARTIFACTS_____ FLOTATION 189 SOIL 188 CHARCOAL 187,188 OTHER

00143

Figure 5.8. Example of a feature form. Features usually will be recorded separately in addition to whatever mention is made of them on the standard excavation unit form. Again, the same feature form normally will be used for anytime a feature is encountered, be it in Phase II, Phase III, or even in those rare cases where Phase I shovel testing bumps into something. The reverse side of the form is gridded for scaled plane drawings and profiles.

Feature records are treated similarly. A feature inventory sheet lists feature number, unit location, level and depth where first defined, date, and nature of feature. Other notes such as Munsell colors may be recorded as well.

Transit and mapping notes should be presented on a standard page form in the project binder. Most Phase II testing exercises generate a large number of photographs. Those photographs include general views of the project area as well as specific photographs of unit walls and of features. The photo log needs to include roll number and film type (for film cameras), exposure number/frame number, and nature of image. Direction of view should always be indicated, as should the metric scale in the image.

A bag inventory is essential. Each artifact bag should be assigned a bag number or field specimen number. There should be a master list in the field notebook that coordinates those numbers with the unit, level, and/or feature. The list may include empty bags, with a note alongside saying "empty" or "no artifacts recovered." This forces each test-unit excavator to turn in a number of artifact bags equal to the number of levels removed and helps avoid bags being misplaced.

If soil samples or flotation samples were taken, these should be tracked in the same manner as artifact bags.

Post-Field

The post-field phase of the project is similar to that of any traditional archaeological research effort, except that it must be finished by a fixed date not of the investigator's choosing. It also may have many people working on different parts of the project at the same time. On returning from the field, the tasks to be done are similar to those for a Phase I project. The biggest differences are in analyses and the literature review for the background research.

Level of Analyses Expected

The Phase II analysis is a detailed interpretive analysis of a given archaeological site, in terms of its depositional structure, its archaeology, and its place in local and regional culture history. The testing performed rarely is sufficient to provide final answers to standing research questions as set forth in the state historic preservation plan or present in the literature, but the results *are* sufficient to contribute to the basic understanding of the region's history or prehistory. As such, new knowledge will be produced and presented in the report, knowledge that furthers understanding of the area's past. It is possible that the information will be redundant and lacks the potential to provide a unique contribution to our understanding of the past, but it is just as possible that it does have such potential. The only way to tell is if the analysis itself is sufficiently detailed.

The analysis should provide the following:

- detailed treatment of the site matrix so that questions of depositional integrity can be addressed;

- identification of diagnostic artifacts, including relation to a specific period or culture, and depositional context;

- basic measurements and descriptions of appropriate artifacts;

- location of components vertically and horizontally across the site, with the distributions verified statistically;

- statistical relationships among artifacts and features; and

- relationships between the contents of the site and the larger body of research about the history or prehistory of the region, including linkages to standing research questions in the literature and in the state plan.

Specialized analyses may be warranted to advance particular analytical sets. For example, high-magnification use-wear analyses may be done on the lithic applications industry to relate tool use to site function and to intra-site activity areas. Questions of seasonality and settlement pattern may be handled through the specialized analysis of flotation samples, if such samples were specified in the SOW. Radiocarbon dates may have been requested as well.

Addressing the Basic Phase II Issues

The basic Phase II issue is whether or not the site is eligible for listing on the National Register. Broadly speaking, there are two sets of criteria. One has to do with the site's integrity relative to the reasons it would be listed. The other set of criteria is the nature of the site's association with the past. The determination of Register eligibility will be made by the lead agency.

As mentioned in chapter 2, integrity is a complex issue. For Register-eligibility purposes, it basically means how true the cultural resource is to the reason it might be considered for listing. For example, is this really the log cabin in which Abraham Lincoln was born? And is the log cabin really where it was originally located?

For buildings and such being considered for listing on the National Register, integrity may well have to do with how true the cultural resource is to what it originally was like. The issue gets a bit fuzzier for archaeological sites lacking structures, since one aspect that differentiates an archaeological site

---

Discard Protocols

Not everything brought back from the field can be, or should be, kept. Some items need only to be counted and maybe weighed. After that, those items will be discarded, depending upon the nature of the project, SHPO/THPO and SOW requirements, and the concerns of the project manager.

Many Federal SOW require that all artifacts recovered in the field be retained, regardless of their age, size, or abundance. Further, Federal regulations prohibit discarding artifacts that have been accessioned. Therefore, some Federal agencies frequently allow the materials collected in the fill to be culled before accessioning. This can make quite a difference, especially on historic sites. For example, we once encountered 20-cm-thick lenses of broken window glass when doing a Phase II testing project, the site being the debris cleared from when the town burned in the 1860s. The glass represented something like 1,120 kg for each of the six test units. We spoke with the Federal agency about the lack of research need for the world to curate almost seven metric tons of broken plate glass. The agency agreed and suspended its artifact retention policy, and the bulk of the glass was discarded on site.

In many areas of the country, fire-cracked rock will be counted, weighed, then discarded. For some projects, though, it may be important to first track the kind of stone involved. In areas of the country with huge volumes of prehistoric pottery, sometimes any body sherd smaller than a certain size is weighed and discarded.

All projects and firms will have a discard policy. It is important to know not only what that policy is, but what it is meant to accomplish relative to the needs of the project.

---

from a mish-mash of stuff is that the site has the artifacts and features in their original context and association. Integrity, then, can and often does involve the question of how undisturbed the archaeological deposit is.

Site depositional integrity usually forms the independent criterion in making a recommendation about Register eligibility. In situations where Register eligibility involves the site's ability to contribute to research questions, then integrity often has to do with how intact or undisturbed the deposit is. If the integrity of the deposit has been compromised, then the information potential of that deposit is likely compromised to some degree. The question is, though, is it compromised relative to what already is known?

Integrity is a two-variable issue. The first is physical disturbance, which would include plowing, fill events, and similar disruption. The second issue for integrity is that of relativity. How disturbed is the site *relative to* other examples. A heavily plowed Late Prehistoric site in Alabama, where only the bottom 10 cm of some post-hole stains survive and everything else is in the plowzone, probably would not be recommended for listing on the Register. There are plenty of much-less-disturbed examples already known. A Paleoindian site with exactly the same physical attributes *would* likely be eligible, since Paleoindian sites that have even partially intact deposits are unusual in the eastern United States. Depositional integrity partly depends on knowledge about similar sites within the jurisdiction of the SHPO.

Cultural resources are managed at the state or local government level, and comparisons need to be made based upon those bounds. Eligibility is on a case-by-case basis; evaluation of the merits of a property does not hinge on consideration of other historic properties. This might seem to contradict what we just said about "relative integrity," so we had better clear that up.

Just because a given type of site is already listed on the National Register—say that undisturbed Mississippian site we just mentioned—does not mean that other undisturbed Mississippian sites are not Register eligible. They most likely would be. It is sort of like an unspoken threshold exists that, once reached, means that the site can join the others in the glory of National Register-dom. However, to carry that threshold image a little further: Severely disturbed sites simply would not merit consideration, since equivalent undisturbed sites do exist.

We learned about archaeology from that . . . Providing Adequate Documentation: Secondary Deposition at Cowanesque

The Cowanesque Reservoir in extreme north-central Pennsylvania is maintained by the U.S. Army Corps of Engineers. Expansion necessitated Phase I, Phase II, and Phase III projects, mostly conducted by different firms. We directed a Phase II project that illustrates the importance of substantiating conclusions presented within the compliance report.

Two Phase I surveys had indicated the presence of a prehistoric site with what seemed to be data potential on a floodplain terrace about 2 m above the Cowanesque River. Each had recommended Phase II testing, although it appeared that the site was indeed Register eligible. The SHPO agreed with that recommendation, and it fell to us to do the Phase II and examine the potential Register eligibility of the site.

Testing, consisting of shovel tests and small units, recovered prehistoric waste flakes and historic coal, window glass, and ceramics, from the upper 30 cm of the units closest to the edge of the terrace. We concluded that the site lacked data potential or integrity: All of the cultural material came from what had been the plow-zone, and that material was not diagnostic. The site was not, in our view, eligible for the Register. We then reported that, concluding that no further work was needed.

These results contradicted the Phase I reports, and the Pennsylvania SHPO legitimately challenged them: How could *two* Phase I reports conclude that the site had data potential and integrity, while our Phase II assessment concluded the opposite? Our draft report was returned to be revised in accord with Phase I conclusions. Clearly, more details were needed.

A total of 53 artifacts were recovered; 41 (77 percent) of which came from the Ap horizon. We found that their average weight was between 0.1 g and 0.2 g (0.01 g to 0.3 g range). Further, none of the materials recovered in Phase I were in their original context. We, therefore, argued that the prehistoric and historic cultural materials had been carried downstream by the river and redeposited on the terrace during a flood, and that this had occurred after valley clearance and the start of cultivation. The reason that all of the artifacts, regardless of age or material, weighed the same was that they had been size-sorted during the flood and deposited at the same time.

The materials were found together in the plowzone because historic land clearance increased runoff and river velocity sufficiently for floods to have enough force to pick up and move cultural materials. When water crossed the terrace at the end

---

We learned about archaeology from that . . . Providing Adequate Documentation: Secondary Deposition at Cowanesque *(Continued)*

stages of the flood, the flow velocity decreased, and the larger particles, like the flakes and glass, dropped out. This also explained why everything was in the plowzone. The event or events carrying the prehistoric and historic materials downstream had happened *after* Euroamerican settlement of the watershed.

This is a cautionary tale. The response of the SHPO to the Phase II draft report was proper. It is the responsibility of the Phase II project to supply thorough documentation on why the site is or is not eligible for the National Register.

Comparisons with other properties become even more of a factor in dealing with mitigation. Just because a site or other historic property is listed on the National Register does not mean it cannot be destroyed. Rather, it means that its existence needs to be taken into account before work proceeds. If there is no way to avoid destroying that property, then usually the recommendation will be to recover enough information about the property—be it an archaeological site or a standing structure [colloquial sense]—before it disappears. But if there is a situation where there is limited funding and more than one Register-eligible archaeological site that will be lost, the decision—a triage decision, really—will be to abandon to fate the site or sites if there are a bunch of equivalent examples elsewhere.

After treating the question of data potential, the second broad issue is whether the information content of the site could contribute to what is known about the past, be it people, events, ways of making or doing things, or how people lived. Historic sites usually involve any of those four options; prehistoric sites usually involve only the last, also called "data potential."

The professional archaeologist does not make a determination of National Register eligibility, but does make a recommendation of what the lead agency should do. The agency generally will follow the archaeologist's advice. The issue comes down to this: Is the site worth a full-scale data recovery excavation? The answer will be "no" if there are comparable sites with similar or better information already known; the answer will be "yes" if there are no comparable sites.

General Structure of Report

The Phase II report contains background information, methods, analyses, results, and recommendations. The general structure of a report is addressed in chapter 7.

The two options for recommendations are that the site is eligible for listing on the National Register, or it is not. If the site appears eligible, the report indicates whether or not the proposed project would compromise that eligibility, that is, create an adverse effect. For example, putting an asphalt parking lot over a site that is 40 cm below the surface might do more to protect the site than damage it and might not be seen as an adverse effect at all. Thus, the question is if there will be adverse effects from the undertaking. If the property is not eligible, then any impacts to it are not "adverse" in the regulatory sense.

If the project would have an adverse effect on a site, the options are either to redesign the project to avoid damaging the site, or to recover enough information from the site so that the continued existence of what remains will be redundant. The adverse effects can be resolved or mitigated through changes to the project or through data recovery.

Sometimes the project cannot be redesigned to avoid adverse effects. In that case, the Phase II report will recommend Phase III data recovery to mitigate the adverse effects of the project.

Chapter Summary

The Phase II testing and evaluation process is the second part of the good-faith effort expected of agencies in their required accounting for cultural resources—here archaeological sites—that could be listed on the National Register. With Phase I, the professional archaeologist will have gone over the area that could be adversely affected by the proposed undertaking. Some archaeological sites may have been previously reported; others, heretofore unknown, may have been found. The question now is: Are any of those eligible for the National Register?

Phase II testing is similar in many ways to traditional archaeological site testing. Some background research will be done, but that research will be focused more on the kind of site that will be examined and less on the region as a whole. The broader work would—or should—already have been done during Phase I. The background issues now are those specifically associated with questions of Register eligibility as summarized in 36 CFR 60.4 [a–d]: association with nationally, regionally, or locally important events [36 CFR 60.4 (a)] or people [36 CFR 60.4 (b)]; an exemplary example of a style or craftsman's work [36 CFR 60.4 (c)]; and/or potential to address important research questions [called "data potential"; 36 CFR 60.4 (d)]. Phase II might best be thought of as a diagnostic step; the background research provides the context for the diagnosis.

Preparation for a Phase II project differs a little for a Phase I survey. Most Phase I surveys are short and done close to the home office. Phase II testing exercises often take more time and may end up being done a long way from the office. Logistics planning often includes billeting and per diem as well as transportation both for equipment and crew. In those respects, a Phase II project is like a traditional archaeological excavation project, although smaller and briefer.

The field component of a Phase II testing exercise is similar to any archaeological testing regime. The only differences—aside from how quickly the work will be done—involves a need to confirm any landscape history based upon vegetation and soils, and often a bias toward digging the more artifact-/feature-rich parts of the site. Of the four National Register criteria listed in 36 CFR 60.4 [a–d], the first three—association with events, people, craftsmanship/style—often can be resolved with historical research. When they cannot, the issue turns essentially forensic and evidentiary, and in many respects data needed to address that turn of argument are the same as those needed to assess research potential. Put a bit more simply, the idea is to get as much information on the artifacts, features, and matrix of the site as can be had that may have a bearing on why the site might be Register eligible, but with the least amount of digging. Thus, Phase II testing often tries to dig in the richest—in terms of artifacts and features—part of the site.

The analysis done on a Phase II archaeological site is the same as for any full-scale excavation, although usually there is a lot less to worry about. The detail and resolution of analyses are the same. Thus, radiocarbon dates are not uncommon, nor is high-magnification use-wear analyses of prehistoric lithics. The resultant Phase II report is usually comparable to a standard archaeological site monograph. Phase II site monographs normally represent primary empirical excavation data for the archaeology of their region.

However, the main reason that Phase II testing is done is to evaluate a site, identified during Phase I, to see if it might be eligible for listing on the National Register. The report, while also reporting the research archaeology, still is slanted to addressing—yea or nay—that core compliance question.

The Phase II report will contain all of the information, along with the archaeologist's own sense of what is present, to allow the government agency to make a determination of Register eligibility. As with the Phase I report, a draft will be submitted to the agency (and often, with prior agency approval, to the SHPO/THPO as well) for substantial in-house peer review. And, as with Phase I, payment of a portion of the contract award will depend upon approval by *both* the agency and the SHPO/THPO (another reason why the rather simplistic protests that professional archaeology is enslaved by profit are naive; it is the agency and the SHPO/THPO that will decide if the work is adequate and therefore if the contract has been satisfied).

The archaeologist in the Phase II report will conclude either that the site does not have the quality of significance as defined in 36 CFR 60.4 [a–d], and therefore is not eligible for listing on the National Register, or the archaeologist will conclude that the site does meet those criteria and should be considered eligible. If the agency and the SHPO/THPO agree the site is not eligible, the compliance issue ends; the artifacts, field notes/records, and final report are turned over to an appropriate curatorial facility; and the project is over.

If the agency and the SHPO/THPO agree that the site is eligible, the process becomes much more formal and deliberate. With a Register-eligible site, the issue is to "take it into account," meaning work around it if at all *practical* and recover from it enough information to make the existence of the threatened portion redundant if avoidance is *not* practical. The Phase II report will contain recommendations about how to proceed. Those recommendations will become the basis of any Phase III data recovery plan.

Additional Readings of Interest

Kelso, William M., and Rachel Most, editors. 1990. *Earth Patterns: Essays in Landscape Archaeology*. University Press of Virginia, Charlottesville. Not all

Phase II test excavations need to go deep; historic sites have comparatively shallow deposits and all that may be needed is to open a large area to see if there are signs of outbuildings or gardens. Kelso and Most have assembled here a wonderful introduction into how landscape archaeology—in the sense of digging to understand how landscapes were set up—can be done. Kelso, by the way, is the person who has found the original Jamestown Settlement (see www.apva.org).

U.S. Army Corps of Engineers. 1996. *Safety and Health Requirements Manual.* EM 385-1-1. U.S. Government Printing Office, Washington, D.C. Unlike Phase I survey work, Phase II testing can and often does go deep into the ground. This raises issues of shoring. The COE *Manual* sets out much of what is needed to be known about excavation shoring. The Manual also provides basic information on project/construction site safety. Such procedures need to be followed on Federal projects anyway. Good managers will follow them even on non-Federal projects.

CHAPTER SIX

THE PHASE III PROCESS: MITIGATION THROUGH DATA RECOVERY

Initiation of a Phase III Process

I f the Phase II testing leads to a determination that the archaeological site is eligible for listing on the National Register, the Section 106 Process calls for a series of formal steps (36 CFR 800):

- determinations of adverse effect;

- distribution of past assessment results (often Phase I and Phase II reports) to all consulting parties and invitation for public comment;

- production of a Memorandum of Agreement (MOA) specifying steps to mitigate or resolve any adverse effects of the undertaking; and

- mitigation of those adverse effects either through redesign of the project (avoidance) or through archaeological data recovery.

Phase III data recovery commences if mitigation or resolution of adverse effects can be done only through excavation or comparable archaeological investigation where avoidance is not reasonably possible. Phase III attempts the recovery, analysis, and dissemination of the anthropological (human behavioral) information stored within the threatened part of the site matrix. The idea is to make the continued existence of the portion of the threatened site *redundant*. If successful, the site's information potential is captured by the process and contained in the archaeological assemblage, field records, laboratory analysis records, and report.

Phase III data recovery is similar to the formal, full investigation of a site conducted by researchers from a university or museum. However, it differs in three ways. First, the Phase III site has been selected for data recovery by circumstances (e.g., a pending development or undertaking) rather than because it could address a pre-existing research design held by a particular investigator. The site will be examined because it, or part of it, soon will be destroyed.

The second difference is limits on funding and time. Not everything that one might want to do can be done. Funding and time are limited by many factors, such as accruing interest on loans and planning variances. Instead it is almost always best to stick to the tasks outlined in the SOW, since the work or level of analysis stipulated there was designed then bid to take into account the time and funding limits of the project. The professional must also remember that it is the client who is underwriting the exercise and who has set budget relative to the Phase III SOW. The archaeologist does the best that can be done given the limits in funding and time.

The third major difference is in the consequences faced if the work done is not exceptional. Like archaeologists in a university or museum, the private-sector archaeologist accepts responsibility for what he or she has produced. Unlike them, errors in the private sector, even errors made in good faith, are much more likely to result in immediate and tangible penalties, ranging from delays in final payment on the project to major suits and fines. Similar penalties exist for failure to finish a project within the schedule outlined in the SOW.

Responsibilities and Perspectives

It is well at this stage to make some comments on how Phase III data recovery, as both a compliance exercise and a research project, works. There has been a lot of misunderstanding among academic archaeologists about this, a confusion that has been passed to students that has surfaced time and again among new hires—especially those with advanced degrees—in private-sector firms and in government agencies. All of cultural resources archaeology practiced in a professional setting is so unlike the way in which archaeology has been taught that some remarks are needed.

First, it is important to remember that the client is the entity underwriting the data recovery exercise. The client is doing so—from its perspective—as part of the overall permitting process. Costs are not being borne to satisfy the archaeologist's intellectual whims of inquiry; costs are being borne by the operating margin built into the client's overall financial structure. Sometimes a plat notation or a protective covenant, resulting in no further construction, will make better economic sense than funding a Phase III exercise in order to continue the project. In cases like that, the developer or contractor can take the reduced value of the property (because its development potential is limited) as a business loss or use the protection to mitigate other impacts.

However, it must be remembered that any developer or contractor is not in the business of taking losses. Further, the line between built-in operating costs and profit margin is very thin; some Federal agency contracts, for example, limit the profit that government contractors can take. If costs become prohibitive, the client may just cut-and-run. This is, perhaps, a real-world application of Lewis's *limited good*: There will come a point where every dollar spent by a client to work around a compliance problem will be a dollar taken from payroll. No company wants matters to reach that point. A good company manager will want to avoid endangering employees.

Scheduling and finance limits result in the data recovery being designed to get the maximum information from the imperiled resource with

Some Options for Avoiding Adverse Effects

Phase III data recovery is also called mitigation because full-scale excavation is seen to mitigate or offset the adverse effects of the proposed undertaking. However, an excavated site is still a destroyed site even if much of the information is saved. Data recovery is always to be viewed as the option of last resort; if there is a way to avoid having the site or its threatened portion destroyed, then it is preferable to adopt that strategy. There are many options. Some of the more common involve:

- redesigning the project so that it does not damage the site;
- restructuring the use of the property so that the site cannot be damaged;
- trading one portion of the property to the public jurisdiction in exchange for another portion; or
- selling or giving the land to a land trust or other conservator.

the available means. Into this will enter the SHPO/THPO or analogous agency, charged with protecting the cultural resource data base. The SHPO/THPO is made up of people with agendas often at variance with those of the developer, sometimes at variance with those of the private-sector archaeologist and the Federal agency, and—rarely—even at variance with those of the ACHP.

Professional archaeology has been at a cross road ever since the Section 106 Process emerged. There are serious issues involved, and this is as good a place as any to mention them. A common statement among the academic community for many years, seldom mentioned in print, was that the professional was "in the pay of" a particular client and therefore would do what needs to be done to get the client to avoid paying any more than necessary. While it is still found in a number of archaeology and introductory Anthropology textbooks, that charge reflected an ignorance of how the entire process works. This danger was anticipated when the regulations found in 36 CFR 800 were first worked out; it has never really become a problem.

How is this potential conflict of interest avoided? It is avoided primarily through the review process. There are two issues here that get mixed up: doing what is best for the client in terms of costs, and doing what is best for the client in terms of how the client's actions will be judged by the review agencies. The potential conflict is avoided by separating the steps in the decision-making process, while at the same time keeping the client's interests and needs at heart.

What is best for the client in terms of costs is always what is best in terms of how the archaeologist's work, as a subcontractor, will reflect on the client. For the client's project to continue requires that the archaeological work performed by the professional archaeologist be completely approved by the state's or the tribal land's apologist for the cultural resources: the SHPO or the THPO. And to be so approved requires not only completion of a stringent peer-review by the SHPO/THPO archaeologists, but often an equally stringent peer-review by agency archaeologists. The review agencies have the power to pull permits; the review agencies have the power to stop the client. The client already has locked into bank loans and has people on payroll. The client cannot afford to sit still. The professional archaeologist must provide a research design (for the Phase III data recovery), an analysis, and a report that will meet the requirements of the review agencies. The better the report, the faster the review and consequent permitting. The final arbiter in the compliance process is the government review agency; the archaeologist works and writes not for the client, but for the review agency, which then will decide the client's fate.

Memoranda of Agreement (MOA)

A second element that enters the scene when Phase III mitigation is envisioned is the "Memorandum of Agreement." A Memorandum of Agreement or MOA is a signatory contract regarding the continued pursuance of the cultural resource process. It is meant to be a formal agreement, between the agency and the SHPO or the THPO,

(1) stating that a Register-eligible site or sites were identified during the Phase II process (or agreeing that the site already is listed or eligible for listing on the National Register),

(2) considering if the planned undertaking will have an effect on that site or sites, then

(3) summarizing what needs to be done to mitigate the effects on the site or sites from the undertaking, should those effects be considered adverse.

An MOA is executed when cultural resources eligible for listing on the National Register are identified within the area of potential effects during the Phase II testing process. In such a situation, the Criteria of Adverse Effect [36 CFR 800.5 (a)] will be applied. It will be the Federal agency, working with the SHPO/THPO, that applies the Criteria of Adverse Effect. This ultimately results in one of two conclusions: the undertaking will significantly change the character of the resource (that is, have an adverse effect), or it will not.

If the agency and the SHPO/THPO agree on the effects of the undertaking (adverse or not) as well as on any necessary actions, then an MOA will be composed, a copy along with any other summary documentation sent to the Advisory Council for Historical Preservation (ACHP), and the undertaking will continue. In this situation, the agency and the SHPO/THPO are signatories to the MOA.

If the SHPO/THPO disagrees on the terms of the MOA or refuses to sign the MOA, then the agency will ask the ACHP to join the consultation. The ACHP must receive documentation relevant to the situation for a 30-day review period while the Federal agency advises the SHPO/THPO.

In the case where the SHPO/THPO cannot agree and/or refuses to sign, the ACHP will become the final arbiter [36 CFR 800.7]. If it agrees with the Federal agency (or suggests changes that the Federal agency accepts), then the Federal agency needs only to comply with whatever it was the MOA (with any changes) set out. The ACHP instead of the SHPO/THPO becomes one of the two signatories to the MOA, and in effect the SHPO/THPO will be overruled. However, if the ACHP objects to the Federal agency's conclusions and the agency does not agree to the proposed changes, then the effects will be considered adverse and some kind of mitigation of those adverse effects will be required.

Only the signatories—the agency, the SHPO/THPO, and/or the ACHP—have the power to amend, execute, or end an MOA. Other of the consulting parties may be invited to sign, too ("invited signatories"), but their refusal to concur or to sign the MOA does not invalidate the MOA.

In nearly all cases, the Federal agency and the SHPO/THPO will be in agreement. Both will work together to develop a way that offsets what otherwise would be adverse effects to the character of the cultural resources. That solution may be a redesign of the project, or it may be some kind of data recovery. It will be that agreement that is set forth in the MOA, and that will initiate the formal process of Phase III data recovery, if so required and agreed.

Data Recovery Plan

The *data recovery plan* may be developed in the Phase II report or it may be a separately assembled, stand-alone document. If it is the latter, then it may have been solicited through a competitive RFP. The data recovery plan forms the basis for the Phase III RFP and SOW.

The data recovery plan addresses six topics, usually in this order:

(1) an outline and background of the project history;

(2) a brief review of the environmental setting for the site and project area;

(3) a summary of the discovery and exploration of the site thus far;

(4) a summary of the prehistory and history as they pertain to the site;

(5) a detailed description, probably repeating the Phase II arguments, of how this particular site addresses the research questions listed; and

(6) a plan for actually getting the data from the site to address the research questions.

Project History and Background

A data recovery plan begins by summarizing the history of the undertaking, the structure of the local and regional environment, and the previous archaeological research. The history of the undertaking puts the proposed data recovery in the context of the larger project design. It shows why data recovery and not redesign of the project is the only way to mitigate adverse effects.

The data recovery plan also presents a synopsis of the environmental setting. What is the nature of the vegetation? The faunal community? The soils? The geology? What were these like in the past, especially around the time the site was occupied? What are conditions like now? The environmental background does two things. First, it puts the archaeological information into a broader ecological context so past life can be best understood. Second, it details the physical structure of the site and the nature of the deposit.

Finally, the background section of the data recovery plan summarizes previous investigations of the site. What work has been done at the site? When was it done? Who did that work? What were the conclusions? What was the nature of the deposit? What work has been done to consult with Indian tribes and other cultural groups? This part of the data recovery plan generally is not very long. It naturally organizes itself in the chronological order of the site investigations. The methods of previous investigations are covered: What was the nature of the Phase I or Phase II programs? What are the field conditions for the site? If prior subsurface work was done, how much was excavated to what depth and in what way? How and where were the test units or shovel tests placed? How was the fill processed? What was found? In addressing those questions, the archaeologist reviews everything previously written and discussed about the site.

Place of Site in Overall History/Prehistory

With the background reviewed, the data recovery plan then details how the site fits into the overall understanding of the greater area's history and/or prehistory. What kind of site is it? How old is it; or more specifically, with what cultural historical period is its Register eligibility associated? How does it relate to standing questions about the past, such as seasonal movements, expansion of settlement frontiers, or structure of emerging social classes? This involves assembling a refined background on the history and prehistory that pertains to the contents of the site. This will require

- reviewing the standard local, regional, and national journals;

- examining monographs and other booklike publications in professional or academic libraries;

- contacting the local libraries for manuscripts and other records that may have a bearing on the site; and

- accessing the compliance reports, located at the appropriate SHPOs/THPOs or state site files, of similar sites (a substantial part of the existing literature on the archaeology of an area is now located in compliance reports).

Assembling this part of a data recovery plan is just a standard scholarly literature search.[1] The data recovery plan requires a detailed discussion of

---

[1] The advent of Internet access has altered what is meant by "standard scholarly literature search." "A standard literature" search means locating as many as possible of the published sources that directly treat the particular issue at hand. In the past, this meant wandering into the university library or the SHPO report files, as well as pulling down all of your own professional journals, then patiently going through the journal table of contents or the titles on the SHPO shelves to see if there was something that had a bearing on the issue at hand.

Unfortunately, at some point this will still have to be done anyway, despite Internet capabilities. This is because journal and compliance report files listed on the Internet are not complete, and of course older monographs probably will not be present at all. Internet journal listings are notorious for stopping after 10 years before the year in which the search is being done. This means that the field work published in the 1930s or the 1960s or the 1980s, which often remains critical to understanding the archaeology of an area, will be missed. Reviewers tend to be familiar with that literature, meaning not just that those earlier sources are expected to be cited in the report, but that if important earlier citations are absent, then the entire report may be sent back to the firm for correction.

what is known about the archaeology for the cultural-historical period with which the site is associated. For single component sites, this is comparatively easy. For multicomponent sites, this approaches a sustained synopsis of what is known for the period—and associated cultures—represented by the site. Compliance reports are a particularly valuable source since they contain the bulk of information gathered in modern field research. The literature review for the data recovery plan requires more than locating and sensing the contents of previously written material. The material must be drawn together into a cogent whole relative to the site being considered.

Research Issues and How the Site Can Address Them

The status of a site's known historical or prehistoric archaeology sets a context. How does the site itself relate to that context? What questions does it appear capable of answering? The two issues addressed at this point by the data recovery plan are the nature of the site relative to standing research questions and the core reasons why this particular site is considered significant in terms of the Section 106 Process.

Having reviewed what the site is known to contain and the history or prehistory relevant to the site, the next step is to explain what the site could do to expand our understanding about the past. This step depends on the literature search and on the research questions in the state historic preservation plan.

The Phase II report gives the reasons why the site is eligible for listing on the National Register. The report also should have identified the research questions that can be addressed by the site. The data recovery plan will specify the data needed to answer the questions. The methodological framework may be inductive, specifying the type of information to be gathered in assembling an image of the past, or it may be deductive, identifying the particular evidence needed to address formal hypotheses.

Physical Characteristics of Site and Data Recovery Plan

The last section of the data recovery plan sets out a detailed procedure to extract the data that will address the research questions that have been identified for the site. Two factors are addressed:

- the nature of the site matrix (this is the physical structure of the medium for which the archaeologist must develop a data extraction strategy); and

- the best approach for recovering the archaeological data contained within that matrix.

The first issue involves the structure of the site itself, and how the actual excavation should proceed: What has previous work revealed about the physical character of the deposit? What was indicated about the horizontal dimensions relative to the overall project area? The vertical dimensions? Will shoring be needed because deposits extend below 1.2–1.5 m? What is the height of the water table in the wettest season? How should the fill be processed: dry-screening, water-screening, air-screening? What is the nature of preservation? Is the site contained within a soil, is it contained within a buried soil, is it contained within a cultural or natural sediment? Did anyone check to see the extent to which artifacts sank through the soils at the site?

All of the information on the physical characteristics of the site should be contained in the Phase I and Phase II reports. This may be augmented by reference to soil survey reports and perhaps engineering boring logs or percolation tests, especially if there is an issue of a shifting or high water table.

The second issue involves engineering the archaeological methods needed to extract the information stored within the archaeological site. The data recovery plan will propose specific field methods that are best suited for recovering the archaeological data contained within the site. An archaeological site is a form of information storage on past human behavior. The archaeologist is the expert in extracting that information. Extraction will involve excavation, analyses, then writing the report.

At this point in the data recovery plan the archaeologist makes extensive use of the method-and-theory literature as it bears upon data recognition and recovery. This is the topic of numerous texts as well as of standard archaeological method-and-theory and field courses.

Project Structure and Pre-Field Preparation

Developing a concerted plan for archaeological methods best represents the kind of military-campaign approach to archaeology formulated and advocated by General Pitt-Rivers (see Daniel 1962) and Sir Mortimer Wheeler (1954).

Site and Regional Documentation

The Phase III data recovery project requires an intimate understanding of the current status of research as it would apply to the site considered for investigation. Addressing this requires that the professional archaeologist perform a two-part background research exercise prior to performance of the work.

The first part of the background research centers on basic culture history applicable to the site. The second part involves the identification and investigation of the research questions that the site could address.

For example, the core question for a region might be the impact of climatic change on population size. A site, as an undisturbed sixteenth-century example, may well indicate if the particular culture was collapsing under the combined impact of the Neo-Boreal climatic minimum and European-introduced small pox. Yet, ancillary questions may include, for example, the nature of the pre-fired ceramic technology (an unresolved question for prehistoric North America north of Mexico), persistence of a microlithic compound tool industry (a major issue in lithic applications technology throughout the midwestern and eastern United States), and frequency of elk in the deposits (critical for further supporting Kay's [1994, 1996, 1997] argument about aboriginal overkill and National Park Service wildlife management practices in the Rocky Mountains).

The archaeologist must know about the human history/prehistory as it pertains to the site and be at least *aware* of the immediately related issues involving wildlife and plant ecology, climatic change, soil science, and similar disciplines whose research questions might involve information stored within the archaeological site.

Local Contacts, Public Relations/Education

Phase III data recovery represents full-scale archaeological investigation of a particular site or sites. The scale is quite large and potentially disruptive. However, the nature of the archaeology itself often is captivating and compelling. People are fascinated with archaeology, especially with the kind of work involved with most Phase III projects. The Phase III project, then, does not just require sound local contacts and good public relations, it can greatly benefit from such efforts.[2]

In terms of public contacts, Phase III may require expanded contact with local or regional officials as well as Federal, state, and local government archaeology regulators. The Section 106 process emphasizes the importance of consultation between Federal agencies and Indian tribes, Native Hawai'ian organizations, and other cultural groups [36 CFR 800.2(c) and other subsections]. Those consultations are meant to take into account issues of cultural/religious sensitivity. The need for much of this should have been anticipated during the planning stages for data recovery.

In terms of publicity, the public relations/education needs will vary by the nature of the project and the wishes or policy of the government agency, local officials, the landowner, and the client. For example, many people do *not* want to put up with the fuss of television reporters wandering about over their property, much less want to have it widely known that a large archaeological project is being done across their backyard. Further, additional publicity may create a security problem for the client. Collectors and looters very likely could descend upon the site and pillage it, particularly if there are chances of old bottles or early prehistoric projectile points being present. How publicity will be handled needs to be planned for ahead of time.

Note that Federal agencies normally prohibit public discussion of Phase III (or even Phase I or Phase II) projects, except by authorized personnel under pre-determined conditions. The Corps of Engineers maintains a general policy that no one may discuss any aspect of the project with nonagency personnel. Exceptions to this, such as planned media days or public briefings, are specified in the SOW or the RFP.

In non-Federal situations, public discussion may not be an issue: For example, the landowner may not mind, or the location of the project may be such that this publicity is no problem, while the agency or SHPO may have agreed to publicly discuss the work. For example, Vermont and some other states ask their archaeologists to give public presentations on their

---

[2]For detailed discussion on public relations and how they bear upon Phase III compliance projects, see Neumann and Sanford 2001:212–214.

work to local town officials, historical societies, and the like. Such actions represent notable public relations/education opportunities.

In the end, what is done in the way of publicity will depend upon the nature and circumstances of the project. A large Phase III project in a small community may attract and benefit from the interest of local government officials. However, a comparatively small Phase III project mitigating the adverse effects of a rural bridge may draw little attention and have no special public relation needs.

Labor Estimates

As with Phase I and Phase II, the proposal budget prepared for the Phase III data recovery provides the figures for estimated labor. The firm will have basic figures applicable to Phase III work, but each Phase III is different. Phase III projects have the same basic five project stages found in Phase I and Phase II (start-up, field work, analysis, draft report preparation/review, and final report delivery).

The Phase III may involve more extensive field work than previous phases. Arrangements may be needed for any environmental permitting associated with the data recovery process, plans for public education programs requested by the SOW or for public relations exercises, scheduling site security (and perhaps locating a security guard), and arranging for sanitation facilities for the crew while they are in the field. Federal projects and some states require that a safety plan be in place.

Phase III also involves more in the way of analysis, and often labor estimates include outside specialists. The labor estimates for specialists are based upon their individual rate schedules combined with a sense, from the Phase II work, of how much of their efforts will be needed. These estimates may be given as line items, set in the same general category as radiocarbon dates and other kinds of specialized processing, or converted into hourly rates for the sake of the original bid.

Staffing Needs

Phase III staff categories are similar to those for a Phase II, although usually the amount of labor needed is much greater. Phase III projects require assembling a research team. The core personnel will come from within the firm; however, additional field technicians and analytical specialists will be hired from the outside.

It will be the duty of the project manager to identify specific project needs then locate people to fulfill those needs. This will need to be done within a given budget and within a given time frame. Equally important is personnel management. The project manager not only handles the project, he or she must handle the team assembled to accomplish the goals of that project.[3]

Field Logistics: Housing, Per Diem, Transport

The logistical needs for the field portion of the Phase III project often involve arranging field accommodations and transportation for crew. A per diem allowance may well be needed, particularly if people will be billeted for any period. This can be true even if the site itself is close to the office, since many Phase III projects require adding staff for the duration of the field work. Otherwise, field logistical needs are identical to those outlined for Phase II projects.

Equipment and Supply Needs

As with a Phase II testing project, the equipment and supply need categories of a Phase III data recovery project are similar to those of a full-scale archaeological excavation. The differences between Phase II and Phase III project needs are in scale of the exercise, the time commitment for the equipment, and a possible requirement for special equipment. A long stay in the field requires on-site equipment maintenance. Large shelters may be needed to work during inclement or harsh weather. Ramps may be required. Large, open areas may need temporary plywood covers. Finally, the project may require items specific to data recovery, such as intake hoses for a water screen, pumps to remove water from units, shoring materials, and space heaters.

Field

The field part of a Phase III data recovery differs in four ways from traditional academic research work. First, it is a continuation of a larger compli-

---

[3]Personnel management and the management of professionals is required throughout all of archaeology, and especially in the Phase III process. A discussion of this is given in Neumann and Sanford 2001:218–220, 222, and 230–233.

ance process. Second, the field technique is abbreviated because of time and budget limits. Third, usually some if not all of the unexcavated part of the affected deposit will disappear after the Phase III work ends. Last, the entire Phase III project, from field work through analysis to submission of a peer-reviewed final report, must be done within pre-set budget and time limits.

Preparatory Work

Four sets of information need to be consolidated and understood before the Phase III field work is started or at least well under way:

(1) reconciling of previous historic and excavation maps with the current physical site;

(2) mapping;

(3) history of land use where the site is located; and

(4) site and deposit dynamics.

Together, these summarize the conditions that the professional archaeologist will face as the data recovery plan is implemented in the field.

Previous maps of the site need to be brought into line with the physical existence of the site itself. Since the planning for the Phase III is often based on where things were said to be located in the Phase II testing (and the Phase I survey), it is important to make sure where those mapped land features actually are. To save time and the costs of having a crew on stand-by, the maps should be reconciled at the start of the project.

As with any excavation, a site map is needed. Even though a Phase II map should exist, unless the Phase III project is being done by the same firm, a new map must be prepared. Except in cases where previous test units must be relocated or a plowzone must be removed, site mapping can be done as the field work itself begins.

Land-use history in Phase II helps assess site integrity and assists in devising a data recovery plan. For Phase III data recovery, land-use history is used to understand specifics about the deposit. This can range from the obvious issue of past plowing to the archaeology of how the land was used, such as formal gardens, orchards, and pastures. Further, the history may reveal other important information such as undocumented hazardous waste dumps either on the site, or sufficiently close to the site that groundwater contamination may create safety problems for the crew.

The fourth body of information required for Phase III is a knowledge of the site's physical structure. The county soil surveys and the Phase I and II reports should have most of this information. There are three issues to consider:

(1) how the deposit will affect the mechanics of excavation, both digging and matrix processing;

(2) how internal processes in the site matrix have influenced the data quality of the site; and

(3) what are the engineering parameters for the excavation.

The physical characteristics of the site matrix will determine the rate at which fill is processed, as well as the appropriate way to process the fill: Dry-screening? Water-screening? Air-screening?

The second issue involves data integrity: Is the deposit conducive to good bone preservation? Has it been below the water table, resulting in good organic preservation? To what extent have artifacts continued to sink in the semi-fluid represented by the soil?

The third issue involves engineering the archaeological data recovery. What are the structural properties of the site matrix? This alone will determine the nature of any shoring needed. At what depth does groundwater appear? This influences both excavation wall strength as well as need for pumps. Does the groundwater level fluctuate (usually indicated by soil horizon mottling)? That will influence not only artifact preservation, but also the potential for groundwater seepage at levels closer to the surface than perhaps encountered during Phase II testing.

Excavation Management

Excavation management requires:

- a thorough understanding of the problem being addressed (structure of the site and research issues involved);

- knowledge of the physical characteristics of the site;

We learned about archaeology from that . . . The French Drain

Our most humorous data recovery experience was at the Weston Site in central New York, where a proposed development contained an early historic Onondaga refugee camp. The land had been plowed, and the soil was seasonally wet and characterized by perched water tables. The Phase III field procedure was to strip the plowzone from six parallel east-west trenches, shovel scrape them to expose features and post-hole stains, then map and recover exposed features.

Figure 6.1. Detail of French Drain Showing Base Construction. Flat stones were placed over these cobbles. Groundwater draining into the drain system originally flowed under the flat rocks. The area between the cobbles was silted-in when exposed, but the water continued to flow across the top surface of the flat stones. Trowel points north; scale is 1.0 m.

In the southernmost trench, we detected post-hole stains from the walls of four houses and a narrow cobble band roughly parallel to one of the house's walls. The

> ### *We learned about archaeology from that . . . The French Drain (Continued)*
>
> band ran across the trench and appeared to be set into a narrow ditch. In several places, there was dark earth, suggestive of post holes, instead of cobbles. "Wall trenches," long trenches into which vertical posts for longhouse walls are placed, were known for contemporaneous sites in southern Ontario and Middle Mississippian sites, but were unknown in central New York. We imagined a village surrounded by a narrow, cobble-packed ditch into which the main stockade wall posts were placed.
>
> We anticipated that the cobble band continued on a straight line, projected where it would appear in the trenches to the north, and followed the bands we found. Over 4.5 ha, we traced a W-shaped pattern of cobble-filled ditches merging into one that continued downhill. We took apart the lower section of cobbles and ditch and discovered that we had been tracing . . . a French drain system. A French drain is a sloped trench dug below the normal height of the water table and filled with gravel and cobbles to collect water and carry it away.
>
> We should have asked ourselves, given soil known to be seasonally wet and containing perched water tables, how had the developer gotten a building permit and however did the field get cultivated productively? Had we thought about the landscape clues, we should have anticipated a subsurface drain system. Lessons learned from this experience include *thinking* about the implications of landscape features and taking things apart. It also reinforced the importance of understanding landscape history, knowing historic land management practices, and recognizing the archaeological signatures of those practices.

- awareness of the logistical limits on excavating the site; then

- carrying out a data recovery plan.[4]

The excavation management plan provides a schedule of tasks. It must consider the budget, contingencies such as weather and a change in site or deposit characteristics. Each detail of the Phase III should be considered. These range from logistics through supply to processing the deposit. Much of this should exist in the excavation plan that was prepared in response to the Phase III RFP. Considerable managerial expertise is required in dealing with the excavation crew, support and technical staff, and the general public.

---

[4]For a detailed discussion of Phase III excavation management, see Neumann and Sanford 2001:233–239.

Official Site Visits

Phase III data recovery projects may receive visits by agency and SHPO/THPO archaeologists. Some will show up with video or film cameras. This is quite appropriate. Part of a regulatory archaeologist's role, and certainly the purpose of such a visit, is to make sure that public money is being properly used and that the project is being performed at a high standard.

Since field visits are likely to occur, and to occur on short notice, it is important that an air of professionalism be maintained about the site, particularly in terms of appearance. The issue is not so much one of being fussily fastidious as it is being neat and organized. Sir Mortimer Wheeler's maxim that "an untidy excavation is a bad one" works in reverse as well: A project area in order suggests that the archaeology also is sound.

At the end of such a visit or inspection, the project manager and field supervisor each should complete detailed written accounts of what occurred. Those accounts will be placed in the field notebook under "Records of Communications."

Field notes are organized in the same manner as for Phase II projects. There will be substantially more information devoted to features and to tracking matrix/flotation samples. If the project is very large or has multiple sites, there will be multiple field note binders. Quality field notes are more important for Phase III projects than for Phase I or II because even the unexamined part of the archaeological deposit soon will be

Reviewing Field Notes

The field notes from a project are one of three sets of permanent records, the other two being the photographs from the site and the artifacts recovered. Even then, the artifacts become virtually useless unless the field notes are sound.

Field notes are crucial for all phases of the compliance process, of course, but they are most critical for the Phase III data recovery project. This is because, unlike the Phase I or Phase II, the portion of the site undergoing mitigation through data recovery will cease to exist. Field notes must be kept to the highest standard possible. Daily review of notes is not micro-management. Rather, it reflects the intense and irreversible nature of the archaeological data recovery process. Review provides a second pair of eyes looking out after the quality of the work.

destroyed by the activities associated with the undertaking. The site, or at least the portion compromised, will exist only as the assemblage recovered, the field notes, and the final report.

Closing Field Operations

The Phase III project is the last field step. Phase I and Phase II work really is diagnostic and evaluative work; the idea is to get a sense of what is present, then, if appropriate, recommend additional work. Closure of the field part of the project usually is little more than backfilling.

Closing the field aspect of a Phase III project presents different issues. Not only is there the physical closing of excavation and the returning or refurbishing of equipment, there also will be the demobilizing of project-hires along with the reassigning of permanent employees who served as field staff.

Field closure can vary by what is going to happen next with the overall undertaking. Sometimes the excavation is backfilled and the land returned to its original condition. However, just as often the excavations are left open and serve for the planned construction as a head-start in their own excavation needs. In either case, a post-closure inspection should be held to ensure the site is stable and in compliance with permits and contracts.

The end result with the closing of a Phase III project is that there will be a lot of equipment and supplies that will need to be returned, stored, or dealt with somehow. And there will be a lot of people who will also need to be reassigned. It is the project manager's responsibility to attend to the needs represented by both.

Post-Field

At the end of the field portion of the Phase III data recovery, there are four tasks that need to be handled. First, the field equipment needs to be refurbished, stored, and/or reissued. Second, the field personnel need to be reassigned or, in the case of project-hires, hopefully directed to continued employment with another project or firm. Third, the field notes and other records need to be consolidated. And last, the materials from the site need to be analyzed and a final report on the project produced.

The final tasks of the Phase III project are to produce a detailed written analysis of the archaeological site that meets compliance needs as set forth in the SOW and prepare the artifacts and site/analysis records for permanent curation.

Collections Processing

Phase III data recovery projects return from the field with three general categories of physical data: artifacts, fill or matrix samples intended for additional processing, and field records. Coordination of the first two, which represent the collection from the site, is the responsibility of the laboratory director. The project manager is responsible for the third.

Artifact processing will involve cleaning (when appropriate), cataloguing, labeling, then rebagging. The laboratory will also produce a master artifact inventory at this time.

The processing of flotation and matrix samples depends upon their nature and upon requirements in the SOW. Such samples may be from features or from general excavation fill. Flotation samples may be reduced in-house to light and heavy fractions that are then sent to subcontracted specialists for detailed study. Matrix samples are fixed-volume samples removed in their entirety from the excavation unit. These samples aid in understanding the physical properties of the deposit. Matrix samples may be sent in their unprocessed entirety to a subcontracted specialist for detailed analysis, or they may be curated and not processed at all.

Analysis and Report Production

The last step is the analysis of the archaeological materials then assembly of the final report. Analysis corresponds to what is expected of any full-scale, formal excavation. This is what is discussed throughout the method-and-theory literature (e.g., Renfrew and Bahn 2000).

Phase III reports are comprehensive site monographs. In addition to reporting the standard research results, the Phase III product must address any and all issues raised in the SOW and in the corresponding data recovery plan. The Phase III report is a thorough analysis of the portion of the archaeological site examined. It is not always an exhaustive analysis, nor is that the goal. However, additional work sometimes can be squeezed in within the budget limits; many project managers will check and recheck the status of their analysis budget to see what more can be done to make the report as thorough as possible. The general structure of the Phase III report is outlined in chapter 7.

Chapter Summary

Phase III is the last stage in the compliance process. Variously referred to as data recovery, mitigation, or resolution, the purpose of the Phase III work is to offset pending destruction of the Register-eligible property—here, the archaeological deposit—through some kind of data recovery. A phrase often used that captures, albeit colloquially, what is desired at this stage is "to achieve data redundancy." That is, by doing full-sale excavation on an archaeological site, not only will the adverse effects of the project be offset or *mitigated*, but the continued existence of that part of the site would be largely *redundant* upon proper data recovery.

Phase III data recovery projects obviously begin with the determination by the lead agency, in light of the Phase II testing results, that the site is eligible for listing on the National Register. With such a determination, the process becomes more formal. One of the first steps involved, at least with the Federal Section 106 Process, will be the execution of a *Memorandum of Agreement* or *MOA* between the lead agency and the SHPO/ THPO.

The MOA will set out that the parties agree that the site is eligible for the National Register, that the undertaking will have adverse effects, and that the only practical solution to mitigate or resolve those adverse effects will be some kind of data recovery. Although other parties may be invited to comment and even to sign the MOA, only the Federal agency, the SHPO/THPO, and/or the Advisory Council on Historic Preservation have authority to amend, execute, or end the MOA.

Phase III data recovery will also have a *data recovery plan*. The data recovery plan will provide a detailed research design for doing the Phase III data recovery. That design will vary by nature of the site, but will include research questions to be addressed just as much as recommended field and laboratory procedures to collected the needed data.

Phase III archaeological work is similar to what one would expect for any kind of full-scale archaeological excavation. The staffs tend to be larger than testing exercises; the amount of time in the field can be long;

and there usually will be a large collection as a result. Like all full-scale excavations, the actual field strategy—and the tactical options used to achieve strategic goals—vary for each Phase III project.

The Phase III project is a sustained effort, and often it will be done at a distance from the home office. There will be a need in most firms to hire on additional personnel for the duration of the field work; there will be a need to arrange for crew billeting. In some particularly large and long-running projects, there may be a need to establish a field laboratory. In most Phase III projects, there will be a need to plan for the huge amount of artifacts and site matrix samples that will descend on the laboratory back at the home office.

Phase III data recovery, as a compliance exercise, does differ from the more traditional archaeological excavation in five important ways. The first difference is that excavation is restricted to the parts of the site within the overall project area. Archaeologists who have not faced this kind of limit before find such a "boundary restriction" to be quite unsettling. The Phase III data recovery project does not excavate beyond project boundary limits.

The second difference is that field work must be finished by a specified date. The general contractor will have scheduled subcontracting tasks for the overall land-alteration project in such a way that the archaeology people are expected to be out of the way by a given date. If that does not happen, the contractor has a large number of people standing idle, has the project completion date pushed back, and faces cost overruns and additional interest on the business loan enabling the work.

The third difference is that Phase III data recovery will be done regardless of most weather conditions. Being able to work under conditions that, in noncompliance situations, results in a sensible suspension of field work requires that the archaeologist have a very good understanding of what the archaeological data are and what can or cannot be done in the field to retrieve those data without compromising them. This is why compliance archaeology is so professionally demanding and is so appealing to archaeological generalists: Flexibility and adaptation are the keys; there is selection against specialization.

The fourth difference between more traditional archaeological excavation projects and the Phase III data recovery project involves funds. Most contract awards for compliance work are paid out in increments, say when a given stage of the project is done or at the end of a given period provided the work has been finished. This means that the compliance firm may well have to underwrite the project for a short period until work is done or the month ends. The money for that has to come from somewhere, and if it is not yet coming in from the agency or firm paying for the overall Phase III mitigation project, then it will have to come from the archaeology firm's own cash reserves, from a business loan, or from the pockets of the workers until such time as they can be reimbursed.

The last difference is unemployment. When the field portion of the project is over, those hired for that stage of work will need to find employment. Normally a firm's staff is sufficient to handle the analysis and reporting parts of the project, and in any case has as its primary obligation continuing employment of its full-time people.

Again, as with traditional large excavation projects, the Phase III data recovery project requires collections to be cleaned, labeled, catalogued, and analyzed. The procedures will be pretty much the same; the specifics will be quite a bit different. Those differences come down to time, available funds, and curatorial requirements. The analyses must be done by a given date, which means that only those analyses set out in the original data recovery plan normally will be done. Further, the finished project report must be submitted to the Federal agency and to the SHPO by a given date, and that date usually is within (often quite well within) a calendar year. As a result, Phase III analyses are basic in the sense of routine-sophisticated-for-any-full-excavation analyses. The idea is that, if more could be done with the material, the collections and field notes will be there for whoever wants to work on them.

That brings up the issue of curation. Private-sector firms do not curate collections. Rather, they prepare collections for curation, then get them out of the door just as quickly as professional standards and project schedules allow. The collections need to be prepared for curation in accord with current museum curatorial guidelines; if generated from a Federal project, they will need to be curated in a facility that meets criteria set forth in 36 CFR 79. All that will be left of the archaeological site after Phase III will be the field records, the analysis records, and the collections. Their curation is a paramount issue.

Finally, like any archaeological field project, there is a required report for the Phase III exercise. Perhaps here is the greatest difference with noncompliance archaeological research. Archaeological ethics require that any excavation—Phase I, Phase II, or Phase III—be written up. This is as true of the academic world as it is of the professional work, and is a legacy of WPA archaeology, when sites rarely were written up after being dug.

However, for the Phase III report, it must not only be a complete, stand-alone archaeological research document, it must like the Phase I and Phase II reports preceding it survive extraordinarily stringent peer review, first from the lead agency and then from the SHPO/THPO. It is stringent not just in terms of the quality of the work; it is stringent because final payment on the contract award will not be received until a peer-acceptable document is in the agency's and SHPO/THPO's hands.

Further, more often than not, that report—in what would be called "camera-ready condition"—must be done within a year of the end of field work, all the while that the same principals compiling that report are compiling a number of others. Assembly of compliance reports is discussed in chapter 7.

With the acceptance of the report, the Phase III project ends with a turning over of the collections, field and laboratory notes, the final report, and other related documents to an appropriate curatorial facility.

Additional Readings of Interest

Hester, Thomas R., Harry J. Shafer, and Kenneth L. Feder. 1997. *Field Methods in Archaeology*. Seventh edition. Mayfield, Mountain View. This latest avatar of what began in 1949 as *A Manual of Archaeological Field Methods* put together by a bunch of undergraduates and graduate students at UC-Berkeley [including chapters by W. Y. Adams, Chester Chard, Robert Heizer, and William C. Massey], originally served as a field methods handbook focused on California. It went through a series of changes since, at first under the authorship of Heizer as *A Guide to Archaeological Field Methods* through the 1950s, later as *Field Methods in Archeology* in 1975 (by then the sixth edition) with Hester and John A. Graham joining Heizer in authorship. The seventh edition underscores the volume as an ongoing project, passed along and revised by the field as needed, and continues its focus on specific, detailed this-is-how-it-is-done consideration of archaeological field methods.

King, Thomas F. 2000. *Federal Planning and Historical Places: The Section 106 Process*. AltaMira Press, Walnut Creek, CA. A comprehensive discussion of the Section 106 Process from the planning perspective, including detailed advice on assembling things like Memoranda of Agreement (MOAs).

Neumann, Thomas W., and Robert M. Sanford. 2001. *Practicing Archaeology: An Introduction to Cultural Resources Archaeology.* AltaMira Press, Walnut Creek, CA. The section on Phase III investigations includes a discussion on personnel management, both in terms of general staff and in terms of professional personnel.

Renfrew, Colin, and Paul Bahn. 2000. *Archaeology: Theories, Methods, and Practice.* Third edition. Thames and Hudson, London. Although it is not anthropological in orientation, nor is it written with Americanist archaeology in mind, we still feel this is probably the best overall method-and-theory text available at the moment. It presents in a well-illustrated, well-written, and well-organized way the various interpretive and conceptual tools required of archaeologists designing and interpreting full-scale excavations.

As wonderful as the Renfrew and Bahn volume is—and it really is—it should be cautioned that its discussion of compliance archaeology is abbreviated and, where pertaining to the United States, generally incorrect (that, though, will be true for many current methods and method-and-theory texts).

REPORT PREPARATION AND PRODUCTION

Purpose and Objectives

Two overlapping tasks take place after the field portion of a compliance project: processing and analysis of the recovered materials, and preparation then submission of the project report.

The Laboratory: Structure, Processing, Analysis

All firms that do professional archaeology maintain an in-house archaeology laboratory. The purposes of that laboratory are to provide space and facilities for analysis, as well as space for temporary collections storage. For every person-hour of labor spent in the field, we have found that another two to three person-hours will be spent in the laboratory. Much of the work that will be done will be similar to what is found in any standard archaeology laboratory. With a couple qualifications unique to the professional workplace, the purposes will be the same as well: to identify, record, label, and curate the archaeological collection; to answer questions about the site/project area *relative to* the compliance needs of the particular project; and to provide a basic analysis and interpretation of any archaeological deposits encountered.

The idea of the processing and analysis steps is to leave the collection in such a state that future workers can come into the assemblage and, armed with the field and laboratory notes, pick up the research from where it left off. This, too, is very much a reaction of how collections were left during WPA archaeology.

Basic Laboratory Structure

Corporate archaeology laboratories provide facilities for processing the materials as they come in from the field (which includes washing and labeling), very basic analyses, and short-term storage until the collections can be turned over to a permanent curatorial facility.

The amount of physical space involved varies by corporation, both in terms of its physical plant and its internal division of labor. Some firms devote upward of a third of their floor space to the laboratory, and nearly all analytical work will be done there. Other firms use the laboratory more for cleaning, labeling, and inventorying, while much of the actual artifact analyses are done at the desk of the principal investigator.

Regardless of how the firm goes about allocating space, all firms will have the basic tools needed to get through fundamental analyses. Thus, scales, micrometers, dissecting microscopes, and similar items will be available. On occasion, the corporate laboratory will have an in-house electrolysis system for stabilizing small metal (meaning iron in most cases) artifacts before they are finally prepared for curation. Most will have the capacity to process flotation samples, at least to the light-fraction (botanical organics)/heavy-fraction (everything else that does not float) stage.

Figure 7.1. Interior of typical corporate laboratory. Photo courtesy of Paul Brockington and Brockington and Associates, Inc.

Because the lab is not meant to be all things to all people, more so-phisticated analysis normally will be contracted. Some firms do have the capacity to do high-magnification lithic use-wear analyses, or to do so-phisticated paleoethnobotanical analyses; most, however, do not. Usually what will happen, especially with Phase III data recovery and some more intensive Phase II evaluation exercises, is that a virtual laboratory will be put together. This is where the project director or principal investigator will assemble a set of research specialists to handle different parts of the analysis. It is a virtual laboratory because it exists only on paper and only for the duration of the project: The specialists themselves usually live in widely scattered locations, and may be strangers to each other. Those in-dependent subcontractors, each with the expertise and equipment needed, will be sent materials for analysis.

Corporate archaeology laboratories usually have excellent access to field vehicles. The labs also serve as a kind of garage-equipment-storage-cum-general-gathering-place. In most firms, though, the lab is "back" in the facility.

Processing Materials from the Field

Collections brought in from the field will come under the jurisdiction of the laboratory director. The director will first make sure that the

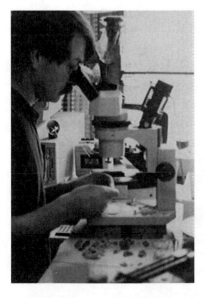

Figure 7.2. Certainly for Phase II and Phase III analyses, all prehistoric flakes should be examined under a dissecting microscope. Approximately 15 percent of flakes classified as "unmodified" from prehistoric archaeological sites in the eastern United States are, in fact, heavily used microliths. Photo courtesy of Pocket Park–Wentworth Analytical Facility.

Figure 7.3. More often than not, the typical archaeology firm is located in an office park. Photo courtesy of Paul Brockington and Brockington and Associates, Inc.

artifact-bag inventory matches the actual bags handed over. With that accomplished, the next step is to process the collections.

How the collection is "processed"—meaning cleaned or otherwise prepared for analysis and ultimately curation—depends on instructions given in the SOW. Those instructions will have been dictated in part by agency protocol and in part by state/SHPO/THPO protocol. Sometimes all of the artifacts will be washed; sometimes only some will be, with the remainder left uncleaned in the hope that future researchers might be able to get more information from what was left on the surface of the object (residue and phytolith analyses come to mind). It will be at this stage that whatever conservation/stabilization measures are needed will be done.

With the artifacts cleaned or otherwise "processed," the artifacts and other parts of the collection, such as matrix samples, will be labeled. Labeling will be done according to museum archiving standards. At the same time that labeling is being done, a general artifact inventory will be prepared as well.

With the collections cleaned and labeled, the collection will then be placed in archivally stable bags (usually 4-mil clear-plastic pressure-locking bags, within which will be labeling and provenience information written on an equally stable material), which in turn will be placed in

On Cleaning Artifacts

Whether or not artifacts are cleaned, and how they are cleaned, depends upon the guidelines of the SHPO as set forth in the SOW. Traditionally, artifacts are washed under running water with gentle brushing, then set to one side to dry. However, some contracts specify that a percentage of prehistoric applications-industry tools (e.g., utilized flakes or projectile points) or unflaked stone tools (e.g., palette stones or metates) *not* be washed. This restriction is meant to permit future residue or phytolith analyses.

Artifacts can be cleaned either by dry brushing, by brushing under running water, or by soaking in a deflocculating solution like sodium hexametaphosphate (e.g., Calgon™). The deflocculant process is usually faster and potentially less damaging than scrubbing in water (Neumann and Sanford 1998).

Figure 7.4. It is critical that the archaeology laboratory be accessible to field vehicles. Office parks are designed for this. In this picture, the "garage door" is the right-hand opening. The equal-sized area to the left is the tinted glass for the firm's laboratory, shown in Figure 7.1. Photo courtesy of Paul Brockington and Brockington and Associates, Inc.

archivally stable boxes that are well-labeled. All of this attention to curation also is in reaction to some of the incredible curatorial disasters that attended some WPA collections.

Figure 7.5.   Example of a labeled artifact. The best kind of artifact labeling system is one that provides all of the basic provenience information. Here, the artifact is labeled with the site number, unit stake number, and ordinal level number. Even lacking the field notes, a person could make some sense of the labeled assemblage.

Figure 7.6.   Labeled artifacts will be placed in 4-mil self-locking plastic bags for curation. The bags will be labeled by site, unit, and depth, as well as by type of artifact. Inside the bag that same information will have been written on an archivally stable label slip.

Levels of Analysis

There are two steps in the analysis of any archaeological assemblage. The first involves recording the information about the artifacts and other materials recovered and will be done in the laboratory or at the principal investigator's desk. The second involves manipulating that body of information. That second step uses the records generated in the laboratory and manipulates those data and will be done as part of the process of preparing the written report.

Levels of Analysis: Laboratory Recordation

All laboratory analyses will do basic identification of the artifacts, including classificatory and typological assessment. All will do counts. Beyond that, the level of analysis done depends upon the nature of the compliance project.

For Phase I survey projects, the laboratory analyses are meant to provide sufficient information on the archaeological assemblage to allow its cultural-historical placement, number of components (horizontal, or vertical within testing depth), and basic site function. Generally, analyses for Phase I sites rarely involve anything more complicated than identification, classification, counting, and, where appropriate, weighing. It is with the identification of many temporally sensitive artifacts that some kind of provisional date or cultural-historical association can be given to the archaeological site.

Phase II testing exercises require more detailed analyses. Many of the questions involve structure of the site, how the site was used in the past, and what the information potential of the site is relative to our knowledge of the past of which it was a part. Thus, laboratory analyses are similar to what one would find in an abbreviated full-scale archaeological investigation: Artifacts will be measured, identified, classified. On prehistoric sites, high-magnification lithic use-wear analyses will be done, and, if flotation samples were recovered and processed, paleoethnobotanical analyses will be done. On historic sites, the fine details of historic glass or historic ceramics will be presented. Most Phase II analyses are capable of standing on their own as finished, complete archaeological research reports. They are meant to be approached that way so that questions about Register eligibility can be answered on behalf of the lead agency.

Phase III data recovery analyses are comprehensive analyses limited only by the SOW and the budget. The laboratory aspect will vary by the kind of site, nature of the assemblage, and resources to do the work. The comprehensive nature reflects in large measure the realization that the deposit will be severely compromised—if not disappear entirely—after field work is done. The Phase III report will be the final narrative on the deposit.

Levels of Analysis: Data Manipulation

The laboratory analyses provide a condensation of the artifactual evidence from the site. The information in effect is transformed from individual physical elements to a series of inventories and tables representing classes of objects. Some of that will be produced by the laboratory staff; a fair amount will be generated by the principal investigator and any specialists hired on for the project. All of that information will then be consolidated into the "Results" section of the report. That will require data manipulation. It does not hurt to think of this step being the scientific equivalent of an exercise in rhetoric, since the goal is not just to make a recommendation, but to justify it.

For Phase I and II projects, the data manipulation is meant to address the compliance needs of the project just as much as it is meant to make archaeological sense of the site. For Phase I projects, the primary questions are: (1) can depositional integrity be ruled out; (2) what is the cultural-historical affiliation; and (3) what is the horizontal and, with limited subsurface testing, vertical extent of the deposit? Behind all of this is the basic question: Should we have someone come back out and check to see if this site really *is* Register eligible?

Although abbreviated in analysis, Phase I data manipulation requires that the professional archaeologist substantiate claims about the deposit. For example, one does not just say "the site is disturbed" and let it go at that, or "the site has artifacts in the B horizon under the plowzone." Rather, one notes that the vegetation and soils, along with historic records, indicate that the site had been extensively plowed. Or again, that while artifacts were found in the B horizon, a chi-squared statistical test indicated that there was no reason to think the subplowzone assemblage independent of what was found in the plowzone.

For Phase II, the primary questions will be the physical integrity of the site, the cultural-historical affiliation, and the vertical/horizontal distribution of the artifacts. However, the analysis also will explore in its own right the nature of the artifactual patterning as well as site function and internal dynamics. All of this is aimed at being able to recommend—yea or nay—to the lead agency that the site is eligible for listing on the National Register.

Phase III data recovery analyses are as sophisticated and thorough as the project budget allows. The kind of data manipulation expected for a Phase III project is what normally is described in method-and-theory texts for the analysis of a site.

Turn-Over

The actual last step in the entire compliance project is *turn-over*. Turn-over is the term used for the handing over of the archaeological collections, field records, analysis records, and copy of the final report to an appropriate curatorial facility. Turn-over takes place when the final report for the project is accepted and produced.

In situations where the Federal government is also the client, the collections belong to the Federal government—meaning, they belong to us as citizens. This in turn means that the collections belong to the nation at large. In situations where the project was Federally enabled but actually done by private parties, whoever owns the land generally owns the artifacts (and probably whoever paid to have the field and analytical work done also owns those parts of the collection, too). This varies by state, by the way, and it is wise to check with the SHPO or equivalent agency. Similarly, states have equivalent procedures for projects where the state is the client.

When collections have been generated by a Federally enabled undertaking, the location for curation must conform to the criteria set out in 36 CFR 79. This is stipulated in 36 CFR 79.3 (a). Those requirements focus on physical plant capabilities, such as fire suppression systems, regular and thorough pest management, security, and climate control. However, they also require the presence of an individual with at least three years' experience equivalent to museum curation overseeing the curation of those collections.

With turn-over completed and all project materials are turned over to a curatorial facility, the final bill for the project will be submitted to the client for payment. Except for financial management issues involving the project—outstanding bills, per diem reimbursement, and the like—payment of that final bill marks the "official" end of the project as far as most archaeologists will be concerned.

The Report: The Final Product

The last step in the cultural resources project will be the production of a final report. The final report does two things: It gives government regulators sufficient information for determinations of effect/adverse effect, and/or of Register eligibility, to be made; and it provides a stand-alone results-of-research document.

The last delivered product will be the final project report. However, the cultural resources process requires reporting on the results of the field work. Often the principal investigator provides short reports on the status of the project. These are variously called *progress reports, management letters*, or *management summaries*, and will be sent out to the client or the agency at given stages in the project, say when a monthly bill is submitted or when field work is completed.

Written reports, be they short or long, are referred to as *deliverables*. These physical products will have been requested within the SOW, and are to be finished physical products before any payment is made on the contract. Other deliverables include education materials, videos, and even community service activities. Most states have information about assessment report formats on their Web sites. Some have entire guide manuals that can be downloaded.

The discussion here focuses on final report assembly and production. Management summaries and other short reports really are like long letters.

The compliance report not only treats cultural resource management and basic research issues, it also provides long-term information storage of the archaeological deposit. The report is a summation of the archaeological research. Federal regulations, particularly 36 CFR 79 and the Secretary of the Interior's Standards and Guidelines, list the compliance report as part of the overall archaeological collection (see also Appendix A). The report produced must be sufficient in detail and quality such that agency and SHPO/THPO archaeologists particularly can judge for themselves the merits of the conclusions reached by the authors. This is because the Federal agency will base its determinations, such as of Register eligibility, mainly on the conclusions of that report, while the SHPO/THPO will assess the legitimacy of those agency determinations by what it has understood from that same report.

The compliance report is not only a regulatory and planning document, it is also an archaeological research document. The report must be sufficient to allow another investigator, armed with the field notes, to continue research on the deposit from the point where the report ends. To do this, the report will contain details regarding site location, condition, pedology and/or stratigraphy, and field and analytical methods. The maps have to be accurate enough to enable another person to locate the previous surface-collection areas, test units, shovel tests, or whatever examination was employed.

From an archaeological perspective, the compliance report is a fundamental source of information. Indeed, it is now impossible to do adequate archaeological research in the United States without referring extensively to the compliance reports for the particular region or cultural-historical tradition. But that is only part of the reason that such a document exists. The primary reason that the compliance report exists is because, as a consequence of the Section 106 process or its counterpart at the state or local level, it represents a planning tool and a form of compliance documentation.

Overall Report Structure

An archaeological compliance report consists of three pieces that are all brought together. There is the background information, like the history and prehistory of the area, assembled before the field work began. There are the results from the field work and subsequent laboratory analyses. And there are all of the figures and photographs meant to further illustrate the points made in the report. Bringing all of these pieces together into a cogent report requires that the principal investigator or project director be adept at managing people, be familiar with what each task requires, and be keenly aware of what those pieces are meant to do relative to the purposes of the compliance report.

How all of this is meant to work can best be understood by having a sense of what the final product will contain. Table 7.1 summarizes the contents of a basic archaeological compliance report.

Compliance reports will begin in a quasi-formal way. That is, there will be ways in which the cover and title are expected to be done. The expectations may be corporate; they may be agency or SHPO/THPO protocols. Nevertheless, the information on the cover and on the title page will be formalized.

Unlike archaeology articles and monographs in more traditional publications, archaeological compliance reports usually require the signature of the principal investigator on the cover page (Figure 7.7). Some Federal agencies also use a form that summarizes the nature of the document.

Some mention should be made about titles. There are a variety of ways to title reports. The title page should contain the site number, county, and state. A descriptive title or subtitle is helpful, for example:

Phase II Archeological Investigation of the Johnson's Spring Site (21HU35), Houston County, Minnesota

or

Test Excavations of a Late Archaic Base Camp: Phase II Archeological Investigation of the Johnson's Spring Site (21HU35), Houston County, Minnesota

Titles in this style allow people doing literature searches to quickly get a basic idea of what the report treats, the level of the investigation, and where the site is or was located.

Normally, the first chapter will be a variation on the SOW, since it will address why the project took place and what was hoped to be accomplished.

The next chapters deal with background information. Sometimes these are combined into one chapter; at other times or in other firms, they are not. Most of the background information will have been prepared in advance of the project. For firms with historians on staff (and most firms, even stand-alone archaeology firms, employ a few B.A. or M.A. historians), those people will have written up some sort of historical background.

One purpose of this background chapter is to show how the work that was done at the site relates to standing research questions about the past. Where appropriate, the research design should be discussed at this point in terms of the state historic plan as well as research questions raised by the literature or identified in the SOW.

Table 7.1. Basic Contents of a Compliance Archaeology Report

Cover, Title Page, Contents, Forms: In addition to the title, author(s), firm or organization, client, and date, the cover of the compliance report sometimes requires specific information in accordance with the sponsoring agency. It also contains the contract number and a clearance statement, such as "Confidential Archaeological Site Information," or "Unclassified. Distribution is Unlimited." Most cover pages require the signature of the principal investigator.

Abstract: Summarizes the nature of the project and its conclusions; this will be the first section of the report that the agency reviewers will read, with the second section being the "Conclusion" section.

Acknowledgments: Lists the agency and client personnel contacted, along with local individuals and resources checked; provides as well a list of professionals involved in the project.

Introduction: States where project is located, what kind of impact activity is planned, and who the contracting/review agency or agencies are. The research design may be included here, and/or in the Methods section. Identify the relevant statute or regulation necessitating the report.

Environmental Background: Summarizes the vegetation, soils, geology, and other noncultural elements of the region and the project area. The focal point is always the project area, and this is essentially an exercise in physical geography.

Cultural Background: Summarizes the history and prehistory of the region, with special reference to the project area; it may include a map and table showing locations and nature of known historic and prehistoric sites/structures within a set distance—usually 2 km—of the project area.

Methods: Outlines the field and laboratory methods and also states where materials, project documentation, and other items will be curated.

Results: Presents in detail the results of the background investigations and of the field work as they bear upon the particular compliance exercise; there will be an interpretive discussion here as well.

Conclusions and Recommendations: Summarizes the report's conclusions and reasoning leading to those conclusions; this section will be the second section agency reviewers will read in the report. Phase I reports need to recommend whether or not further examination is needed of any identified sites. Phase II reports need to state whether or not the examined site or sites satisfy criteria for listing on the National Register.

References Cited: References usually are cited in standard anthropological literature format and will include informants and maps along with the more traditional types of sources used.

Appendices: Includes new or amended site forms; tabulation of artifacts recovered (if any); and for some projects, summary of interviews, a copy of the scope of work, and qualifications of project personnel.

ARCHEOLOGICAL TESTING OF THE MOREHEAD SITE, 8BY804, BAY COUNTY, FLORIDA

Contract Number 1443PX500094490

Prepared for and Funded by:

United States Air Force
Tyndall Air Force Base
Florida

Administered by:

National Park Service
Southeast Regional Office
Atlanta, Georgia

By

Thomas H. Gresham, R. Jerald Ledbetter and Thomas W. Neumann, Ph.D.

Thomas H. Gresham
Thomas H. Gresham
Principal Investigator

July 22, 1994

SOUTHEASTERN ARCHEOLOGICAL SERVICES, INC.

P.O. Drawer 8086
Athens, Georgia 30603

Figure 7.7. Example of a typical compliance report title page. Information includes agency for which the work was done, the contract number, and similar administrative information. Also included will be the signature of the individual who served as principal investigator for the project.

A lot of the background material eventually gets repeated from report to report. This reused material is called *boilerplate*, and usually is lifted in toto from one report and dropped, with a few modifications, into the next. There is nothing wrong with this, by the way, always providing that people make sure that those parts that were specific to the previous project have been removed or changed relative to the current project. The project director/principal investigator will be responsible for making sure that these sections are "clean" before the draft is submitted for agency review.

The "Methods" chapter is often a mixture of new material and boilerplate. The new portions usually involve the specifics of the field work itself. The boilerplate almost always includes how the laboratory analyses were done and how curation was handled. Like the background sections, much of this will already exist in some form from previous projects. The principal investigator will cull and rework for the new project's needs; the lab director, who will be responsible for the laboratory methods part, will do the same.

Normally, there will be a "Results of Investigations" chapter separate from the "Summary and Recommendations" chapter. Both will be assembled new for the project report. The former will be a results report just like any basic archaeological results section of a traditional site report.

The recommendations chapter, though, will differ. The recommendations follow from the summary. It will draw on the results of the field and laboratory work then recommend in light of what was mentioned at the start of the report (and in the SOW) what the client's next steps should be relative to the archaeological resource. Based upon the results of the field investigation, and following from what was revealed during the background research, the archaeologist makes recommendations (*never* determinations; see 36 CFR Part 63 - Determinations of Eligibility for Inclusion in the National Register of Historic Places). Likely recommendations are summarized in Table 7.2.

Scattered throughout the report will be figures and other illustrations meant not only to further clarify the research arguments, but also to serve as basic research reporting. The more basic kinds of figures are listed in Table 7.3.

Most firms, regardless of whether the archaeology is the entirety of the company or just a division among a bunch of architects, engineers,

Table 7.2.   Summary of Recommendation Options for Compliance Reports

Phase I:

- No materials present and no further work is needed (Agency interpretation: Therefore no possible adverse effects); or

- Materials present, but the disturbed physical context and/or absence of data potential indicates that the site does not satisfy criteria for listing on the National Register, and therefore no further work is warranted (Agency interpretation: Therefore, no adverse effects); or

- Materials present, and there is sufficient evidence to suggest that the site might satisfy criteria for listing on the National Register; either further testing is recommended (Phase II) or the project should be redesigned to avoid the site (Agency interpretation: Therefore there may be adverse effects); or

- Materials present reflecting the previously documented presence of a listed or eligible site; either further testing is recommended (Phase II) or some kind of project redesign is needed to avoid the site (Agency interpretation: There may be adverse effects).

Phase II:

- Further testing from the Phase I project indicates that the site does not satisfy the criteria for listing on the National Register, and no further work appears warranted (Agency interpretation: There will be no adverse effects); or

- The site does satisfy criteria for listing on the National Register, and either data recovery (Phase III) is recommended to mitigate those adverse effects, or the project needs to be redesigned (Agency interpretation: Therefore there will be adverse effects).

Phase III:

- Usually the only recommendation within a Phase III report will be where only part of the site was lost because the project was redesigned. In that situation, the recommendation usually involves protecting in perpetuity the undamaged portions of the site.

geologists, and environmental scientists, will have a graphics department. The graphics department will be responsible for making the camera-ready figures for the compliance report.

Production and Assembly of the Draft Report

Looking back at what we have written so far in this text—and not just this chapter—we perhaps have neglected to mention something about compliance archaeology that has a lot to do with report production. In any firm at any given moment, the people—be they the field or lab techs with their recent undergraduate degrees, or the senior people with master's or doctorates—will all be working on a number of projects at the same time. For the principal investigator, there probably will be 6 to 10 projects each year, each of which will require a final report. Traditionally, when archaeology was still the sole province of universities and museums, the archaeologist worked on one site or project at a time and would finish off one monograph before starting another. Not always, but this has long been what those of us in university settings ideally expected to happen. That is

Table 7.3. Basic Figures Commonly Included in Reports

General Location of the Project or Undertaking: All reports will have a figure showing where the project was located within the state. This will consist of a general map of the state as an inset and a more detailed locale map, usually based on the USGS quadrangle map.

Map or Plans for the Proposed Project: All reports have a map of the proposed undertaking. This usually is a photocopy reduction of the developer's or agency's plans.

Regional Map Showing Locations of Known Cultural Resources: Some SHPOs want a regional map showing eligible or listed structures and sites, since it gives a sense of what is known in the area. Others do not want such a map made, since it may compromise the privileged information contained in the site files. If there is to be such a figure, often it will be complemented by a table listing the sites shown on the figure, along with their cultural-historical affiliation, National Register status, and previous investigations and reports.

Map of State or Regional Physiographic Provinces: Sometimes, a map of the state or region's physiographic provinces is included in the section of the report treating the environmental background. Some states request such inclusion; others do not.

Historic Maps: Historic maps document the presence or absence of possible historic structures and archaeological sites. Usually such maps are expected as part of Phase I highway corridor surveys and bridge replacements.

Historic Photographs: Photographs showing previously standing structures or land use are particularly useful for historical archaeological sites.

Map of the Project Area Showing Field Tests Locations: The map of the project area usually doubles as a base map showing locations of surface/subsurface examination areas and approximate site boundaries if appropriate.

Unit Profiles and Feature Drawings/Photographs: Unit wall profiles are drawn and photographed for Phase II and Phase III reports. Some states also require a line drawing or photograph of a typical shovel-test profile for Phase I survey projects.

Artifacts: Examples of all diagnostic artifacts should be photographed for all reports.

not true in the professional work place. The private-sector archaeologist may turn out quite a few full-length archaeological monographs each year. Some will be co-authored with one or two other people; many will be single-authored.

In addition to all of that multiple monograph writing, project directors and principal investigators often produce two or three conference *papers* along with a few research articles each year, too.

The mechanics in assembling a report under contract deadlines requires fine choreography. The pieces break down into the writing, the figure production, the table production, the report layout/production, the duplication and assembly, and finally the delivery.

Writing and table generation are exercises in word-processing. Figure production has been mentioned. By the way, one pleasant advantage for manuscript production enjoyed with archaeological reports is that nearly all archaeologists are excellent at producing camera-ready graphics, and therefore can figure well what the graphics division/department needs to do. Many Federal agencies have a preferred formatting style for the draft report, including line spacing, placement of headings and page numbers, and margins sizes. All of this normally will be mentioned in the SOW.

Report layout and production really is an exercise in desk-top publishing. In smaller firms, this task may be coordinated either by the office secretary or by the principal investigator. In larger firms, there often will be an in-house editor-cum-desk-top-publishing-specialist who will be responsible for taking the different pieces of the report and putting them together into a physical whole.

The compliance report is planned to be produced in two stages: a draft report, that is meant to be reviewed by the agencies and hopefully the SHPO/THPO; and a final report, which will be the report curated with the collection. The specifics of report production will be outlined in the SOW. In some cases, the report will be produced as a physical hard copy that will then be taken to the client or the agency (and often enough, to the SHPO, even though one would think that normal chain-of-command and business-etiquette protocols would not have that done; doing so, though, reflects the joint belief all of us have in the process, combined with the commonsense realization that the more comments by the SHPO/THPO handled early on, the more likely the project will be completed to everyone's satisfaction). In some cases, the draft report will be submitted electronically. This depends upon jurisdiction, the firm's and the state's computer capabilities, and so on.

The Review Process

The archaeological compliance project is both a research exercise and a regulatory/planning exercise. The work done and the report produced to represent it will be subjected to a searching and rigorous peer-review. Part of that review will involve the scientific merit of the report, be it in the methods used or the results presented. A goodly measure of that review, though, will focus on the core compliance issues. These will depend upon if the project is a Phase I survey, a Phase II testing and evaluation, or a Phase III data recovery exercise.

Section 106 Review

For Section 106 projects, the lead agency will have staff archaeologists or a historic preservation specialist who will review the draft report. The draft report will be returned to the firm with comments. Those comments will be addressed, either through changes in the report or a detailed explanation of why they were not made.

A second and usually final report will be prepared that meets agency conditions. That report will be passed along to the SHPO/THPO. The SHPO/THPO has 30 days to comment if the agency argues a finding of no adverse effect. If no comment is received in 30 days, then the SHPO/THPO is deemed to have accepted the results "without comment," and the agency has satisfied its obligations under Section 106 [see 36 CFR 800.5 (c)(1)]. This comment period holds true for notification to any other consulting parties.

If the finding is of an adverse effect, and SHPO agrees, the situation moves along smoothly with the drafting of a Memorandum of Agreement (MOA) [36 CFR 800.6; see also King 2000].

Non-Section 106 Review

The review procedure for non-Federal regulations and projects varies by the jurisdiction involved. Typically, a compliance report for a private-sector or government agency client is presented on behalf of that client to the SHPO/THPO and to a state/local government planning commission or equivalent. Often, a formal presentation is made by the professional archaeologist before a local regulatory body such as a community planning board. The non-Federal situation is generally less structured but has wide latitude in the range of questions and type of authority.

TIPS: Hearings

The archaeological project may require a presentation before a planning commission on behalf of the client. The archaeologist, as a specialty witness, should be prepared to inform the public about a subject often shrouded in mystery and misconception. Here are a few tips for presentations ranging from formal hearings to informal public meetings:

- If using additional witnesses, prepare a list of them in addition to a short summary of yourself. All witnesses should be identified in terms of their affiliations, qualifications, addresses, and telephone numbers, and availability to answer questions.

- All witnesses should have been to the project location or archaeological site. This is true even for experts on a particular analytical technique, such as thermoluminescence, who may have been brought in to assist at the hearing. The public (and other decision makers) appreciate the real-world connection.

- Prepare a written and oral outline of the presentation and testimony. Include the main points to be covered and by whom.

- All potential witnesses and speakers should participate in a dress rehearsal. This is particularly reassuring to the client, plus it lets you see whether or not the team members can communicate effectively and credibly.

- Witnesses and speakers should use references and plans that illuminate main points or help the audience get its bearings.

- Practice the viewing distance for interpreting maps, photos, and drawings. Typically, information is presented at too small a scale for effective viewing for an audience member in the back seat. One approach is to make photos of large drawings and illustrations. These can be handed out (and included in the official exhibits in the case of evidentiary hearings).

- Prepare an $8\frac{1}{2} \times 11$–inch copy of your reports and testimony.

- Prepare a single-page fact sheet of critical information about the archaeological aspects of the project. This background information can help the reader interpret your testimony.

- Prepare proposed draft *findings of fact*, agreements, or conditions to help the members of the hearing panel determine if the project meets the applicable regulations.

- Bring extra copies for alternates, staff, clerks, and the audience, including the opposition.

- Visit the hearing room to determine acoustics, behavioral issues, and availability of presentation equipment. Locate a place to stand where the audience and the decision makers will be addressed simultaneously.

Final Report and Dissemination

With completion of agency reviews and the return of the draft report along with the comments on it, the final report is put together. The SOW will have specified how many copies were to be made of the report. In some cases, that may also include an unbound copy so that the agency or client has a master copy available for future production.

Finally, the report is distributed. A core requirement of Federal guidelines is that the compliance report be made available to the interested public (e.g., Secretary of the Interior's Guidelines for Archeological Documentation: "Results must be made available to the full range of potential users" [48 FR 44737]). How this distribution is done varies by the nature of the agency and its policies, and the nature of the state. Usually, hard copies of the report will be distributed at minimum to the client, the lead agency, the SHPO, the state site files (if separate from the SHPO), and the curatorial facility (since a copy of the report is to be part of the collections turned over to that facility); authors/contributors; and the principals identified in the acknowledgments section. In some cases, additional copies will be distributed to a mailing list of professional and academic archaeologists within the state. Copies might also go to local public and college libraries.

Some agencies will have removed the pages or blacked-out the sentences giving locations of sites before giving reports to libraries or the media. As a substitute, they might have the archaeologist prepare a condensed version of the report for public relations/education use. This reduces controversy over seeing blacked-out words or noticing that pages are missing.

Some agencies maintain a publication series that distributes some or all of the studies: The Georgia Department of Transportation, for example, maintains its *Occasional Papers in Cultural Resource Management*. In other cases, the reports are available on demand for the cost of duplication and shipping. Compliance reports may even be scanned into a master computer file accessible through the Internet.

For most states, the SHPO will serve as a *de facto* if not formal clearinghouse for access to compliance reports. There should be a list of the reports available (hence the importance of providing a descriptive and suitable title).

Chapter Summary

Two overlapping tasks take place after the field portion of the compliance project ends: processing and analysis of what was found; and preparation then submission of the project report.

All archaeology firms maintain an in-house archaeology laboratory. That laboratory is designed to handle basic processing and analysis tasks. Thus, the laboratory has facilities for cleaning then labeling artifacts and for cataloguing those artifacts. Most professional laboratories also have the equipment needed to deal with the more common archaeological analyses. They will have binocular dissecting microscopes, various mensuration aids, and computers. Less common will be the equipment required of specialized analyses, such as high-magnification lithic use-wear analyses. If the need for such analyses comes up, specialists will be contacted to do the work.

The nature of analysis varies by the demands of the project relative to compliance needs. While protection of the resource is important, the compliance exercise exists as part of a larger planning process. The work done must see to those planning issues. For Phase I analyses, the needs are cultural-historical and classificatory. For Phase II analyses, the needs are documenting data potential or, if historical research has failed to do so, establishing association with important people, events, or designs/styles. And for Phase III analyses, the needs are to make substantial head-way into what the deposit tells us about how people lived in the past.

The lab serves as a place for short-term storage before the material associated with the archaeological site is turned over. Part of the responsibility of the person running the archaeology lab is to prepare the collection for long-term storage; that is, to prepare it for *permanent curation*.

The last step in a cultural resources project is the production of a report. In its final form, the project report serves as a planning document as well as a research document. As a planning document, it will provide sufficient information to government regulators so that determinations of Register eligibility as well as effect/adverse effect can be made without having to do the field work themselves. As a research document, the final report presents the data and conclusions from the cultural resource recordation process. For archaeological research, the final report consists in large measure of an archaeological research monograph. It is from the research conclusions reported in the monograph that the reasoning for planning recommendations, made by the authoring archaeologist, can be appreciated by the government regulators.

For an archaeological project, the final report will be one of five sets of records of the cultural resources investigation. The other records will be various project documents like the SOW, the field notes, the field photographs, and the laboratory notes and artifact inventory. The final report ties all of those other records together and represents a cogent summation of what the entire project was about. This, too, is a legacy of WPA archaeology, when so many archaeological sites were excavated but never written up. At the end of every archaeological compliance project there is a written report. Further, that written report will have first undergone a very thorough and stringent peer-review by agency and SHPO archaeologists, and their recommendations for changes will have been addressed and normally incorporated, before it is produced in final form.

Most of the archaeological research done after the late 1970s in the United States is reported in compliance reports. It is now the core location for basic empirical research in the field.

Compliance reports assemble project background information (see chapter 3), results from field investigations and subsequent analyses (see chapters 4–6), and various figures and other graphics. The reports themselves are organized in pretty much the same way, regardless of the nature of the project or area of the country. Broadly speaking, the report will have:

- a front section with title, cover, contents, abstract, and acknowledgments;

- a chapter summarizing the nature of the project and reasons for why it was done;

- a chapter or sometimes two chapters reviewing past and present ecological systems as well as the prehistory and history associated with the project area or site;

- a chapter explaining field and laboratory methods;

- a chapter presenting the results of the field investigations and laboratory analyses; and

- a chapter summarizing the project then taking the results of the research and using them to justify recommendations made to the agency or client regarding the project area and any associated cultural resources.

The report will also have a list of references and often a set of appendices.

The first and last chapters generally are the main part of the report's role as a planning document. The interior chapters that set the research up then report on it form the heart of the report as a research document.

The actual assembly of a compliance report involves writing, figure and table generation, compilation as a publishable document, duplication and assembly, then delivery. Most of the writing, figure production, and table generation will be done at the same time by different members of the research project in association with office staff. Compilation as a publishable document is an exercise in desk-top publishing, and may be done by a specialist on staff, by the secretarial staff, or by the project manager.

The report usually will go through two stages: a draft report that is reviewed, followed by a final report. It will be the draft report that the client or agency will receive, and it will often be that report that will be shared with the SHPO/THPO. The idea of the draft report is to make sure that everything is sorted out, while also letting all of the formal consulting parties know how things look to turn out. The agency and the SHPO/THPO will comment on the report and send their comments back to the professional archaeologist. Those comments will be addressed, a final report will be assembled, and with the delivery of that report and the other parts of the project (notes, collections, and so on), the project will end.

It is more and more common for draft reports to be submitted electronically. This does make life a lot easier for everyone. However, final reports represent a curated part of the final archaeological collection and will be produced in hard copy form even if there is a final electronic version.

Additional Readings of Interest

Groff, Vern. 1990. *The Power of Color in Design for Desktop Publishing*. Management Information Source Press, Portland, OR. A straightforward discussion of document layout, particularly in terms of color use. Although more marketing oriented, still the volume is good both for sensitizing to the use of color as well as for ideas.

McLean, Ruari. 1997. *The Thames and Hudson Manual of Typography*. Thames and Hudson, London. An extremely thorough discussion of how to present text on a page. McLean considers issues of type-face readability (serif type faces are usually best for extensive text), how text is read (people read entire words and read those words generally based upon the upper halves of the letters), number of words per read line (eight words or less is best, otherwise the eye gets confused), and the history and structure of type faces. A very useful volume for those, like professional archaeologists, caught in the desk-top publishing world.

Neumann, Mary Spink. 1994. *Developing Effective Educational Print Materials*. Centers for Disease Control and Prevention, Division of STD/HIV Prevention, Training and Education Branch, Atlanta. A general discussion for developing print materials for nonprofessional audiences, particularly those with at most a high school education. Mostly a how-to-get-the-job-done document, it contains (p. 26) a clear discussion on how to compute reading level of written text. We have found Neumann's formulae to be more accurate than the Flesch-Kincaid algorithm used in the Word and WordPerfect grammar checks.

South, Stanley. 1977. *Methods and Theory in Historical Archeology*. Academic Press, New York. Essential reading for anyone facing historic deposits. Perhaps dated in some way, but South originated the basic ways in which the assemblages from historic sites can be handled relative to the people—or society—that produced then used those assemblages.

Sutton, Mark Q., and Brooke S. Arkush. 1998. *Archaeological Laboratory Methods: An Introduction.* Second edition. Kendall/Hunt Publishing, Dubuque, IA. A serviceable text that provides discussion on all aspects of basic archaeological laboratory procedure. It includes a chapter on how to design, set up, then run a university archaeology laboratory.

Tschichold, Jan. 1962. *Treasury of Alphabets & Lettering* [Translation by Wolf von Eckardt of *Meisterbuch der Schrift*]. Norton, New York. The Tschichold volume is considered one of the main sources for deciding on the suitability of a print face. As with the McLean volume above, also contains a discussion of suitability of type face for different tasks.

FEDERAL REGULATIONS, STANDARDS, AND GUIDELINES ON DOCUMENTATION

The role, nature, and quality of the archaeological compliance report have been set forth in Federal regulations and guidelines. It is important at the outset to understand the roles of the report, what is expected of it, and how it fits into the larger compliance process.

Archaeological Documentation: Kind

36 CFR 800.11 (d) and (e) involve what *kind* of documentation is required to allow the consulting parties in the Section 106 Process to make determinations of adverse effect. Those requirements are to provide sufficient documentation in the following areas:

- a description of the undertaking, specifying the Federal involvement and its area of potential effects, including photographs, maps, and drawings as necessary [**36 CFR 800.11 (d)(1)** and 36 **CFR 800.11 (e)(1)**];

- a description of the affected historic properties, including information on the characteristics that qualify them for the National Register [strict sense of the term; see chapter 2] [**36 CFR 800.11 (e)(3)**];

- a description of the efforts made to identify historic properties if there is a finding by the agency of no adverse effect [**36 CFR 800.11 (d)(2)**], as well as an explanation of why there will be no adverse effect [**36 CFR 800.11 (d)(3)**]; or an explanation of why the criteria of adverse effect were found applicable or inapplicable, including any conditions or future actions to avoid, minimize, or mitigate adverse effects [**36 CFR 800.11 (e)(5)**]; and

- copies or summaries of any views provided by consulting parties and the public [**36 CFR 800.11 (e)(6)**].

Similar documentation is required where the SHPO/THPO and the lead agency have not been able to agree or generate a Memorandum of Agreement, and the Advisory Council for Historic Preservation has been asked to comment [**36 CFR 800.6 (g)**].

Archaeological Documentation: Intent and Structure

36 CFR 800 sets out the specific procedures and rules for implementing Section 106, including documentation. The National Park Service Archeology and Historic Preservation, Secretary of the Interior's Standards and Guidelines [48 FR 44716-44742] explains how that documentation is intended to be used, and therefore of what it should consist. It also sets forth the standards expected for that documentation and related work, so that it will serve its intended need. This is done by setting the standards for who is allowed to do the documentation.

The Secretary's Standards and Guidelines are an explication of the historic preservation planning process; Section 106 and related sections are meant to be planning instruments. The central part of planning involves developing the necessary plans, identifying historic properties (strict sense), evaluating those properties, registering those properties, then treating those properties. This involves not only archaeology, but also history and the built environment. Part of the planning process, then, requires some form of field work, various kinds of field surveys, sampling, and the like. This is all part of the documentation process, the final product being some form of report or, in the case of historic architecture and engineering, measured drawings, plans, photographs, and similar records.

The investigations done by the practicing archaeologist usually involve four parts of that process: identification of historic properties, evaluation of historic properties, historical documentation, and of course archaeological documentation. The Secretary of the Interior's Standards and Guidelines sets forth specific standards and guidelines for the execution of each of those procedural steps. The standards, given here, set forth what is expected of the compliance work; the guidelines actually stipulate of what in a general sense that work should consist.

Phase I survey work and, to a lesser extent, Phase II testing come under the Secretary of the Interior's Standards for Identification [48 FR 44720–44721], which are:

- *Standard I. Identification of historic properties is undertaken to the degree required to make decisions;*

- *Standard II. Results of identification activities are integrated into the preservation planning process;* and

- *Standard III. Identification activities include explicit procedures for record-keeping and information distribution.*

Assessing identified properties is addressed by Secretary of the Interior's Standards for Evaluation [48 FR 44723], which are

- *Standard I. Evaluation of the significance of historic properties uses established criteria;*

- *Standard II. Evaluation of significance applies the criteria within historic contexts;* and

- *Standard III. Evaluation results in a list or inventory of significant properties that is consulted in assigning registration and treatment priorities.*

These standards require some form of historic and prehistoric background research to be done and for those backgrounds in effect to be couched in terms of the state's historic preservation plan (which will have set out the requisite historic contexts).

For the historic research that will be done, certainly as part of the Phase I or Phase III project, Secretary of the Interior's Standards for Historical Documentation [48 FR 44728-44729] apply. These are:

- *Standard I. Historical documentation follows a research design that responds to needs identified in the planning process;*

- *Standard II. Historical documentation employs an appropriate methodology to obtain the information required by the research design;*

- *Standard III. The results of historical documentation are assessed against the research design and integrated into the planning process;* and

- *Standard IV. The results of historical documentation are reported and made available to the public.*

For archaeological documentation, be it Phase I, Phase II, or Phase III, the Secretary's Standards for Archeological Documentation also stresses its planning role:

[Archeological documentation] is guided by a framework of objectives and methods derived from the planning process, and makes use of previous planning decisions, such as those on evaluation of significance [48 FR 44734].

There are four standards:

- *Standard I. Archeological documentation activities follow an explicit statement of objectives and methods that responds to needs identified in the planning process;*

- *Standard II. The methods and techniques of archeological documentation are selected to obtain the information required by the statement of objectives;*

- *Standard III. The results of archeological documentation are assessed against the statement of objectives and integrated into the planning process;* and

- *Standard IV. The results of archeological documentation are reported and made available to the public.*

Archaeological documentation consists of the background, field, and laboratory research. The resultant data and other products of that documentation then are applied to the specified planning needs. Those results are then to be reported.

Part of the guidelines is devoted to *Reporting Results* [48 FR 44736-44737], which notes that:

Archeological documentation concludes with written report(s) including minimally the following topics:

1. Description of the study area;

2. Relevant historical documentation/background research;

3. The research design;

4. The field studies as actually implemented . . .;

5. All field observations;

6. Analyses and results, illustrated as appropriate with tables, charts, and graphs;

7. *Evaluation of the investigation in terms of the goals and objectives of the investigation, including discussion of how well the needs dictated by the planning process were served;*

8. *Recommendations for updating the relevant historic contexts and planning goals and priorities, and generation of new or revised information needs;*

9. Reference to related on-going or proposed treatment activities . . .; and

10. Information on the location of original data in the form of field notes, photographs, and other materials.

The report, the guidelines add, must be made available "to the full range of potential users."

The reason that the archaeology is being done is to assist in the historic preservation planning process. The archaeological documentation becomes the entire sequence of work associated with archaeological research: research design, background work, field work, analysis, report production, and curation of the products of the investigation (records as well as artifacts). To be sufficient, though, the archaeological report not only must be a research document, it also must address planning and preservation concerns. There are, then, additional concerns in a compliance archaeological report that are not of moment to most university and museum archaeologists.

Archaeological Documentation: Standards

Assuring the quality of the archaeological documentation, including that of the report, is done in two ways. The first is by specifying the level of training, amount of supervised and supervisory experience, and the kind of degrees. These standards are set forth for all involved in the historic preservation process, including archaeologists, both in 36 CFR Part 61 [36 CFR Part 61 Appendix A (b)] and again in the Secretary's Standards and Guidelines [48 FR 44739]. By specifying minimum training standards, the regulations attempt to guarantee a minimum level of professional work. Included in those training and experiential expectations is the requirement that the practicing professional archaeologist have demonstrated the ability to carry research to completion, which will include producing a final, peer-review quality research document of monograph scale.

The second way that quality is assured is in the report review process as set out in 36 CFR 800. The archaeological report is to be used as part of the planning process. Its approval depends upon the approval of the enabling agency as well as the SHPO/THPO.

Role of the Report and its Distribution

The archaeological report serves not only as a planning document and as a research compilation, it also serves as a summary storage of the data recovered from the archaeological site. This is reflected not only in the expectation that, after each step in the field evaluation process—here labeled Phase I, Phase II, and Phase III—a written report is required, but that such a report is to be considered a part of the curated collection from the site.

36 CFR Part 79 focuses on curation. It, in effect, expects the existence of a written report on the site from which the archaeological materials came. The definition of a *collection* from an archaeological site [36 CFR 79 (a)(2)] includes not only the material remains recovered, but also the records of that recovery and interpretation. These records specifically include the manuscripts and reports produced as part of the archaeological investigation [36 CFR 79 (a)(2)(i)]. Just as important, 36 CFR 79 directs repositories holding Federally generated collections to make that collection available, to qualified individuals, for scientific and education purposes [36 CFR 79.10]. Obviously, if part of the collection is the report on the archaeological site, then that report must be made available. This is an extremely round-about way of requiring that such documents be available. Such reports are, though, public records and usually do not have restrictions placed on access or distribution.

The Secretary of the Interior's Standards and Guidelines for Identification *Reporting Identification Results* [48 FR 44723], Guidelines for Historical Documentation *Reporting Results* [48 FR 44730], and Guidelines for Archeological Documentation *Reporting Results* [48 FR 44737] all require that the results of the investigations be made available to the full range of potential users (although the information provided during the identification needs to consider whether such a release of information would threaten the resource). This is to be done in part by publishing the results in articles or monographs, or by distributing the compliance report to libraries and technical clearinghouses.

CODES OF CONDUCT AND STANDARDS OF RESEARCH: THE MEANING OF "PROFESSIONAL"

A code of ethics is what helps define members of a discipline or occupational group as professionals. There are two sets of ethical codes of interest for archaeologists: one from the Register of Professional Archaeologists (RPA), the other from American Cultural Resources Association (ACRA). Each is presented below.

Code of Ethics for the Register of Professional Archaeologists (RPA)

The Register of Professional Archaeologists (RPA) is a voluntary professional registration program. Its members have a graduate degree in archaeology or related discipline and agree to abide by the following statements.

Archaeology is a profession, and the privilege of professional practice requires professional morality and professional responsibility, as well as professional competence, on the part of each practitioner.

The Archaeologist's Responsibility to the Public

1.1 An archaeologist shall:
Recognize a commitment to represent Archaeology and its research results to the public *in a responsible* manner; Actively support conservation of the archaeological resource base; Besensitive to, and respect the legitimate concerns of, groups whose culture histories are the subjects of archaeological investigations; Avoid and discourage exaggerated, misleading, or unwarranted statements about archaeological matters that might

induce others to engage in unethical or illegal activity; Support and comply with the terms of the UNESCO Convention on the means of prohibiting and preventing the illicit import, export, and transfer of ownership of cultural property, as adopted by the General Conference, 14 November 1970, Paris.

1.2 An archaeologist shall not:
Engage in any illegal or unethical conduct involving archaeological matters or knowingly permit the use of his/her name in support of any illegal or unethical activity involving archaeological matters; Give a professional opinion, make a public report, or give legal testimony involving archaeological matters without being as thoroughly informed as might reasonably be expected; Engage in conduct involving dishonesty, fraud, deceit or misrepresentation about archaeological matters; Undertake any research that affects the archaeological resource base for which she/he is not qualified.

The Archaeologist's Responsibility to Colleagues, Employees, and Students

2.1 An archaeologist shall:
Give appropriate credit for work done by others; Stay informed and knowledgeable about developments in her/his field or fields of specialization; Accurately, and without undue delay, prepare and properly disseminate a description of research done and its results; Communicate and cooperate with colleagues having common professional interests; Give due respect to colleagues' interests in, and rights to, information about sites, areas, collections, or data where there is a mutually active or potentially active research concern; Know and comply with all federal, state, and local laws, ordinances, and regulations applicable to her/his archaeological research and activities; Report knowledge of violations of this Code to proper authorities. Honor and comply with the spirit and letter of the Register of Professional Archaeologist's Disciplinary Procedures.

2.2 An archaeologist shall not:
Falsely or maliciously attempt to injure the reputation of another archaeologist; Commit plagiarism in oral or written communication; Undertake

research that affects the archaeological resource base unless reasonably prompt, appropriate analysis and reporting can be expected; Refuse a reasonable request from a qualified colleague for research data; Submit a false or misleading application for registration by the Register of Professional Archaeologists.

The Archaeologist's Responsibility to Employers and Clients

3.1 An archaeologist shall:
Respect the interests of her/his employer or client, so far as is consistent with the public welfare and this Code and Standards; Refuse to comply with any request or demand of an employer or client which conflicts with the Code and Standards; Recommend to employers or clients the employment of other archaeologists or other expert consultants upon encountering archaeological problems beyond her/his own competence; Exercise reasonable care to prevent her/his employees, colleagues, associates and others whose services are utilized by her/him from revealing or using confidential information. Confidential information means information of a non-archaeological nature gained in the course of employment which the employer or client has requested be held inviolate, or the disclosure of which would be embarrassing or would be likely to be detrimental to the employer or client. Information ceases to be confidential when the employer or client so indicates or when such information becomes publicly known.

3.2 An archaeologist shall not:
Reveal confidential information, unless required by law; Use confidential information to the disadvantage of the client or employer; use confidential information for the advantage of herself/himself or a third person, unless the client consents after full disclosure; Accept compensation or anything of value for recommending the employment of another archaeologist or other person, unless such compensation or thing of value is fully disclosed to the potential employer or client; Recommend or participate in any research which does not comply with the requirements of the Standards of Research Performance.

Standards of Research Performance

The research archaeologist has a responsibility to attempt to design and conduct projects that will add to our understanding of past cultures and/or that will develop better theories, methods, or techniques for interpreting the archaeological record, while causing minimal attrition of the archaeological resource base. In the conduct of a research project, the following minimum standards should be followed.

The archaeologist has a responsibility to prepare adequately for any research project, whether or not in the field. The archaeologist must:

4.1 Assess the adequacy of her/his qualifications for the demands of the project, and minimize inadequacies by acquiring additional expertise, by bringing in associates with the needed qualifications, or by modifying the scope of the project;

4.2 Inform herself/himself of relevant previous research;

4.3 Develop a scientific plan of research which specifies the objectives of the project, takes into account previous relevant research, employs a suitable methodology, and provides for economical use of the resource base (whether such base consists of an excavation site or of specimens) consistent with the objectives of the project;

4.4 Ensure the availability of adequate and competent staff and support facilities to carry the project to completion, and of adequate curatorial facilities for specimens and records;

4.5 Comply with all legal requirements, including, without limitation, obtaining all necessary governmental permits and necessary permission from landowners or other persons;

4.6 Determine whether the project is likely to interfere with the program or projects of other scholars and, if there is such a likelihood, initiate negotiations to minimize such interference.

In conducting research, the archaeologist must follow her/his scientific plan of research, except to the extent that unforeseen circumstances warrant its modification.

Procedures for field survey or excavation must meet the following minimal standards:

5.1 If specimens are collected, a system for identifying and recording their proveniences must be maintained.

5.2 Uncollected entities such as environmental or cultural features, depositional strata, and the like, must be fully and accurately recorded by appropriate means, and their location recorded.

5.3 The methods employed in data collection must be fully and accurately described. Significant stratigraphic and/or associational relationships among artifacts, other specimens, and cultural and environmental features must also be fully and accurately recorded.

5.4 All records should be intelligible to other archaeologists. If terms lacking commonly held referents are used, they should be clearly defined.

5.5 Insofar as possible, the interests of other researchers should be considered. For example, upper levels of a site should be scientifically excavated and recorded whenever feasible, even if the focus of the project is on underlying levels.

During accessioning, analysis, and storage of specimens and records in the laboratory, the archaeologist must take precautions to ensure that correlations between the specimens and the field records are maintained, so that provenience contextual relationships and the like are not confused or obscured.

Specimens and research records resulting from a project must be deposited at an institution with permanent curatorial facilities, unless otherwise required by law.

The archaeologist has responsibility for appropriate dissemination of the results of her/his research to the appropriate constituencies with reasonable dispatch.

6.1 Results reviewed as significant contributions to substantive knowledge of the past or to advancements in theory, method or technique should be disseminated to colleagues and other interested persons by appropriate means such as publications, reports at professional meetings, or letters to colleagues.

6.2 Requests from qualified colleagues for information on research results directly should be honored, if consistent with the researcher's prior rights to publication and with her/his other professional responsibilities.

6.3 Failure to complete a full scholarly report within 10 years after completion of a field project shall be construed as a waiver of an archaeologist's right of primacy with respect to analysis and publication of the data. Upon expiration of such 10-year period, or at such earlier time as the archaeologist shall determine not to publish the results, such data should be made fully accessible to other archaeologists for analysis and publication.

6.4 While contractual obligations in reporting must be respected, archaeologists should not enter into a contract which prohibits the archaeologist from including her or his own interpretations or conclusions in the contractual reports, or from a continuing right to use the data after completion of the project.

6.5 Archaeologists have an obligation to accede to reasonable requests for information from the news media.

(Source: Internet site for Register of Professional Archaeologists, http://www.rpanet.org/, reprinted with permission. Accessed February 2, 2001.)

Code of Ethics for the American Cultural Resources Association (ACRA)

The American Cultural Resources Association (ACRA), an association of consulting archaeology professionals maintains the following code of ethics and professional conduct:

Preamble

This Code of Ethics and Professional Conduct is a guide to the ethical conduct of members of the American Cultural Resources Association (ACRA). The Code also aims at informing the public of the principles to which ACRA members subscribe. The Code further signifies that ACRA members shall abide by proper and legal business practices, and perform under a standard of professional behavior that adheres to high principles of ethical conduct on behalf of the public, clients, employees, and professional colleagues.

The ACRA Member's Responsibilities to the Public

A primary obligation of an ACRA member is to serve the public interest. While the definition of the public interest changes through ongoing debate, an ACRA member owes allegiance to a responsibly derived concept of the public interest. An ACRA member shall:

1) Have concern for the long-range consequences of that member's professional actions.

2) Be cognizant of the relevance to the public of that member's professional decisions.

3) Strive to prevent the results of significant research to the public in a responsible manner.

4) Strive to actively support conservation of the cultural resource base.

5) Strive to respect the concerns of people whose histories and/or resources are the subject of cultural resources investigation.

6) Not make exaggerated, misleading, or unwarranted statements about the nature of that member's work.

The ACRA Member's Responsibilities to Clients

An ACRA member is obligated to provide diligent, creative, honest, and competent services and professional advice to its clients. Such performance must be consistent with the ACRA member's responsibilities to the public interest. An ACRA member shall:

1) Exercise independent professional judgment on behalf of clients.

2) Accept the decisions of a client concerning the objectives and nature of the professional services provided unless the decisions involve conduct that is illegal or inconsistent with the ACRA member's obligations to the public interest.

3) Fulfill the spirit, as well as the letter, of contractual agreements.

4) Not provide professional services if there is an actual, apparent, or perceived conflict of interest, or an appearance of impropriety, without full written disclosure and agreement by all concerned parties.

5) Not disclose information gained from the provision of professional services for private benefit without prior client approval.

6) Not solicit prospective clients through the use of false or misleading claims.

7) Not sell or offer to sell services by stating or implying an ability to influence decisions by improper means.

8) Not solicit or provide services beyond the level or breadth of the professional competence of its staff or project team.

9) Solicit or provide services only if they can responsibily be performed with the timeliness required by its clients.

10) Not solicit or accept improper compensation for the provision of judgments or recommendations favorable to its clients.

11) Not offer or provide improper compensation as a material consideration in obtaining or sustaining client or prospective client favor.

12) Disclose information identified as confidential by its client only if required by law, required to prevent violation of the law, or required to prevent injury to the public interest.

The ACRA Member's Responsibilities to Employees

As an employer, an ACRA member firm has certain responsibilities to its employees, and shall strive to:

1) Comply with all applicable employment/labor laws and regulations.

2) Provide a safe work environment in compliance with all applicable laws and regulations.

3) Appropriately acknowledge work performed by employees.

4) Provide opportunities for the professional growth and development of employees.

5) Develop clear lines of communication between employer and employee, and provide employees with a clear understanding of their responsibilities.

6) Consistently maintain fair, equitable, and professional conduct toward its employees.

The ACRA Member's Responsibilities to Professional Colleagues

An ACRA member shall strive to contribute to the development of the profession by improving methods and techniques, and contributing knowledge. An ACRA member shall also fairly treat the views and contributions of professional colleagues and members of other professions. Accordingly, an ACRA member shall:

1) Act to protect and enhance the integrity of the cultural resources profession.

2) Accurately and fairly represent the qualifications, views, and findings of colleagues.

3) Review the work of other professionals in a fair, professional, and equitable manner.

4) Strive to communicate, cooperate, and share knowledge with colleagues having common professional interests.

5) Not knowingly attempt to injure the professional reputation of a colleague.

(Source: Internet Web site, American Cultural Resources Association, http://www.acra-crm.org/, reprinted with permission. Accessed February 2, 2001.)

GLOSSARY

A horizon: In current soil horizon terminology, this refers both to the near-surface, mostly decomposed organic soil horizon, as well as the dark organic-rich soil horizons above the B horizon or subsoil. The A horizon is known colloquially as the "topsoil." See also B horizon.

ACHP: Advisory Council on Historic Preservation. Also known as "The Council." The ACHP is an independent Federal agency that carries out duties assigned by NHPA. Its mission is "to balance historic preservation concerns with Federal project requirements."

ACRA: *See* American Cultural Resources Association.

Adverse Effect: An effect on a property, eligible for listing on the National Register, that could render said property no longer eligible.

Aggradation: The building up of material at the surface, through deposition. The opposite of degradation.

AHPA: Archaeological and Historic Preservation Act of 1974 (16 USC 469-469c).

Alluvial deposits (alluvium): Material deposited by flowing water. Examples include floodplains, alluvial fans, and deltas. Coarser material is nearer the source than are the finer-grained particles.

American Cultural Resources Association (ACRA): A professional association of consulting archaeologists.

Ap or Ap horizon: Pronounced "A-P." The "at-surface" part of the soil that has been plowed, now usually around 25–30 cm below the surface. Also called "plowzone."

APE: *See* Area of Potential Effects.

Area of Potential Effects (APE): Defined in 36 CFR 800.16[d] as the "geographic area or areas within which an undertaking may directly or indirectly cause changes in the character or use of historic properties, if any such properties exist. The area of potential effects is influenced by the scale and nature of an undertaking and may be different for different kinds of effects cause by the undertaking."

ARPA: Archaeological Resources Protection Act of 1979, as amended (16 USC 470aa-mm).

Assemblage: The total set of artifacts from a site.

B horizon: Soil horizon usually below the A or E horizons and having less organic content because it is more weathered. The B horizon is known, colloquially, as the "subsoil."

Blue line map or blue line drawing: Architectural or engineering rendering of a project, intended for planning purposes.

Boring log: Record of drilling and similar subsurface testing done by engineers to determine the physical properties of the area.

C horizon: The essentially unaltered material that is seen to be the mineral source for the overlying soil (the A and B horizons, collectively known as the solum).

Certified Local Government (CLG): As defined in 36 CFR Part 61.2, CLG is a local government (municipality, city, county, borough, township, parish) that has been certified to carry out the purposes of the National Historic Preservation Act, as amended, in accordance with section 101(c).

CEQ: Council on Environmental Quality.

COE: U.S. Army Corps of Engineers.

Collection: The actual materials recovered from a site along with the records of recovery and interpretation [defined in 36 CFR 79 (a)(2)].

Colluvial debris or colluvium: Debris, such as soil or rock, moved downslope by gravity. This is also known as "slope wash." The resulting pile at the bottom of the slope is called a "talus slope."

Compliance archaeology: General reference to all aspects of archaeology done in response to ("in compliance with") historic preservation laws.

Compliance project: A particular archaeological response to government regulations done "in compliance with" historic preservation laws.

Component [archaeological]: An archaeological component is seen to be a single, continuous, and uninterrupted occupational/depositional event. The important part is "continuous." A single component site is one where the archaeological assemblage appears to be more or less continuous and contemporaneous, never mind that it may represent a couple years or a couple thousand years. A tricky term, component may be thought of as the debris left at an archaeological site from a continuous and uninterrupted occupation.

Contract archaeology: The performance of archaeological services under contract and in response to government regulations. This term is a little outdated; "compliance archaeology," "private-sector archaeology," or, best, "professional archaeology" are preferred and more commonly used terms.

Correlation matrix: A statistical summary of the artifacts and their location levels from different test excavation units, used to indicate behavior patterning. The researcher uses the matrix to help understand variation of distributions of different artifact classes.

Council: *See* ACHP.

Council on Environmental Quality (CEQ): The Federal entity responsible for the formulation of NEPA regulations, guidelines, and policies.

Cultural resource: A generic term for archaeological and built-environment properties. Although not a term formally defined in NHPA or associated regulations, it is commonly used as a synonym for the formal term "property" as used in historic preservation regulations.

CRM: *See* Cultural Resource Management.

Cultural Resource Management (CRM): Research, conservation, and management of cultural resources within a regulatory framework. Within anthropology, CRM is used as a synonym for professional archaeology.

Culturally sterile: Used in reference to the part of the tested volume that does not contain cultural remains.

Data recovery plan: The plan for a Phase III data recovery or mitigation project.

Datum: A fixed, permanent, and readily relocated position used in mapping, be it an archaeological site or project area.

dbh: *See* Diameter at breast height.

DEIS: Draft Environmental Impact Statement.

Diachronic: Literally, "through time." Archaeology is diachronic cultural anthropology, meaning cultural anthropology through time. *See also* Synchronic.

Diagnostic: Usually in reference to an artifact or feature distinctive of a particular culture or cultural period.

Diameter at breast height (dbh): The diameter of a tree taken at 4.5 feet above average ground level around the base of the tree.

Discoverable document: A document entitled to review by an opposing party in a legal proceeding.

Effect: In historic preservation code, an impact or alteration to a cultural resource. If adverse, it changes the nature of the resource. (Note the difference between "effect" and "affect." "To effect" means to cause to happen. "To affect" means to influence; it is less casual. Usually, "affect" is used as a verb while "effect" is used as a noun; the first involving the influences that bring change about, the second is the outcome of that action. Thus, "adverse effects" means a change—an effect— that has happened by an undertaking that "affects"—influences—the physical character of the area.)

E horizon: In current soil horizon terminology, the horizon located immediately below the A horizon (which is kind of like the undifferentiated leaf litter). In the older literature, the E horizon would be called the A2 horizon, and would be roughly synonymous with "topsoil."

EIS: *See* Environmental Impact Statement (EIS).

Environmental Impact Statement (EIS): A written report in response to an environmental assessment activity required under Federal legislation (NEPA).

Faunal analysis: Examination of the animal remains in an archaeological assemblage.

Feature: A nonportable, human alteration of an archaeological site, such as a pit, foundation, or hearth. Cannot be removed without loss of physical integrity.

FEIS: Final Environmental Impact Statement.

Flotation: In archaeology, a method of obtaining seeds and other organic materials from the fill of an archaeological site, or portion thereof (e.g., feature), through suspension in water.

Fluvial deposits: Materials deposited by flowing water.

Froth flotation: In archaeology, a specific flotation method involving the agitation of water.

Ground truth: Verification of remotely sensed data by immediate, hands-on measurements or observation. Also generally refers to verification of externally supplied site data.

Ha: Abbreviation for Hectare. *See also* "m."

Hectare (Ha): Metric unit for area. One hectare is 10,000 m². This is approximately 2.47 acres.

Historic property: Regulatory term meaning a property that is eligible for listing on the National Register of Historic Places.

Integrity: Degree to which a site, structure, feature, or collection is undisturbed or unaltered relative to currently known examples.

Lithic: Of or pertaining to stone tools.

m: Abbreviation for "meter." The use of metric measurements is required by all professional archaeology organizations. Unknown to most, the metric system is established by law as the official measurement system of the United States. A meter was originally defined as one 10-millionth of the distance between the equator and the North Pole. *See also* meter and metric.

Matrix: The surrounding material in which archaeological materials are found.

Memorandum of Agreement (MOA): A formal document indicating an agreement between one or more parties concerning the treatment of an archaeological material or resource; has specialized meaning within the Section 106 Process.

Meter and metric: System of weights and measures defined during the French Revolution that is based upon a series of Earth-based equivalencies, such that one 10-millionth of the distance from the equator to the North Pole is a meter, one cubic centimeter (a centimeter being one billionth of that distance from the equator to the North Pole) of standard water weighs one gram, while a 1,000 cubic centimeters of water represents both a liter and a kilogram.

Microlith: Tiny stone tools that were mounted in handles or paddles.

Mitigate: To offset the effects of.

MOA: *See* Memorandum of Agreement.

NAGPRA: Native American Graves Protection and Repatriation Act of 1990 (25 USC 3001-3013).

National Register of Historic Places: Defined in CFR Part 61.2 as the national list of districts, sites, buildings, structures, and objects significant in American history, architecture, archeology, engineering, and culture, maintained by the Secretary of the Interior under authority of Section 101(a)(1)(A) of the NHPA.

NEPA: National Environmental Policy Act of 1969 (42 USC 4321). Requires Environmental Impact Statements for major Federal undertakings.

New Archeology: An approach to archaeology that emphasized a deductive-nomothetic methodology and the elucidation of cultural processes.

NHPA: National Historic Preservation Act of 1966 as amended (16 USC 470-470t, 110) and subsequent modifications. The basic historic preservation legislation requiring Federal agencies to check for properties eligible for the National Register before a Federally enabled undertaking proceeds. Takes precedence over NEPA.

Overburden: Material overlying a deposit. For an archaeological site, includes material, consolidated or not, found over a site.

Palynologist: A specialist in the study of plant pollen and spores. Pollen and spores can help in the reconstruction of past environments.

Party: A property owner, government agency, cultural group, or other entity having the right or permission to participate in the review or formulation of a government undertaking.

Pedology: Study of soils.

Per Diem: "By the day." Refers to a daily allowance meant to offset out-of-pocket living expenses.

Phase I Process: The first stage in the archaeological cultural resources process, involving identification of archaeological properties within any area of potential effects. May also be termed "survey" or "inventory." The purpose of a Phase I is to make a good-faith effort to identify archaeological resources within an undertaking's area of potential effects.

Phase II Process: The second stage in the archaeological cultural resources process, Phase II focuses on evaluating archaeological resources in terms of their eligibility for listing on the National Register of Historic Places as well as what the impact of the undertaking, as planned, will be on those resources.

Phase III Process: The final stage in the archaeological cultural resources process, where archaeological resources eligible for listing on the National Register will suffer adverse effects from the undertaking. In most cases, Phase III consists of a formal excavation of an archaeological site, the purpose of the excavation being to recover as much information about the site—or the portion threatened—as possible before it is lost. Phase III excavation is meant to offset those adverse effects of the undertaking through excavation, hence it is also called "mitigation" and "data recovery."

Physiographic: Pertaining to the natural features of land surface, including fauna and flora.

Phytolith: Literally "plant-stone." Phytoliths are silica deposits within a plant and are sufficiently unique to a species that they are used, like pollen, to identify the presence of past plants and to reconstruct environments. Phytoliths are also the reason why lawn mower blades become dull.

Professional archaeology: The practice of archaeology outside of an academic setting, usually in response to historic preservation law.

Provenience: The location of an artifact or feature within an archaeological site matrix.

Reconnaissance: See Phase I Process.

Register of Professional Archaeologists (RPA): A professional association that provides a voluntary certification for its members.

Remote sensing: Noninvasive reconnaissance and surface survey techniques used to determine the extent and nature of buried archaeological materials and environmental features.

Request for Proposals (RFP): An invitation to respond to the articulated need for research or professional services. Usually in the form of a bid for a contract.

RFP: *See* Request for Proposals.

RPA: *See* Register of Professional Archaeologists.

Scope of Work (SOW): The range and details of professional services and activities to be provided by the contractor.

Section 106: That portion of the NHPA—specifically 16 USC 470f—requiring Federal agencies to identify then take into account any adverse effects on properties eligible for listing on the National Register that may be located within the area of an agency-enabled undertaking.

Section 106 Process: Procedure set out in 36 CFR 800.3 - 800.13 in response to NHPA Section 106, meant to identify then resolve any adverse effects likely to be caused by a Federally enabled activity.

Sheet litter: A continuous spread or "sheet" or archaeological material.

SHPO: *See* State Historic Preservation Officer.

Shoring: Bracing used to keep excavation walls from caving in.

Significance: The quality of significance, set out in 36 CFR 60.4, means that the archaeological site or element of the built environment can be listed on the National Register of Historic Places.

Solum: The biologically and chemically active parts of a soil, usually corresponding to the A and the B horizons, that is, to the topsoil and the subsoil.

SOW: *See* Scope of Work.

State Historic Preservation Officer (SHPO): The official within each state who has been appointed by the governor to administer the state historic preservation program.

Survey: An archaeological reconnaissance of an area. See also Phase I.

Syllogism: Deductive reasoning based on a major premise, a minor premise, and a conclusion (e.g., "Only Paleoindians had fluted points, this point is fluted, therefore this point is Paleoindian"). In more common usage, syllogistic reasoning is logical, step-by-step reasoning.

Synchronic: Literally "at the same time." Synchronic anthropology, which consists mainly of ethnography, social anthropology, and linguistics, studies people living at the same time as the investigation. See also Diachronic.

THPO: *See* Tribal Historic Preservation Officer.

Tribal Historic Preservation Officer (THPO): A designated tribal official with the equivalent function of a SHPO in reviewing the potential effects of actions on or immediately adjacent to tribal lands.

Undertaking: Defined in 36 CFR 800.16(y) as "a project, activity, or program funded in whole or in part under the direct or indirect jurisdiction of a Federal agency, including those carried out by or on behalf of a Federal agency; those carried out with Federal financial assistance; those requiring a Federal permit, license or approval; and those subject to state or local regulations administered pursuant to a delegation or approval by a Federal agency."

Use-Wear: The striations, polish, and other types of abrasions of stone tools associated with particular tasks.

Viscosity or viscous: In reference to fluids: Short of an engineering definition, viscosity has to do with how thick or slow-moving/fast-moving a fluid is. A thick, slow-moving oil is a viscous oil.

WPA: *See* Works Progress Administration.

Works Progress Administration (WPA): President Franklin D. Roosevelt's New Deal response to unemployment between 1935 and 1943 that supported a large number of public works projects, including excavation of archaeological sites.

REFERENCES

Advisory Council on Historic Preservation (ACHP)
   1991 *Treatment of Archaeological Properties: A Handbook.* National Park Service/Department of the Interior, Washington, D.C.

Ambrose, Stephen E.
   1996 *Undaunted Courage: Meriwether Lewis, Thomas Jefferson, and the Opening of the American West.* Simon and Schuster, New York.

Barber, Russel J.
   1994 *Doing Historical Archaeology: Exercises Using Documentary, Oral, and Material Evidence.* Prentice Hall, Englewood Cliffs, NJ.

Bradley, James W.
   1979 *The Onondaga Iroquois: 1500–1655: A Study of Acculturative Change and Its Consequences.* Ph.D. dissertation, Syracuse University. University Microfilms International, Ann Arbor.

Bradley, James W.
   1987 *Evolution of the Onondaga Iroquois: Accommodating Change, 1500–1655.* Syracuse University Press, Syracuse.

Brady, Nyle C., and Ray R. Weil
   1998 *The Nature and Properties of Soils.* Twelfth edition. Prentice Hall, Upper Saddle River, NJ.

Chesterman, Charles W.
   1979 *The Audubon Society Field Guide to North American Rocks and Minerals.* Knopf, New York.

Coates, Earl J., and Dean S. Thomas
   1990 *An Introduction to Civil War Small Arms.* Thomas Publications, Gettysburg, PA.

REFERENCES

Daniel, Glyn
1962 *The Idea of Prehistory.* Penguin, Baltimore.

Davis, George B., Leslie J. Perry, and Joseph W. Kirkley
1983 *Atlas to Accompany the Official Records of the Union and Confederate Armies.* U.S. Government Printing Office, Washington, D.C. Republished as: Davis, George B., Leslie J. Perry, and Joseph W. Kirkley. Compiled by Calvin D. Cowles. Introduction by Richard Sommers. 1983 [1891–1895] *The Official Military Atlas of the Civil War.* Gramercy Books, New York.

Drury, W. H., and I. C. T. Nisbet
1973 Succession. *Journal of the Arnold Arboretum* 54:333–367.

Fagan, Brian M.
1997 *In the Beginning.* Ninth edition. Longman, New York.

Feder, Kenneth L.
1997 Chapter 4. Site Survey. Pp. 41–68 in *Field Methods in Archaeology*, by Thomas R. Hester, Harry J. Shafer, and Kenneth L. Feder. Seventh edition. Mayfield, Mountain View, CA.

Firth, Ian J. W.
1985 *Cultural Landscape Bibliography.* National Park Service/Southeast Region Office. U.S. Government Printing Office, Washington, D.C.

Fish, Paul R.
1980 Federal policy and legislation for archaeological conservation. *Arizona Law Review* 22:681–699.

Fish, Suzanne K., and Stephen A. Kowaleski, editors
1990 *The Archaeology of Regions: A Case for Full-Coverage Survey.* Smithsonian Institution Press, Washington, D.C.

Foss, J. E., F. P. Miller, and A. V. Segovia
1985 *Field Guide to Soil Profile Description and Mapping.* Second edition. Soil Resources International, Moorhead, MN.

Fowler, Don D.
1982 Cultural Resources Management. Pp. 1–50 in *Advances in Archaeological Method and Theory, Volume 5*, edited by Michael Schiffer. Academic Press, New York.

Fox, Robin
1996 State of the Art/Science in Anthropology. Pp. 327–345 in *The Flight from Science and Reason*, edited by Paul R. Gross, Norman Levitt, and Martin Lewis. Annals of the New York Academy of Sciences, Volume 775.

Groff, Vern
1990 *The Power of Color in Design for Desktop Publishing*. Management Information Source Press, Portland, OR.

Gross, Paul R. and Norman Levitt
1994 *Higher Superstition: The Academic Left and Its Quarrels with Science*. Johns Hopkins University Press: Baltimore, MD.

Hamermesh, Daniel S.
1996 Not so bad: the annual report on the economic status of the profession 1995–1996. *Academe* (March–April):14–37.

Hay, Conran, James W. Hatch, and J. Sutton
1987 *A Management Plan for Clemson Island Archaeological Resources in the Commonwealth of Pennsylvania*. Pennsylvania Historical and Museum Commission, Bureau of Historic Preservation, Harrisburg, PA.

Hester, Thomas R.
1997 Chapter 5. Methods of Excavation. Pp.69–112 in Hester, Thomas R., Harry J. Shafer, and Kenneth L. Feder, *Field Methods in Archaeology*. Seventh edition. Mayfield, Mountain View, CA.

Hopke, William E.
1993 *The Encyclopedia of Careers and Vocational Guidance*. Ninth edition. Ferguson Publications, Chicago.

Hosmer, Charles B., Jr.
1981 *Preservation Comes of Age: From Williamsburg to the National Trust, 1926–1949*. Two volumes. National Trust for Historic Preservation in the United States/University Press of Virginia, Charlottesville.

Hothem, Lar
1999 *Indian Artifacts of the Midwest. Volume III*. Collectors Books, Paducah, KY.

Hubka, Thomas C.
1984 *Big House, Little House, Back House, Barn: The Connected Farm Buildings of New England*. University Press of New England, Hanover, NH.

Illinois Archaeological Survey
1983 *Professional Standards*. Illinois Archaeological Survey, Springfield, IL.

REFERENCES

Internal Revenue Service (IRS)
    1998 *Your Federal Income Tax for Individuals.* Internal Revenue Service Publication 17. U.S. Government Printing Office, Washington, D.C.

Internal Revenue Service (IRS)
    1999 *Per Diem Rates.* Internal Revenue Service Publication 1542. U.S. Government Printing Office, Washington, D.C.

Jameson, John H., Jr., John E. Ehrenhard, and Wilfred Husted
    1992 *Federal archeological contracting: Utilizing the competitive procurement process.* Archaeology & Ethnology Program Technical Brief 7. NPA February 1992.

Johnson, Frederick, Emil W. Haury, and James B. Griffin
    1945 Report of the Planning Committee. *American Antiquity* 9:142–144.

Kanefield, Adina W.
    1996 *Federal Historic Preservation Case Law, 1966–1996: Thirty Years of the National Historic Preservation Act.* A Special Report Funded in Part by the United States Army Environmental Center/Advisory Council on Historic Preservation, U.S. Government Printing Office, Washington, D.C.

Kavanagh, Maureen
    1982 *Archeological Resources of the Monocacy River Region.* Maryland Geological Survey Division of Archaeology File Report No. 164.

Kay, Charles E.
    1994 Aboriginal overkill: The role of Native Americans in structuring western ecosystems. *Human Nature* 5:359–398.

Kay, Charles E.
    1996 Ecosystems then and now: A historical-ecological approach to ecosystem management. Pp. 79–87 in *Proceedings of the Fourth Prairie Conservation and Endangered Species Workshop,* edited by W. D. Wilms and J. F. Dormaar. Provincial Museum of Alberta, Occasional Paper 23.

Kay, Charles E.
    1997 Aboriginal overkill and the biogeography of moose in western North America. *Alces* 33:141–164.

Kelso, William M., and Rachel Most, editors
    1990 *Earth Patterns: Essays in Landscape Archaeology.* University Press of Virginia, Charlottesville.

Ketch, Shepard K, III
1999 *The Ecological Indian: History and Myth.* Norton, New York.

King, Thomas F.
1998 *Cultural Resources Laws and Practice: An Introductory Guide.* AltaMira Press, Walnut Creek, CA.

King, Thomas F.
2000 *Federal Planning and Historical Places: The Section 106 Process.* AltaMira Press, Walnut Creek, CA.

Krech III, Shepard
1999 *The Ecological Indian: Myth and History.* W. W. Norton & Company, New York.

Kohl, Philip L. and Clare P. Fawcett, editors
1996 *Nationalism, Politics, and the Practice of Archaeology.* Cambridge University Press, Cambridge.

Larkin, Robert
2001 *Fabjob.com Guide to Become an Archaeologist.* http://www.fabjoc.com/archaeologist.htm.

Lehmer, Donald J.
1971 *Introduction to Middle Missouri Archeology.* Anthropological Papers 1. National Park Service. U.S. Department of the Interior, Government Printing Office, Washington, D.C.

McAlester, Virginia, and Lee McAlester
1986 *A Field Guide to American Houses.* Knopf, New York.

McLean, Ruari
1997 *The Thames and Hudson Manual of Typography.* Thames and Hudson, London.

National Park Service
1995a *How to Apply the National Register Criteria for Evaluation.* National Register Bulletin 15. National Park Service. Washington, D.C. (http://www.cr.nps.gov/nr/nrpubs.html).

National Park Service
1995b *How to Complete the National Register Form.* National Register Bulletin 16. National Park Service. Washington, D.C. (http://www.cr.nps.gov/nr/nrpubs.html).

REFERENCES

Neumann, Mary Spink
1994 *Developing Effective Educational Print Materials*. Centers for Disease Control and Prevention, Division of STD/HIV Prevention, Training and Education Branch, Atlanta.

Neumann, Thomas W.
1978 A model for the vertical distribution of flotation-size particles. *Plains Anthropologist* 23:85–101.

Neumann, Thomas W.
1985 Human-wildlife competition and the passenger pigeon: Population growth from system destabilization. *Human Ecology* 13:389–410.

Neumann, Thomas W.
1989a Human-wildlife competition and prehistoric subsistence: The case of the Eastern United States. *Journal of Middle Atlantic Archaeology* 5:29–57.

Neumann, Thomas W.
1989b *A Phase I Archeological Investigation of Catoctin Furnace (18 FR 29), Cunningham Falls State Park, Frederick County, Maryland*. State of Maryland/Office of Engineering and Construction/Department of General Services, Baltimore.

Neumann, Thomas W.
1992 The physiographic variables associated with prehistoric site location built the upper Potomac River Basin, West Virginia. *Archaeology of Eastern North America* 20:81–124.

Neumann, Thomas W.
1993 Soil dynamics and the sinking of artifacts: Procedures for identifying components in non-stratified sites. *Journal of Middle Atlantic Archaeology* 9:94–108.

Neumann, Thomas W.
1995 The structure and dynamics of the prehistoric ecological system in the Eastern Woodlands: Ecological reality versus cultural myths. *Journal of Middle Atlantic Archaeology* 11:125–138.

Neumann, Thomas W., Brian D. Bates, and Robert M. Sanford
1998 Chapter 15: Setting up the basic archaeology laboratory. Pp. 343–358 in *Archaeological Laboratory Methods: An Introduction*, by Mark Q. Sutton and Brooke S. Arkush. Second edition. Kendall/Hunt Publishing, Dubuque, IA.

Neumann, Thomas W., William C. Johnson, Jennifer Cohen, and Neal H. Lopinot
1990 *Archeological Data Recovery from Prehistoric Site 36Fa363, Grays Landing Lock and Dam.* U.S. Army Corps of Engineers, Pittsburgh District.

Neumann, Thomas W., and Robert M. Sanford
1985 *A Cultural Resource Assessment of the Proposed Onondaga Senior Center.* Prepared by Neumann and Sanford Cultural Resource Assessments, for the Syracuse/Onondaga County Planning Agency, New York.

Neumann, Thomas W., and Robert M. Sanford
1987 *The Weston Site: Phase III Cultural Resource Mitigation of the Southeast Area.* Prepared by Neumann & Sanford Cultural Resource Assessments, Syracuse, New York, on behalf of Goodfellow Construction, Inc., Jamesville, New York.

Neumann, Thomas W., and Robert M. Sanford
1998 Cleaning artifacts with Calgon™ (sodium [hexa]metaphosphate). *American Antiquity* 63:157–160.

Neumann, Thomas W., and Robert M. Sanford
2001 *Practicing Archaeology: An Introduction to Cultural Resources Archaeology.* AltaMira Press, Walnut Creek, CA.

Neumann, Thomas W., Robert M. Sanford, and James F. Palmer
1992 Managing archaeological cultural resources as environmental resources: An aid for local governments. *The Environmental Professional* 14:117–125.

Neumann, Thomas W., Robert M. Sanford, and Richard L. Warms
1993 Using vegetation successional stages to reconstruct landscape history for cultural resource assessments in south-central Texas. Wentworth Analytical Facility, Lilburn, GA.

Neumann, Thomas W., and Martha R. Williams
1990 *A Phase 1 Archeological Investigation of the Novak Property, Anne Arundel County, Maryland.* Prepared by R. Christopher Goodwin & Associates, Inc., for Brown & Brown Builders, Ltd., Crofton, MD.

Neumann, Thomas W., and Martha R. Williams
1991 *Phase 1 Archeological Investigation of the 230-KV Transmission Line Corridor and Proposed Access Road Corridor, Clover Generating Plant, Halifax County, Virginia.* Prepared by R. Christopher Goodwin & Associates, Inc., for Old Dominion Electric Cooperative, Glen Allen, VA.

REFERENCES

New York Archaeological Council
1994 *Standards for Cultural Resource Investigations and the Curation of Archaeological Collections in New York State*. New York Archaeological Council, Albany.

New York Times
1991 Transco Settles Claims in Alabama. *New York Times*, May 31, 1991:D4.

Noël Hume, Audrey
1974 *Archaeology and the Colonial Gardener*. Colonial Williamsburg Archaeological Series No. 7. The Colonial Williamsburg Foundation, Williamsburg.

Noël Hume, Ivor
1974 *Digging for Carter's Grove*. Colonial Williamsburg Archaeological Series No. 8. The Colonial Williamsburg Foundation, Williamsburg.

Ohio Historical Society
1994 *Archaeology Guidelines*. Ohio Historical Society, Columbus.

Olson, Gerald W.
1976 *Criteria for Making and Interpreting a Soil Profile Description: A Compilation of the Official USDA Procedure and Nomenclature for Describing Soils*. Kansas Geological Survey Bulletin 212. University of Kansas Publications, Lawrence.

Overstreet, Robert M.
1997 *The Overstreet Indian Arrowheads Identification and Price Guide*. Fifth edition. Avon Books, New York.

Parker, Patricia L., and Thomas F. King
1995 *Guidelines for Evaluating and Documenting Traditional Cultural Properties*. National Register Bulletin. National Park Service. Washington, D.C. (http://www.cr.nps.gov/nr/nrpubs.html).

Patterson, Thomas C.
1995 *Toward a Social History of Archaeology in the United States*. Harcourt Brace College Publishers, Fort Worth.

Poirier, David
1987 *The Environmental Review Primer for Connecticut's Archaeological Resources*. Connecticut Historical Commission.

Redman, Charles L.
1999 *Human Impact on Ancient Environments*. University of Arizona Press, Tucson.

Renfrew, Colin, and Paul Bahn
2000 *Archaeology: Theories, Methods, and Practice*. Third edition. Thames and Hudson, London.

Rice, T. D., and L. T. Alexander
1938 The physical nature of soil. Pp. 887–896 in *Soils and Men. Yearbook of Agriculture, 1938*, edited by the Committee on Soils. U.S. Department of Agriculture, Government Printing Office, Washington, D.C.

Rogers, Lori M.
1991 FERC hears gas industry concerns, announces Transco settlement. *Public Utilities Fortnightly*, July 1, 1991:36–37.

Rosenberg, Ronald H.
1981 Archaeological resource preservation: The role of state and local government. *Utah Law Review* 4:727–802.

Russell, Emily W. B.
1997 *People and the Land through Time: Linking Ecology and History*. Yale University Press, New Haven.

Sanford, Robert M., and Thomas W. Neumann
1987 The urban tree as cultural artifact. *Northeastern Environmental Science* 6:46–52.

Sanford, Robert M., Don Huffer, Nina Huffer, Tom Neumann, Giovanna Peebles, Mary Butera, Ginger Anderson, and Dave Lacy
1994 *Stonewalls and Cellarholes: A Guide for Landowners on Historic Features and Landscapes in Vermont's Forests*. Vermont Agency of Natural Resources, Department of Forests, Parks and Recreation, Waterbury, VT.

Sanford, Robert M., Thomas W. Neumann, and Gary F. Salmon
1997 Reading the landscape: Inference of historic land use in Vermont forests. *Journal of Vermont Archaeology* 2:1–12.

Scovill, Douglas H., Garland J. Gordon, and Keith M. Anderson
1977 Guidelines for the Perception of Statements of Environmental Impact on Archaeological Resources. Pp. 43–62 in *Conservation Archaeology*, edited by Michael B. Schiffer and G. J. Gumerman, Academic Press, New York.

REFERENCES

Sharer, Robert J., and Wendy Ashmore
1993 *Archaeology: Discovering Our Past.* Second Edition. Mayfield, Mountain View, CA.

Sloane, Eric
1954 *American Barns & Covered Bridges.* Harper and Row, New York.

Sloane, Eric
1955 *Our Vanishing Landscape.* Harper and Row, New York.

Sloane, Eric
1956 *American Yesterday.* Harper and Row, New York.

Sloane, Eric
1982 *Eric Sloane's America.* Promontory Press, New York.

Soil Survey Division Staff
1951 *Soil Survey Manual.* USDA Handbook No. 18. U.S. Government Printing Office, Washington, D.C.

Soil Survey Division Staff
1975 *Soil Taxonomy.* USDA Handbook No. 436. U.S. Government Printing Office, Washington, D.C.

Soil Survey Division Staff
1981 Chapter 4 from the unedited text of *Soil Survey Manual.* Soil Conservation Service, U.S. Government Printing Office, Washington, D.C.

South, Stanley
1977 *Method and Theory in Historical Archaeology.* Academic Press, New York.

Squier, E. G., and E. H. Davis
1848 *Ancient Monuments of the Mississippi Valley.* Smithsonian Contributions to Knowledge, Volume 1. Washington, D.C.

Sutton, Mark Q., and Brooke S. Arkush
1998 *Archaeological Laboratory Methods: An Introduction.* Second edition. Kendall/Hunt Publishing, Dubuque, IA.

Thomas, Cyrus
1894 *Twelfth Annual Report of the Bureau of Ethnology 1890–'91.* Smithsonian Institution, Washington, D.C.

Thomas, Dean S.
1985 *Cannons: An Introduction to Civil War Artillery.* Thomas Publications, Gettysburg, PA.

Thomas, Keith
1983 *Man and the Natural World: Changing Attitudes in England 1500–1800.* Oxford University Press, Oxford.

Trimble, Michael K., and Thomas B. Meyers
1991 *Saving the Past from the Future: Archaeological Curation in the St. Louis District.* U.S. Army Corps of Engineers, St. Louis District, MO.

Tschichold, Jan
1962 *Treasury of Alphabets & Lettering* [Translation by Wolf von Eckardt of *Meisterbuch der Schrift*]. Norton, New York.

U.S. Army Corps of Engineers
1996 *Safety and Health Requirements Manual.* (EM 385-1-1). Government Printing Office, Washington, D.C.

Ward, Geoffrey C., and Ken Burns
1994 *Baseball: An Illustrated History.* Knopf, New York.

Watts, May Thielgaard
1975 *Reading the Landscape of America.* Revised and expanded edition. Collier, New York.

Wauchope, Robert W.
1966 *Archaeological Survey of Northern Georgia with a Test of Some Cultural Hypotheses.* Society for American Archaeology Memoir 21.

Weichman, Michael S.
1986 *Guidelines for Contract Cultural Resource Survey Reports and Professional Qualifications.* Missouri Department of Natural Resources, Columbia.

Wessels, Tom
1997 *Reading the Forested Landscape: A Natural History of New England.* Countryman Press, Woodstock, VT.

Wheeler, Mortimer
1954 *Archaeology from the Earth.* Penguin, Baltimore.

REFERENCES

Willey, Gordon R., and Jeremy Sabloff
    1993 *A History of American Archaeology*. Third edition. Freeman, New York.

Yamin, Rebecca, and Karen Bescherer Metheny, editors
    1996 *Landscape Archaeology: Reading and Interpreting the American Historical Landscape*. University of Tennessee Press, Knoxville.

Zeder, Melinda A.
    1997 *The American Archaeologist: A Profile*. AltaMira Press, Walnut Creek, CA.

INDEX

ABOUT THE AUTHORS

Thomas W. Neumann received his B.A. from the University of Kentucky, with a major in Anthropology and minors in Physics, Forestry, and English Literature. He received his M.A. and Ph.D. in Anthropology from the University of Minnesota. He established, then directed for many years, the doctoral program in archaeology at Syracuse University, served as a research associate for the State University of New York Research Foundation, and since 1985 has worked as a corporate archaeologist and research administrator. He has taught at the University of Minnesota, Syracuse University, University of Georgia Honors Program, and Emory University. He currently manages the Diachronics Division at the Pocket Park–Wentworth Analytical Facility. Neumann and his wife live in Lilburn, Georgia, where they garden, brew beer, and generally enjoy life in their virtual village.

Robert M. Sanford received his B.A. in Anthropology from the State University of New York College at Potsdam and his M.S. and Ph.D. in Environmental Science from the State University of New York College of Environmental Science and Forestry at Syracuse. Sanford has worked as a consulting archaeologist and as an environmental regulator. He has taught at Antioch New England Graduate School, the Community College of Vermont, Johnson State University, Onondaga Community College, and SUNY College of Environmental Science and Forestry. He is on the faculty of the University of Southern Maine, where he teaches in the Environmental Science and Policy Program. He lives in Gorham, Maine, with his wife Robin and children, Corey, Dan, and Morgan.

Readers are invited to share comments, stories, updates, and anecdotes with the authors by contacting the publisher.